SASKATCHEWAN
The History of a Province

SASKATCHEWAN

The History of a Province

By
J. F. C. WRIGHT

Illustrated by
A. W. Davey

Research Assistant
Alexander Robb

*This original edition is published to commemorate
the Golden Jubilee of the Province of Saskatchewan*

McClelland and Stewart Limited
1955

Printed and bound in Canada by
THE HUNTER ROSE CO. LIMITED

Preface

PROFESSOR George W. Simpson, head of the History Department, University of Saskatchewan, when asked by a doubtful student, "What's the use of history?", replied, "Do you know what happens to people who lose their memory?".

Professor Simpson retains an exacting memory, not only of the essence of his academic studies, but of ploughing with oxen on his homestead south of Swift Current and of days as rural school teacher in a one-room school-house on the treeless, rolling, windswept plain in the vicinity of Ponteix and Val Marie, Saskatchewan. Diligent, scholarly, and reticent, he suggested I should abstain from highlighting his part in the conception and final preparation of "Saskatchewan— The History of a Province". But the acknowledgement is the author's prerogative; without Professor Simpson's understanding encouragement and consistent guidance, this particular book would not have been written.

The project was initially financed by the taxpayers of the province through the Saskatchewan Golden Jubilee Committee, and the author appreciates the research material made available to him as a result of the meticulous and pertinacious work of Alex Robb.

Like many a four-horse outfit of earlier prairie days, the team-work of adviser, research worker, artist (A. W. Davey), and author provided a combination for the cultivation of this field of history.

With Dr. Simpson and Mr. Robb, I wish to thank the following for their cooperation in gathering scattered source material: Miss Barbara Hobbs of the Shortt Library, University of Saskatchewan, Saskatoon; Miss Ruth Murray of the University Library, University of Saskatchewan; Mr. A. R. Turner of the Saskatchewan Archives Office at the University of Saskatchewan; and Mr. J. H. Archer, Legislative Librarian, Legislative Building, Regina.

Details about the part played by Saskatchewan men and women in two world wars were obtained by writing to the following officers at the Department of National Defence, Ottawa: Captain William Strange, Director of Naval Information; Colonel C. P. Stacey, Director of the Historical Section of the General Staff (Army); and Wing Commander F. H. Hitchins of the Air Staff.

Assistance in selecting and collecting material was given by the following in their areas of specialization: Mr. B. Wettlaufer, Archaeologist with the Department of Mineral Resources, Regina; Mr. J. Mitchell, Professor and head of the Department of Soil Science, University of Saskatchewan; Mr. B. W. Currie, Professor and head of the Department of Physics, University of Saskatchewan; Mr. F. H. Edmunds, Professor of Geology, University of Saskatchewan; Mr. Lewis Thomas, Provincial Archivist; Mr. E. G. Drake, formerly Assistant Provincial Archivist; Miss Evelyn Eager, Assistant Provincial Archivist; and Dr. Jean Murray, Assistant Professor of history, University of Saskatchewan (on the fur trade period).

I thank also the various individuals who so readily responded to requests for information relevant to the manuscript. And along with the many associates from whom, over the years, I have had the privilege to learn, I look back to good friends, including especially James Crossley of Minnedosa, Manitoba, my teacher of high school days, an inspiring disciplinarian who encouraged the enquiring mind.

Saskatoon,   Jim F. C. Wright
January 10, 1955

Contents

Introduction

THIS year (1955) Saskatchewan is celebrating the fiftieth anniversary of her establishment as a province of Canada. This history outlines the story of her people, problems, and achievements from the very beginning, of which little is known, to three hundred years ago when this part of North America became linked with dynamic and expanding Western Europe, and down through the period of dependence to the swiftly flowing era of settlements and self-government. Finally it surveys the chief events and trends during the fifty years of provincial development. The names of numerous important communities and many outstanding people the province is rich in have had to be omitted because of limitations of space. These unexploited historical resources, it is hoped, will be cultivated more widely by local chroniclers and specialists. Mr. Wright tells a connected story of Saskatchewan and recaptures its atmosphere and flavour.

In one sense the history of Saskatchewan reflects distantly the pulsations of European history in one of its most vital periods of growth. When Europe wanted furs, a tremor of activity ran along Saskatchewan's rivers, through her forests, and over her great plains. When European commerce expanded, small tributary outlets were extended to these distant regions. As Europe and Eastern America became industrialized, her plains were used for cattle or ploughed up for wheat and other grains; prospectors searched the north for essential metals; and vast new systems of transportation were established to meet the new developing forms of economic life.

European reflection was to be seen not only in economic affairs. Great European wars and diplomatic bargains controlled the fate of far-off lands including the valleys of the Saskatchewan river system. Political conflict, especially in Great Britain, involving the power of kings, parliaments, and people, established trends, precedents, and law which ultimately laid down the framework of our political life. The religious movements and organizations of Europe were carried here by devoted men, while other cultural institutions, vogues, fashions, and trends ultimately reached this western periphery.

Saskatchewan's history, however, cannot be regarded simply as a distant reflection of movements originating elsewhere. It has its own unique quality and pattern. People had to adapt themselves to a distinctive environment which had to be learned and relearned in terms of changing technology. With the means at hand the people had to construct and adapt. The process still continues. Already, however, there is an interesting story of hope, energy, and achievement which rises above frustration, temporary defeat, and miscalculation.

There are a few facts about Saskatchewan that the reader must keep in mind from the beginning. One is the size of the province— greater than the combined area of Germany and Great Britain.

The people of Saskatchewan represent many ethnic groups, races, and nations. Less than half are of British origin. In spite of variety and diversity of origin, the people of the province have developed a common life which in two generations has demonstrated what can be achieved through mutual understanding and co-operation in meeting basic community problems. The many-coloured strands of customs and attitudes being continuously interwoven within a framework of English law and traditional political organization have created a society that is endlessly interesting.

In the first fifty years of her existence as a province, particularly notable have been the dominant place of wheat in her economy and the preponderance of rural over urban life. The most typical Saskatchewan community has been the prairie village with grain elevators. However, the picture has been neither uniform nor static. New economic and social changes are altering the situation, and the swift developments of recent years are modifying the previous pattern.

Saskatchewan's history cannot be written without ample reference to Saskatchewan weather. The contest among the gods of rain, sun, wind, and frost has been carried on without reference to mortals. Like a temperamental woman, Saskatchewan weather has caused both exhilaration and exasperation. Through fortitude and ingenious adaptation, the people have learned to live with the weather and even to like it.

The history of an area is essentially the history of a people. To an exceptional degree the people of Saskatchewan have shown buoyancy, courage, and a readiness to respond to an imaginative or generous idea. These are qualities associated with a newly forming frontier society. In Saskatchewan this general spirit has arisen through those fine men and women who provided leadership to the pioneers at a time when communities were being shaped and fashioned. It is to these pioneers, both the great and the humble, that this history is dedicated.

University of Saskatchewan   GEORGE W. SIMPSON
     April, 1955

Rock, Water, and Soil

In their daring penetration of North America's vast and rugged far northwest, the first explorers and fur traders turned their canoes westward from Lake Winnipeg to find more "beaver country" along a swiftly moving river. *Kis-is-ska-tche-wan* (fast-flowing) the native Cree Indians had named this wide and forest-flanked stream. In the mid and later 1700's the newcomers of British and French origin, thrusting their paddles into the challenging waters, called this swirling highway "the Saskatchewan" after the Indian name.

One hundred and twenty-five years later, on the southern treeless plain, fast-flowing became the westward advance of steel rails, an iron wheel road, followed by a rush of settlers from many lands,

1

who, in one generation, transformed a broad expanse of shortgrass buffalo pasture into fields of billowing wheat.

After passing through several stages of administrative evolution, the area of the Province of Saskatchewan was pencilled out of Canada's vast Northwest Territories in 1905. Its political boundaries are unrelated to geographical regions. Saskatchewan's northland is part of the great Pre-Cambrian Shield, largest in the world, a rugged hardrock, mineral-bearing formation, marked by lake and forest, that extends, similarly exposed, through the northern areas of Quebec, Ontario, Manitoba, Alberta, and the eastern Northwest Territories as well.

No geological or topographical feature, no river, lake, range of hills, or peculiar rock or soil formation marks Saskatchewan's boundary land as distinct from that of adjacent provinces—Manitoba to the east and Alberta along the west.

Parallel of latitude 60 is Saskatchewan's northern boundary. This mathematical line of measurement runs through lake, rock, muskeg, bush country, and sub-Arctic tundra of the Province of Saskatchewan, all similar to the terrain of the contiguous Northwest Territories. Along Saskatchewan's southern border, the 49th parallel, North Dakota's grain land and Montana's grazing country merge so naturally with those of Saskatchewan, a roving horseman might not know whether he was in the Canadian province or either of the American states, unless reminded by a customs or immigration patrol.

From Saskatchewan's southern to northern boundary is 761 miles. The southern east-west boundary is 393 miles in length, the northern 277. The two large geographical regions of the province contain the Pre-Cambrian rock of the northland, and the agricultural soil of the southern open plains.

The Pre-Cambrian rock was exposed by a series of Arctic glaciers, the most recent of which gouged and ground its way southwestward. The depth of subsoil on the plains was built up by crushed rock left by melting glaciers. Four successive ice ages, and possibly five, have been traced by geologists in their study of rock and soil formation.

When geologists speak of ice ages they refer to what is for them comparatively recent times. In their larger perspective of time, reaching back two billion years (2,000 million), the history of the earth is revealed.

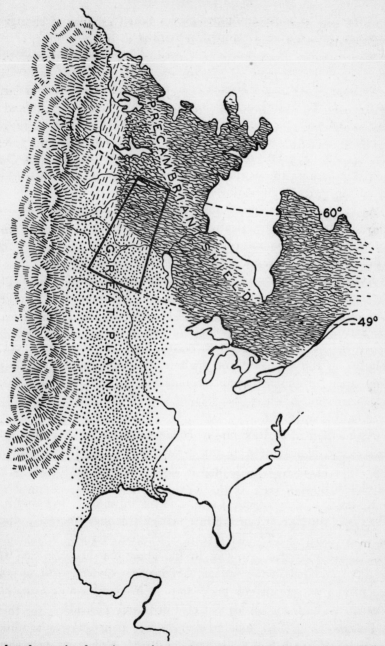

Saskatchewan's location with reference to continental drainage systems, the Precambrian Shield, and the Great Plains

According to some anthropological estimates, human beings have lived on earth during a comparatively brief period of a million years. Humanity's history, prior to the written word, is dimly obscure beyond 5,000 years ago.

Perhaps this immense stretch of time might be most easily grasped in terms of the history of Saskatchewan if we consider the geologist's two billion years as one year only. This hypothetical year begins, as our calendar years do, on January 1. Throughout most of the year the climate of earth remained generally uniform and temperate, probably because the warm crust over a hot interior was surrounded by an impenetrable insulating blanket of cloud.

As long as the rock was intensely hot and fluid, particles of basic mineral elements were relatively free to assemble, and eventually formed various mineral concentrations that later appeared in the solidified rock of the earth's crust.

Later in the hypothetical year, sometime after the end of March, the earth's surface had cooled sufficiently to allow rain to remain and form great oceans. Then most of the land was submerged, as the extrusion of mountain ranges and less spectacular uplifts of land above the sea level were yet to occur. The salts that were held in solution in this immense and shallow sea made for the beginning, long after, of Saskatchewan's commercial potassium salts deposits which remained when the inland sea of Canada's prairie area eventually evaporated.

About the end of June on our condensed calendar (a billion years ago) there appeared in warm ocean basins mineral-eating microorganisms living without benefit of direct sunlight (dense cloud still enveloped the earth).

It was, in the hypothetical year, an eventful summer followed by a still busier autumn, when the first marine trilobites emerged. About mid-November (250 million years ago) giant fernlike trees of the lush forest were fast growing in the great marshes. As the trees matured and fell in the waters, they became covered with silt and, together with remains of huge amphibian reptiles and other life, formed the basis for subsequent coal beds and oil fields.

December 17 (70 million years ago) giant dinosaurs walked erect. Two days before Christmas, the Rocky Mountains were thrust up, as were other very recent mountain chains including the Andes,

Alps, and Himalayas. Mountain building was a factor in altering the climate in such a way that temperature variation increased. Within a few (hypothetical) hours the curved-tusked hairy mammoths were foraging for lichens in weather that would mean pneumonia for tropical elephants of today.

December 31, on other continents, the first human beings emerged (a million years ago). In the late evening of the same day, about 9:40 p.m. (600,000 years ago) came the first great glacier grinding down from the north. At approximately 10:25 o'clock began a second glacial period, followed by a third at 11:15 p.m., and then a fourth and possibly a fifth. Where Lloydminster, Saskatoon, and Yorkton now stand was ice half a mile in thickness. As the ancient glaciers, colossal and relentless bulldozers, reached down from the north, they sheared off great areas of mineralized rock, pulverized huge quantities of it, carried it southward with age-long leisure, and deposited it to form the subsoil of the prairies.

Close to midnight of that last day of this hypothetical year (20,000 to 30,000 years ago), across the Bering Straits from Asia came those nomadic hunters, the prehistoric Indians. Some three seconds before midnight, the first European explorers and fur traders were paddling up the Saskatchewan River. And a fraction of a second before midnight, as if awaiting the cheers to usher in New Year's Day, Saskatchewan became a province of Canada.

Of greater certainty than this admittedly speculative and very approximate time schedule assigned to early geological events, is the expansive route taken by the most recent glacial advance. Over Saskatchewan's Pre-Cambrian Region of hardrock, water, forest, and muskeg, the last great glacier moved in a southwesterly direction. This fact, at least, is revealed to the non-geological eye by the lay of numerous lakes, both large and small.

While almost one-third of the surface of the Pre-Cambrian is freshwater lake and stream, the combined annual precipitation of rainfall and snowfall there is no greater than the average for the province as a whole (15 inches). But the impervious rock basins, gouged out by the glaciers, have prevented the water from penetrating as in the porous surface soil and sedimentary rock of the southern parklands and plains.

That the impervious rock basins and stream channels constitute

*Section of the Pre-Cambrian Shield in northern Saskatchewan show-
ing the direction of the lakes, which indicates the southwestward
movement of the last glacier*

the principal reason for visible water retention becomes evident in the
topography of Saskatchewan's extreme northeast corner. Here is
the southerly edge of the sub-Arctic tundra with an overlay of moss
and lichen-covered sand, allowing moisture to seep below the surface.
Consequently no large lakes, and few small ones, are in evidence,
while the evergreen forest thins to sparse, stunted spruce and pine.

The Pre-Cambrian Region proper is bordered on the south by a
softwood forest of spruce, jackpine, tamarack, and poplar, taller and
larger in circumference as a result of an extended growing season plus
a depth of sandy soil resting on the hardrock. Here are fewer lakes,
because more of the precipitation passes down through the porous
overburden, while the rate of evaporation is increased owing to a longer
summer season and drier winds. Further south, roughly in the

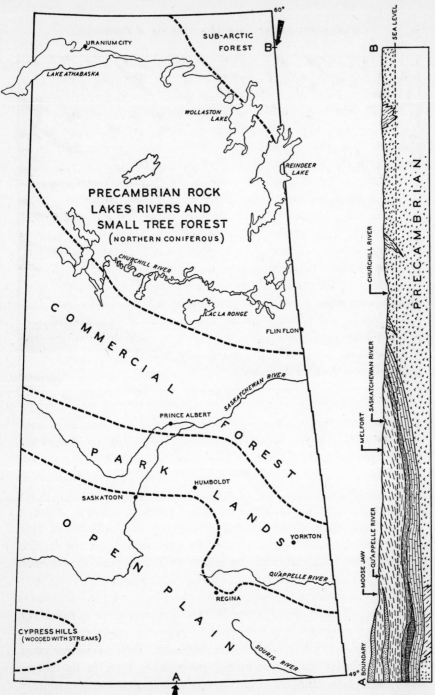

Geographical regions of Saskatchewan. Section in depth across Saskatchewan from south to north showing the Precambrian rock exposed in the north and overlaid by rock strata and glacial deposits in the south

vicinity of Prince Albert, begin the parklands, an intermediary area between the forest and the open plain, where the evergreens diminish in quantity and size, while fast-growing poplars proportionately increase in number, but also decrease in height and diameter.

Still further south, in the vicinity of Saskatoon, begins the treeless open plain, a great grassland, once the northcentral extremity of an immense buffalo range extending southward far beyond the Canadian-U. S. border, through the states of North Dakota and Montana, to Texas, the Rio Grande, and the Gulf of Mexico. Over this entire area the sun shines strongly through generally dry air, while winds are persistent and at times relentless. During prolonged arid periods, moisture evaporation exceeds both rainfall and snowfall, depleting the reserves. Except in river valleys and coulees, trees do not flourish naturally, as their summer leaves would give moisture off more rapidly than their roots could draw it from the drying earth.

But grass, and plants that are members of the grass family (to which wheat, oats, barley, and rye belong), may thrive where trees fail. Some varieties of the grass family have hairlike roots which penetrate six feet and more to reach subsoil moisture, while all varieties have a surface-spreading root system designed to utilize intermittent moisture from rain showers, no matter how meagre. Moreover, the grasses lose moisture through expiration at a rate less rapid than trees. While the native Indians did set fire to the prairie grass, both to stampede the buffalo for a kill and on some occasions to encourage a rapid growth of fresh green grass as an early spring attraction for a roving herd, it is doubtful that a complete absence of prairie fires would have encouraged a forest in a region inhospitable to trees.

Like an oasis on the open plain are the poplar and spruce-clad hillsides with freshwater springs which make up the Cypress Hills lying in the southwest corner of Saskatchewan and extending into Alberta. This elevation, with a maximum height of nearly 4,500 feet above sea level, reaches about 1,500 feet above the surrounding open plain. The most recent glacial action was ineffectual at approximately 4,300 feet, and so, according to geological surveys of this unique area, there was insufficient weight of ice in motion to erase the Cypress Hills.

The flat-rimmed, often dry coulees typical of the open plains

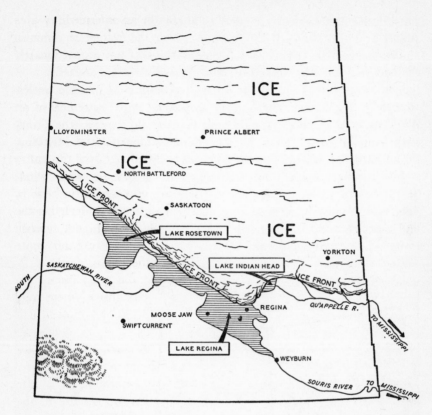

Lake Regina stage in recession of the last glaciation about 18,000 years ago

were once well filled water courses, rushing rivers carrying away the flow from melting ice at the conclusion of the latest glacial advance. At one time the waters of the Saskatchewan River, blocked to the north by glacial ice, flowed into a broad lake which then covered the Regina plains and thence flowed through the Souris River into the Mississippi and south to the Gulf of Mexico. Other lakes important for future soil formation were Rosetown Lake and Indian Head Lake.

As the glacier retreated north, the waters of the South Saskatchewan veered northward, joining a later channel, the North Saskatchewan, to form one fast-flowing stream emptying into Hudson Bay. The

junction of the present channels is about 35 miles east of Prince
Albert.

Throughout the Province of Saskatchewan, January is usually
the coldest month and July the warmest. January's average
temperatures vary from about 10 degrees Fahrenheit in the southwest to 23 degrees below zero in the northeast. Very low temperatures
do occur in December, January, and February. The lowest recorded
vary from 50 to 60 below on the plains and from 60 to 70 below
through the Forest Region to the northern boundary.

July average temperatures vary from 67 degrees across southern
Saskatchewan to 57 degrees across the north, while temperatures in
July and August have been recorded as high as 110 in the south,
and more than 90 in the north. Late frosts in early June and early
frosts in late August do occur.

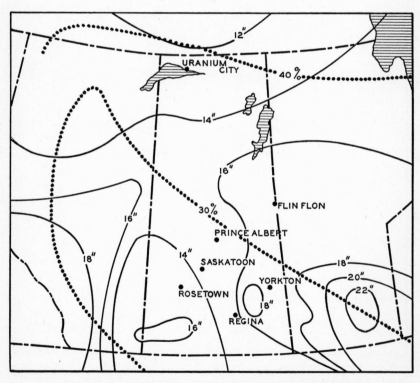

Average annual precipitation and percentage of snow

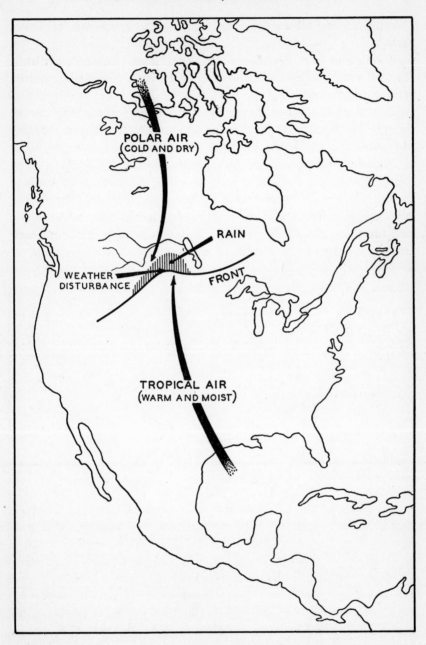

POLAR AIR
(COLD AND DRY)

RAIN

WEATHER
DISTURBANCE

FRONT

TROPICAL AIR
(WARM AND MOIST)

Major air mass movements in contact along a front at which the warm moist air will rise and cool, producing rain

Average precipitation, ranging from 12 to 18 inches, decreases from south to north and increases from west to east. Precipitation in the form of snow increases almost uniformly from about 25 per cent of total precipitation in the southwest to more than 40 per cent in the extreme northeast.

On the restless wings of the wind rides the variable weather of this midcontinental area. Prevailing winds blow from the southeast and from the northwest. Southeast wind from over the Gulf of Mexico brings warm air laden with moisture evaporated from the surface of the tropical sea 2,000 miles and more from Saskatchewan. Where this warm air is pushed upward by cold air masses moving in from the Arctic, the warm air cools, contracts, and releases moisture that falls as rain or snow. Rainfall throughout the summer months is unequal, the month of greatest precipitation being June.

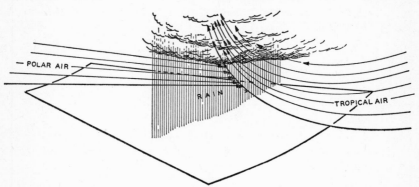

The lifting of warm, moist tropical air by cold, dry polar air to form rain clouds over Saskatchewan

Sometimes in the extreme heat of a summer afternoon or early evening, localized and turbulent air currents cause a rapid and fluctuating elevation of moisture-laden air, and ice pellets develop in mountainous clouds. When updrafts can no longer sustain these ice pellets, they fall earthward in a fury of hail.

The restless winds over Saskatchewan, which usually blow dry, at times bring rain and snow. During sub-zero temperatures people measure the consequence of cold less by the thermometer than by the degree of windchill. On winter days beneath a high blue sky the sun shines strongly on drifted snow while, bathed in light, the landscape varies with the passing clouds. Once experienced, the brilliance of sunrise and the sight of the luring horizon are rarely forgotten.

Throughout thousands and thousands of years the Saskatchewan area remained untouched by man. The first immigrants to arrive on this scene of natural desolation and grandeur saw no footprints other than their own, no sign of human habitation.

Here they began afresh man's answer to the challenge of his environment of rock, soil, and water; heat, cold, and wind.

2

First Immigrants

From Asia, some 20,000 to 30,000 years ago, across the narrow Bering Strait to North America came the first immigrants, the ancestors of the people whom the early European navigators and explorers called Indians. While anthropologists are in agreement that Asia was the land of origin for the first North American inhabitants, they still differ over the approximate time, or times, of migration. From the Siberian mainland across Bering Strait to the Alaskan coast is less than 60 miles, and those miles are punctuated by islands. The strait, a meeting place of the North Pacific and Arctic oceans, is rarely ice-free. Thousands of years ago, when the climate of the area is believed to have been even colder than at present, it is possible that nomadic Asian hunters followed game eastward across a bridge of ice and islands connecting the two continents, or were driven across it as a result of pressure from other nomads.

Evidence points to Eurasia as being the cradle of early humanity, and strongly supports the reasoned supposition that the "Indians" who became the first natives of the New World had, at the time of their arrival, already attained a certain development in the use of stone tools. Two pertinent facts are that spearpoints and other ancient Stone Age weapons and implements similar to those in use by Indians when the first Europeans arrived, have been discovered in excavations throughout the North American continent; and that there has been no discovery in the Americas of any fossilized bones comparable to those remains of more primitive people that have been found in Europe and Asia.

When the ancestors of the Indians came to North America, much of the interior of Canada was covered with glacial ice. It seems probable, therefore, that the first migrants drifted southward along the more inviting Pacific coast or mountain valleys.

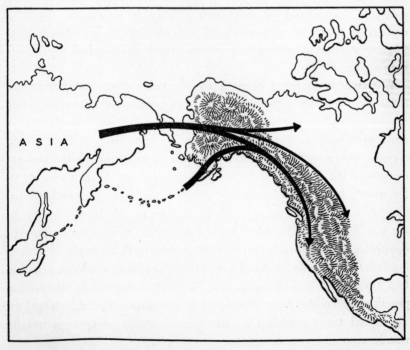

Possible lines of migration from Asia to the Americas

Eventually their descendants reached the Saskatchewan area, but whether they came eastward by gradual stages across the valleys and through the mountain passes of Canada, or whether, after a sojourn in the southern part of the continent, they wandered northward along the foothills of the Rockies, is open to conjecture. Other arrivals may, as the ice fields receded, have approached approximately along the course of the Mackenzie river system, then eastward to the vicinity of Lake Athabasca. Whatever unknown routes they followed during uncounted ages, Indians became dispersed throughout both American continents and, thousands of years later, were seen everywhere by the newcomers from Europe.

Evidence of age-old and sustained culture is found in the development and expansion of language groups which spread to include greater numbers of people ranging over larger areas. Three principal language groups inhabited the Saskatchewan area when the first Europeans arrived. During what period of time and to what extent these three language groups dominated the Saskatchewan scene prior to the impact of European culture is uncertain. What is certain is that the movement of various Indian groupings, after this impact, was accelerated by diverse pressures, including the Whiteman's gun.

Everywhere in what became the Province of Saskatchewan Indians were a hunting people. In fact nowhere in the entire Canadian northwest did Whitemen find Indians engaged to any degree in agriculture such as was practised by natives in warmer or more humid climes. When it is considered that the first literate individuals to encounter the Indians of Saskatchewan were not anthropologists or historians, but men attached to the fur trade or in search of the elusive Northwest Passage— a hoped-for short cut across the top of the world for trade between Europe and the Orient—the vagueness, confusion, and contradiction apparent in various accounts of Indian life become understandable. There remains a core of evidence pointing to a shifting multiplicity of Indian customs, a fluidity of unrecorded practice descending from generation to generation and dependent on 'aboriginal traits modified by the chance conditioning of a usually wandering and intermittently warring people.

While many Indian bands wandered in what they considered

at that time to be their tribal territory, there is evidence that tribal fragments, and sometimes entire tribes, drifted over vast areas of North America. As their culture had not advanced to include a regional system of land tenure, the animals, fish, and birds belonged to those who could most readily procure them. The primary reasons for drifting were probably those that have motivated man in recorded and unrecorded times alike: the necessity for new hunting grounds in the unending search for food, clothing, and shelter; pressure from other men also on the move; and inherent, impelling, but vaguely defined dissatisfactions and searchings that characterize humanity.

Systematic archæological investigation has just begun in Saskatchewan. In the next few decades much of the story of the thousands of years before the coming of the Whiteman will be outlined with greater precision. We may know then when the stone-tipped spear, the stone hatchet, and the bow and arrow were introduced. We will know more about the bison, the larger and more powerful ancestor of the modern buffalo, and even about the skulking wolf or the faithful dog and his early association with man.

Of the early American Indian there is as yet little evidence. When the Whiteman came, the physical traits of the Indians were, within the various groups, common and generally stable. The hair of the head was straight, coarse, thick, and black or sometimes bluish black; the facial and body hair was scant; the eyes were dark and the cheekbones prominent; the chin was not conspicuously developed. More distinctive than the physical differences between groups was the difference in language.

The three broad linguistic groups in the area of the northwest that became Saskatchewan were distributed, at the time of the appearance of the first European explorers, somewhat in relation to the three principal geographical regions. Inhabiting the Pre-Cambrian Region proper of what became northern Saskatchewan, were people of the Athapaskan language group, which includes the Chipewyan, Dogribs, and Yellowknives tribes. Southward in the vicinity of the forest-flanked Saskatchewan River were the Cree Indians, identified with the Algonkian linguistic group; and farther south and west were the parklands and plains Crees, also of the Algonkian group, who for transporting the camp load relied on the dog instead of the

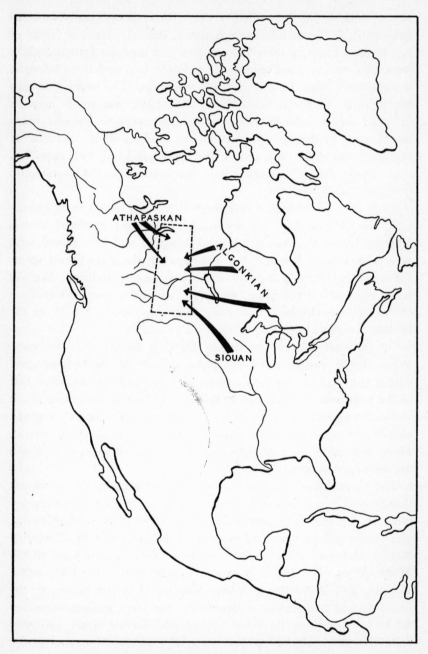

Source of linguistic groups in the Saskatchewan area

canoe used by the forest Crees. Yet farther south were Assiniboian Indians of the Siouan language group.

Various Indian legends about life, death, and life hereafter have been reported and interpreted by literate individuals who arrived in the native habitat after it had experienced the initial impact of a more complicated and less soluble culture from a dynamic Europe. Some of the legends which subsequently appeared in print may have led the English poet, Alexander Pope (1688-1744), to characterize the North American aborigine:

> Lo! the poor Indian, whose untutor'd mind,
> Sees God in clouds, or hears Him in the wind.

Undoubtedly the Indians of the Saskatchewan area, like many primitive people, attributed to the spirit world sights and sounds beyond their comprehension.

In the wind the Indian heard the crunch of the caribou herd travelling over drifted snow of the sub-Arctic tundra, the resounding bellow of a solitary moose in the evergreen forest, and the pounding hooves of buffalo running on the sealike grasslands of the open plain. These were sounds important to the hunter, upon whose skill depended the procurement of food, clothing, and shelter for himself and his family.

The Chipewyan (Athapaskan) natives who roamed in small bands from the Churchill River north to the treeless tundra did most of their moving on foot. Though the Eskimo to the north of the Chipewyans used dogs for transportation, as did the plains Indians far to the south, the Chipewyan men continued to rely on their womenfolk to move camp, an arduous and almost continuous process.

Vital for food and clothing in the Chipewyan economy was the caribou. Compared to the moose, the caribou is not a large animal. Males average 220 pounds in weight, cows about 150 pounds. Antlers on the bulls are multi-pronged and impressively large in relation to the rest of the animal. The caribou is found nowhere else in the Arctic world, and during the annual migration southward the greatest numbers enter Saskatchewan. Throughout the brief but intense Arctic summer, the caribou feed on the moss and sparse grass of

The Barren Lands caribou

the tundra. In August or early September the herds begin their
annual migration southward to Saskatchewan's Pre-Cambrian
Region, there to graze through the winter on frozen muskeg pasture
until April or May when they begin their northward trek back to
the tundra. Thousands travel in a single herd. The Indians, following the herds, killed caribou with bow and arrow or spear, and at
times snared them. Sometimes they retrieved carcasses of animals
that had been drowned when crossing a stream concealed by snow-
covered and treacherous ice.

These far northern Indians depended on caribou hide for robes,
shirts, and leggings, for moccasins, caps, and mitts, and for tents,
nooses to snare with, and nets to catch fish and beaver. Their most
valued tool, used by both men and women, was the stone knife usually
fashioned from granite or other igneous rock by a laborious process
of chipping with a stone hammer and grinding against another piece
of rock.

This northern area was a most difficult terrain, infested moreover

with mosquitoes and black-flies in summer, and in winter snowpacked
and exposed to wind. The Forest Region to the south had more
varied possibilities in the way of adaptation.

For how long Cree (Algonkian) Indians were in nomadic
possession of the forested area between the Churchill and North
Saskatchewan river systems, remains open to speculation. This was

The moose

a territory of the woodland Crees when the first Europeans arrived,
or very shortly after. As with the Crees of the plains to the south, and
the Chipewyans to the north, the diet of the woodland Crees was
meat. When there was no meat they would eat fish, when they could
capture it by jigging a bone hook or spearing through a hole in the
winter ice. The game most sought after was woodland caribou (which
do not migrate, though they are relatively very few in number), moose,

elk, beaver, and bear. When larger game failed, rabbits were snared or shot with bow and arrow; ducks and geese were considered a delicacy and were enjoyed as such whenever they could be taken.

In response to their environment the woodland Crees, in common with natives elsewhere inhabiting areas of forest and stream, developed a practical and beautiful craft for travelling over the water highways

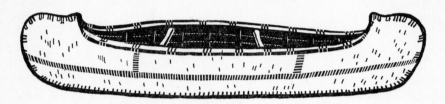

The bark canoe

—the bark canoe. No other type of boat was devised to respond so readily to pressure of paddle for shooting rapids of the stream, while being light enough to be carried easily overland from one waterway to another. Though the fur traders of European origin subsequently constructed larger and stronger (ribbed) canoes, and eventually smaller craft of the native pattern became in evidence at every lakeside resort, the essential streamlined design evolved by the Indians was little improved upon.

Southward in the wooded prairie parklands and out on the open plains of Saskatchewan, Cree and other Indian bands such as the Assiniboian hunted the shaggy buffalo. To the Indians of the treeless plains the great herds of buffalo provided food, clothing, bedding, shelter (tents), and fuel (buffalo chips or dung). In addition to the fresh meat they procured, the Indians preserved meat (pemmican) by drying (dehydrating) thin strips of lean meat in the sun or over a slow fire, and shredding and pounding it into powder, which they then placed in buffalo hide bags sealed with buffalo tallow. The resultant product would, under favourable conditions, keep through many months. For the buffalo-hunting Indians, a goodly store of pemmican staved off hunger and starvation.

When the horse was unknown and when the bow and arrow was the principal weapon, stealthy stalking of lone animals or fragmen-

A jumping pound

tary herds was occasionally resorted to, but for mass slaughter there
were two principal methods: the surround and the impound. The
surround was the simpler method, used on the open plain when
neither time nor material was available for impounding. The en-
circling hunters crept cautiously toward the herd in the hope that,
no matter in which direction the aroused animals might eventually
scatter, some arrows would be effective as the thundering herd
broke the circle. Impounding required the laborious building of
brushwood fence lines converging to a narrow neck opening into a
circular pound of wooden stakes driven into the ground. When a
herd was started running into the wide opening, the animals would
continue on within the crude converging fence, or lines of strategically
placed people and objects, until they reached the circular pound.
There the animals, milling in confusion, were slaughtered. When
local topography was suitable, the narrow neck of the fence would
sometimes be constructed to open over the edge of a precipitous
coulee, called a jumping pound, into which the stampeding animals
hurtled to injury and death. By this method many suffered broken
legs and some were killed by the weight of others falling on top of
them. With spears, knives, and stone hatchets the hunters rushed
in to complete the kill. An additional stratagem, occasionally employed in the impounding technique, was that of an agile young
hunter, dressed in buffalo hide with horns attached, moving ahead
of the herd into the initial opening of the converging fence. Imitating
the walk of a buffalo, he would act as a decoy to the foremost members
of the herd. If the herd followed him, he would, before it advanced
dangerously near, crawl to one side of the brushwood fence, adroitly

The buffalo

discard and conceal his buffalo suit, and lie low behind a brush pile to peer at the animals thundering by.

The plains Indians developed the *tipi,* a practical tent of appealing beauty and of an original design on which the European newcomers were able to make little or no improvement.

In summer, rain or the lack of it determined the movements of the great buffalo herds roaming in search of the best prairie grass pasture. Where the buffalo went, the Indians followed. Dogs, smaller than those used by the Eskimos, hauled much of the camp load on *travois,* a twin-pole frame or shafts attached to the dog's back, with the lower ends of the poles dragging on the ground. What the dogs were unable to haul, the Indian wives packed on their backs.

With the approach of penetrating Arctic winds and the drifting snow of the midcontinental Saskatchewan winter, the people largely abandoned the open plains and took to river valleys, deep coulees, wooded hills, and the parklands, there to seek shelter and firewood.

Prior to the influence of European civilization, it is probable that

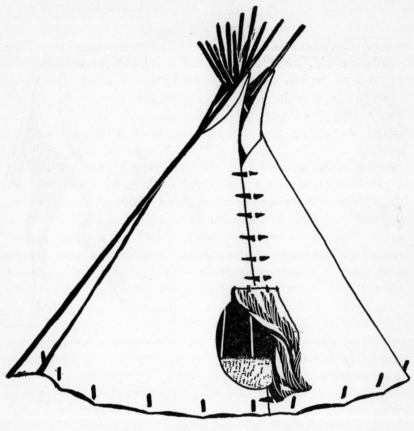

The tipi

aboriginal customs and beliefs were relatively stable. Though the
Whiteman's impact on the Redman resulted in rapid cultural flux,
followed by virtual disintegration of the native economy and the
prehistorical social structure, certain practices were recorded by early
observers of Indian life throughout the area that became the Province
of Saskatchewan. For instance, as successful hunting, then imperative
to survival, was a rigorous occupation, boys were schooled in the
hunt before they reached adolescence. From the age of 10 years,
in fact, they were conditioned to arduous marches, and were trained
in the skill of stalking.

Girl children early began to learn, from their mothers and the other women of the camp, the arts of hide-curing, sinew-making, and sewing. The advent of adolescence was seriously regarded, and frequently the girl, impressed with the importance of her imminent approach to the full status of womanhood, was required to isolate herself for a time in a dwelling apart from the family. Young women were considered of marriageable age from 14 years on, but no outstanding ceremony seems to have marked the wedding event.

Acting in an advisory and prophetic capacity was the *shaman*, or medicine man, who was expected to drive away evil spirits to which illness and accident were attributed. Through dreams he was supposed to reveal the location of game, especially in times of scarcity and dire need. His regular duties included incantations believed to bring good fortune in the hunt and in war. On the plains where the annual sun dance religious festival and celebration attained the maximum development and importance, the shaman led ritual dancing to the rhythm of tribal drums.

Stories of past exploits and disasters were told and retold in legend and song. A stoic people they were, imbued with a fatalistic acceptance of hardship, but camp life was neither dour nor silent, joking and conversation being much enjoyed. Pipe smoking, ordinarily indulged in as a sedative and a social custom, was in addition invested with ceremonial significance. Sharing the *pipe-of-peace* with members of another tribe symbolized a vow, rarely broken, to keep the peace at least for a stipulated period of time or over a specified area. The possession of Indian artifacts by natives far from the source of materials was evidence of some degree of barter and trade between bands, tribes, and different linguistic groups.

In the long course of their regional adaptations, the Indians evolved kinds of food, clothing, shelter, and transportation which were to become essential to the European explorer and trader in his eventual penetration of the vastness of Canada's northwest. Pemmican, moccasins, the tipi, snowshoes, the toboggan, and canoe—these inventions were readily and eagerly adopted.

In the Whiteman's casual report the Indian became a legendary and contradictory figure, denounced on the one hand as bloodthirsty, cruel, revengeful, shiftless, and dirty; and extolled on the other as chivalrous, generous, noble, and highly sensitive to spiritual things. Neither extreme presentation could be fair or accurate. Indians are human beings with the basic faults and virtues of a human race: mainly restless, often kindly, and sometimes ruthless in search of both transient happiness and enduring values. The core of the American Indian's relatively primitive culture became dissolved by the stronger acid of a more complicated, highly organized culture of the older civilization of a dynamic Europe. A comparable process, resulting from the Whiteman's impact, was taking place simultaneously in other lands.

3

Furs, Forts, and Pemmican

THE first cultural thrust into the Saskatchewan area came with Stone Age "Indians" from the far east of the Asian land mass. Thousands of years later the next cultural penetration originated along Europe's western rim of the identical land mass.

Three dynamic centres of civilization—China, India, and the countries of the eastern Mediterranean—had emerged from this, the world's largest land mass. Each had developed characteristic features. The eastern Mediterranean culture, evolving from the ancient Jewish, Greek, and Roman civilizations, had spread throughout Europe and had been modified and shaped by the pervasive, integrating, and vitalizing force of Christianity. But Christian Europeans found themselves isolated in a small corner of the continent by the broad band of Moslem states that stretched from North Africa into India and over the great grassland plateaux and by the deserts that lay between eastern Europe and India and China.

Across this vast land moved the "ships of the desert", the camel caravans, uniting by thin but vital lines of communication three dynamic centres of civilization. Prior to 1492, Europe was neither the wealthiest land nor conspicuously the most advanced. After 1492, with comparative suddenness, maritime Europe made direct contact by sea with the older civilizations and in the exploratory process discovered the two continents, North and South America. These continents of the New World were thinly inhabited and little developed culturally, although several regions, more advanced, involuntarily furnished seafaring invaders from Europe with quantities of precious metals, mainly gold, a medium of exchange valuable almost anywhere and especially in trade with the Orient.

Western Europe now began to accumulate reserves of economic power. The unequal possession of these reserves contributed to political struggles and intermittently to wide-scale warfare between rapidly rising and expansive European empires such as the Spanish, Portuguese, and those of the then smaller Atlantic powers. Initially Spain and Portugal achieved an ascendancy amounting almost to monopoly. Thus, the comparative latecomers—France, England, and Holland—had to engage in a desperate struggle if they were to participate in the new-found wealth. Denied ready access to the gold of Central and South America, they sought alternative and shorter sailing routes, across the Arctic seas, to the far-off, rich centres of trade in the Orient.

Europe's global expansion was not limited to improved communications and economic reserves. A new intellectual vigour became focussed on the exploration and explanation of the physical universe, thus laying foundations of advancing science and emerging technology, which later were to provide European civilization with a material advantage over other cultural areas.

Equally important in this dynamic Europe was the emergence of fresh concepts concerning relations between government and the governed. In England especially, modified relationships between King and Parliament gave rise to hitherto untried theories of government. An emerging concept of political democracy was eventually to dis-

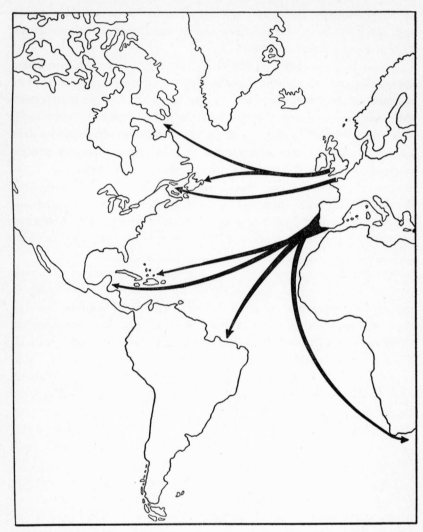

Approaches to the Americas across the Atlantic Ocean

tinguish a dominant Western civilization from the others as sharply as did a developing science and rising industrialism.

From this new Europe, vibrant with energy, the great navigators and explorers sailed westward across the North Atlantic, entered the Gulf of St. Lawrence and the inland sea that is Hudson Bay, pushed westward beyond the latter's sub-Arctic shores of rock and muskeg, and reached up the fresh water of the swift-flowing Saskatchewan river system.

Although, long before, the fierce energy of the Scandinavian Vikings had carried those seafaring warriors across the Atlantic to the shores of North America, this initially promising contact had early been broken.

It was John Cabot, an Italian navigator sailing under English auspices, who in 1497 entered northern waters off Newfoundland to establish England's initial claim to New World territory.

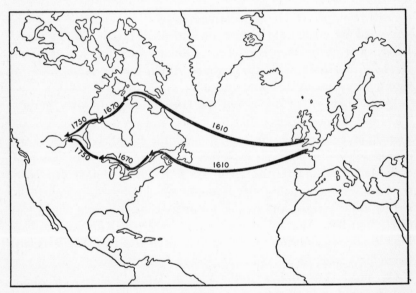

*The lines of approach of the French and English and their conver-
gence in the Saskatchewan area*

Later, and subsequent to voyages of exploration by Jacques Cartier in 1534-35, France established a claim to New World territory, in the same general area as had England. Thus was the basis laid for the ensuing struggle for the possession of most of North America.

England's attempt at overseas expansion took two forms: harassing Spanish shipping on the South Atlantic and seeking desperately to find a northwest passage by which the Spanish monopoly might be circumvented. In 1576-77 Martin Frobisher explored the coast of Labrador, crossed Hudson Strait, followed the coast of Baffin Land, and entered the bay that bears his name today. In 1585 John Davis made his bold bid to find a sea route past North America when he explored the strait separating Greenland from Baffin Land (Davis Strait). Both Frobisher and Davis passed the entrance to Hudson Strait, but it was not until 1610 that Henry Hudson sailed through the strait and explored the eastern coast of the great inland sea which became known as Hudson Bay. Though Hudson's one voyage into the bay ended with his death, exploration was continued by Fox, Button, Baffin, James, and others whose names appear on the map of the area.

Two years before Hudson's famed voyage, the French had finally succeeded in making a permanent settlement on the St. Lawrence River, and were busy exploring tributary streams for extension of their fur trade with the Indians, while not unmindful of the search for a route to the "western sea".

By 1660 they had discovered the Great Lakes and were pushing out from Lake Superior north, south, and west. Active for the French in penetrating the area around the Great Lakes were two coureurs-de-bois—hunters, explorers, and traders—Pierre Radisson and Medard Chouart, the Sieur des Groseilliers. On a trip north from Lake Superior, in 1661, Radisson was impressed by the wealth of furs in the vicinity and by the possibility of taking them out by way of Hudson Bay. Angered at the confiscation by the Governor of New France of most of their "take" of furs from this trip, Radisson and Groseilliers took their bold plan to the English. So it was that in 1668, under the auspices of the English, Groseilliers carried on the first trade in furs in the area of Hudson Bay.

So successful was the expedition of 1668-69 that its backers, including Prince Rupert, cousin of King Charles II, sought a monopoly of trade out of Hudson Bay and its environs. On May 2, 1670, King Charles granted to "The Governor and Company of Adventurers of England Trading into Hudson Bay" a charter which gave them power to hold and alienate lands, plus the sole right of trade in Hudson Strait and the coastal area. This, to be known as Rupert's Land, was considered by the company, commonly called the Hudson's Bay Company, to include all land drained by waters finding their outlet in Hudson Bay.

The charter that set up, on parchment, the first governmental administration in the vast and unexplored area, including what was to become the Province of Saskatchewan, provided for the election of a governor, deputy governor, and managing committee of seven from among the shareholders, of whom there were originally 20. This group guided the company's affairs from London. In practice, by 1690 the management had devolved upon the committee, since the governor at that time, the Duke of Marlborough, brilliant ancestor of Winston Churchill, was too much concerned with continental wars to devote much time to company affairs.

The committee kept firm control of company affairs at home and abroad, dictating policies to its governors, factors, and traders in Rupert's Land. At the outset, a policy of fair dealing to all was laid down, as indicated by the company motto *Pro Pelle Cutem* (skin for skin), and rigid discipline was enforced. Hudson's Bay policy was, at this time, to wait at the bay for the Indians to come downriver with their furs.

With the establishment of the Hudson's Bay Company, the French, aware of this menace to the fur economy of New France, pushed west and south from Lake Superior, seeking always to trade directly with each Indian tribe encountered. Although the French were successful in sending parties overland from the St. Lawrence River to James Bay and by sea to the ports on the Churchill and Nelson rivers, emptying into Hudson Bay, their efforts were nullified by the Treaty of Utrecht, which ended 23 years of almost continuous war between the French and English.

The treaty required the French to give up their activities in the Hudson Bay periphery, but their fur trade in the interior continued to be successful. Here they exploited the Indian weakness for liquor, while adopting in part the Indian way of life. As early as 1690 the Hudson's Bay Company seems to have felt the effect of French contact with tribes west and north of the Great Lakes. In that year, Henry Kelsey, who had joined the company as a boy and was later to rise to the position of Governor in Chief on Hudson Bay, was sent inland by way of the Hayes-Nelson river route to prevail upon tribes of the interior to bring their furs to the bay. Kelsey, who recorded his travels, penetrated the Saskatchewan area beyond the site of Humboldt. He was the first Whiteman to view the Saskatchewan plains where roamed the great buffalo herds.

Competition for the fur trade of the northwest became increasingly intense in the 1700's. Under the leadership of the ambitious and energetic Le Verendrye, the French, while seeking a route to the western sea, built a line of trading forts connecting Lake Superior to Lake Winnipeg in the 1730's, and in the 1740's pushed west from Lake Winnipeg to establish posts on the banks of the Saskatchewan River.

Token money used by the Hudson's Bay Company

To offset the effects of the French intrusion into Rupert's Land, the Hudson's Bay Company modified its policy of "waiting at the Bay". In 1743 Henley House was erected about 150 miles inland on the Albany River. In 1754 Anthony Henday was dispatched on a mission comparable to that of Henry Kelsey. Henday travelled without European companions through hundreds of miles of Indian country, crossing the western plains to the foothills of the Rockies and suffering no violence to his person.

Thus French and English lines of rivalry had been extended to the Saskatchewan rivers. But once again the fortunes of war in Europe had an effect on this vast, lone land. In 1763 the Peace of Paris, ending the Seven Years' War, transferred New France to English sovereignty and the French had to abandon their posts on the Saskatchewan river system. But the French had blazed the trail from Montreal to the northwest, a trail readily followed and extended by aggressive Scottish and English traders who fell heir to the French trading tradition and system when the British took New France by conquest.

Voyageur carrying two ninety-pound "pieces" of pressed fur

These Canadian fur brigades, led mainly by hard-driving Scots and manned by virile French-Canadian voyageurs accustomed to native ways, introduced West Indies rum, processed by New England Puritans, into the fur trade and set up trading forts along the Saskatchewan River and beyond. Established thus on the routes to the bay, the Pedlars (so called by Hudson's Bay Company employees because the Pedlars traded with the natives in their lodges) were in a position to intercept the Indians on their way to Hudson Bay fur forts. Alarmed by the reduced volume of peltries arriving, not only by way of the Saskatchewan River, but also by the more northerly Churchill river system, the Hudson's Bay Company sent Samuel Hearne, the discoverer of the Coppermine River, inland, in 1774, to establish a post. He chose his site well; the strategically placed Cumberland House, on Cumberland Lake, became the first permanent settlement in what was to become the Province of Saskatchewan.

The Hudson's Bay Company had finally abandoned its policy of "waiting at the Bay". In the late 1770's, the intense competition resulted in further duplication of fur forts and extension of trading posts to fur country yet more remote from operational bases, with consequently increasing costs. North of the Saskatchewan River, the Frobisher brothers were trading on the Churchill River and in 1775-76 established a post at Ile à la Crosse. In 1778 that violent visionary from New England, Peter Pond, opened up the fur-rich Athabaska area.

Gun used as an article of trade

To meet the competition of the Pedlars the Hudson's Bay Company included brandy among its articles of trade. Previously the company had served liquor to Indians only as a welcoming gift and had depended for actual trading on guns, powder, shot, tobacco lengths, copper kettles, blankets, and knives, together with needles, awls, and other small articles highly prized by the natives.

In Europe, wine had been fermented and beer brewed during centuries previous to the discovery of distillation, with the result that Europeans had long been conditioned to potent alcoholic drink; but North American aboriginal men and women, exposed abruptly to distilled spirits, were disastrously affected.

The struggle for supremacy in the fur trade of the northwest had its economic roots in Europe's demand for fur, especially beaver,

Tobacco lengths used in trade

plus the Indian's insatiable desire for European products. While the Indians in their Stone Age culture were for the first time being introduced to manufactured articles, Europeans had long valued furs for their soft beauty, utility, and the outward sign they provided of prestige. Though the trade in North America greatly increased the availability of fur in the markets of Europe, the rarer ornamental furs, such as ermine (weasel) and fox, continued costly and consequently their use was confined to the very few. But the fur of the prolific beaver was made into

The beaver

hats in accordance with a fashion dating from
the Middle Ages. Hatters particularly prized the
beaver's downy underhair, because its barbed
and serrated fibres were eminently suitable for
felting, a process in which heat, moisture, and
pressure were combined to strengthen the
natural tendency of fibres to cling together
in a continuous mat without spinning or
weaving. So prominent was the beaver in the expanding fur trade,
its pelt became the standard by which the value of other furs, and
trading goods, was reckoned. For instance, in 1733 the trading value
of a Hudson's Bay woollen blanket was stated at six beaver pelts.
Beaver pelts varied in quality from the light-coloured, coarse-textured
fur found south of the Great Lakes, to the dark-coloured, fine-textured
variety taken in the northern forests. Most suitable for felting was
what the French called *castor gras,* the northern beaver pelt worn by
the Indian for winter warmth, fur side next his skin. The trader,
pushing further into the northwest, found yet more natives in possession of valuable furs and, at the same time, most anxious for
European articles of trade.

The beaver hat

Unlike the French who frolicked with the Indians and in some
instances won their intimate affection, or the Hudson's Bay Company
officials who were at great pains to be proper in their relationship with
the natives, the fast fortune-hunting, hard-driving Pedlars, though
they readily formed unions of convenience with native women, tended
to antagonize the Indian hunters. The Pedlars extended and encouraged the practice of advancing credit in order to keep the Indian
under constant obligation. If, after discharging his debt, he wanted
to pass on with his furs to trade at a rival post, the Pedlar, at times,
resorted to threats and violence to retain the trade. The Indians,
especially the proud people of the plains, did not readily submit to
such unceremonious treatment. In 1779 many Pedlars, singly or in
small groups at isolated posts, became victims of native vengeance, an
outstanding episode occurring at Eagle Hills in central Saskatchewan
where several Montrealers were killed and where the post and trading
goods had to be abandoned. So alarming did the situation become that
the Pedlars welcomed, at first, the smallpox epidemic of 1780-81,

which reduced the numbers of the natives and drove survivors deep
into the forest, from which they feared to emerge for trade.

While the smallpox, brought to North America by Europeans,
relieved the Pedlars of the Indian menace, it was, inevitably, disastrous
to the trade. The resultant loss, together with acts of violence
among the independent traders themselves, caused some of the leading
Montreal-based traders to band together in the North West Company
of 1784. Other trading concerns, together with disaffected North
West Company men, including Alexander Mackenzie, coalesced in
1800 to form the New North West Company, commonly called
the XY Company because of its method of marking trade goods.
Rivalry between the two Montreal-based concerns reached such
intensity and resulted in such serious losses, a need for further union
became both obvious and imperative. Union of the two was effected
in 1804 under the name of the North West Company.

The formation of the North West Company ushered in a period
of even more intense rivalry. The Hudson's Bay Company met the
situation by establishing further trading posts in the interior. The
North West Company also established new posts and consolidated
older ones. It demanded audaciously the privilege of shipping via
the Hudson Bay. When peaceful pressure failed, the new company
resorted even to outright violence. Soon a state of virtual war existed.
This intolerable situation was brought to an end in 1821 when the
two rivals merged under the name of the older establishment, the
Hudson's Bay Company. To effect a union of spirit the pugnacious
Governor Williams was replaced by George Simpson, who was vested
with adequate authority and who combined sufficient energy with
wisdom to accomplish a difficult task.

If we could project ourselves back to the time of intense fur
trade rivalry and could travel up the Saskatchewan river system
with one of the competing fur brigades, we should see clusters of
fur forts, either in operation or recently abandoned, marking every
strategic point along the fast-flowing waterway. Between the present
Manitoba-Saskatchewan boundary and the forks of the Saskatchewan
rivers, nine trading posts would be seen in groups of two or three at
Cumberland House, Hungry Hall, Nipawin, and Fort St. Louis.
Between the forks and the site on which years later Saskatoon was

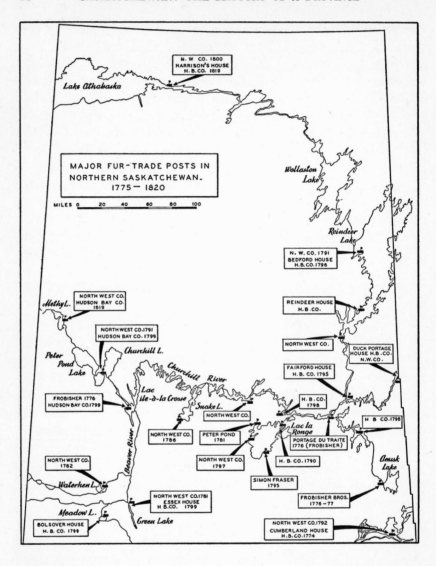

built, were four trading establishments on the South Saskatchewan River, while at Chesterfield House, near the Saskatchewan-Alberta border, was another cluster of forts. West of the forks on the North Saskatchewan River were some eight trading posts.

In Saskatchewan's Pre-Cambrian Region rival fur forts were also established: on Lake Athabaska, Fond du Lac, Reindeer Lake, and the

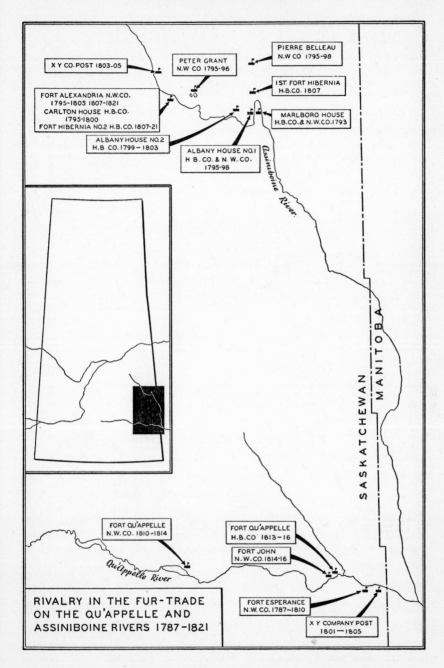

XY CO. POST 1803-05

PETER GRANT
N.W CO 1795-96

PIERRE BELLEAU
N.W CO 1795-98

1ST. FORT HIBERNIA
H.B.CO. 1807

FORT ALEXANDRIA N.W.CO.
1795-1805 1807-1821
CARLTON HOUSE H.B.CO.
1795-1800
FORT HIBERNIA NO.2 H.B.CO. 1807-21

ALBANY HOUSE NO.2
H.B CO. 1799-1803

MARLBORO HOUSE
H.B.CO. & N.W.CO.1793

ALBANY HOUSE NO.1
H.B.CO. & N.W.CO.
1795-98

Assiniboine River

SASKATCHEWAN

MANITOBA

FORT QU'APPELLE
N.W. CO. 1810-1814

FORT QU'APPELLE
H.B.CO 1813-16

FORT JOHN
N.W.CO.1814-16

FORT ESPERANCE
N.W.CO. 1787-1810

X Y COMPANY POST
1801-1805

Qu'Appelle River

RIVALRY IN THE FUR-TRADE
ON THE QU'APPELLE AND
ASSINIBOINE RIVERS 1787-1821

Churchill River, while similar competition was in evidence at Ile
à la Crosse and Green Lake. In the Parklands and Plains regions
there was comparable duplication on the Swan, Assiniboine, and
Qu'Appelle rivers. In all there were more than three dozen strongly
manned posts in an area that, after the union of 1821, the Hudson's
Bay Company operated with little more than a dozen trading
posts, requiring a fraction of the personnel.

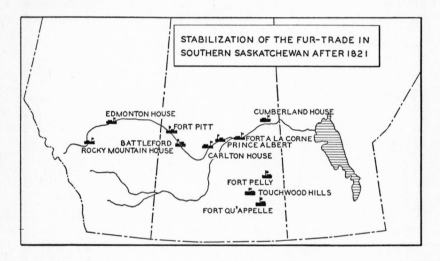

While the union of 1821, a 21-year agreement, ended hostilities
between rival trading companies in the northwest, it did not
settle the form of government in that territory. The adoption of
the name of the older concern, Hudson's Bay Company, was indicative of the desire of all parties to the agreement to enjoy the
benefits of the 1670 charter, the validity of which had so recently
been questioned. By the broadest interpretation of the charter's terms,
the area included could be deemed to extend only to the sources of
rivers finding their outlet in Hudson Bay. Long before 1821 the
relentless energy of the partners of the North West Company had
carried these hard-driving men to the western slopes of the Cordillera
and to the valleys of the Peace, Athabaska, and Mackenzie rivers,
which drain northward to the Arctic Ocean. A system of trading
posts in these areas was one of the main contributions of the North

West Company to the assets of the united concern and in 1821 a special licence for 21 years was granted, extending trading privileges of the Hudson's Bay Company to the Pacific.

While no attempt was made to define the area covered by the charter, government acceptance, in 1822, of company plans for a system of administration and law in the area under its control, including the District of Assiniboia, south of Lake Winnipeg, could be considered tacit acknowledgement that the Red River settlement was within the chartered area.

In the initial organization of the union period, Sir George Simpson was governor of the Northern Department, which extended from Hudson Bay to the Pacific Ocean. As such he was superior to the governor of the Southern Department, a smaller area south of the bay. A third department was set up to oversee Hudson's Bay Company interests in Montreal. The tremendous Northern Department, which eventually established its headquarters at Norway House at the north end of Lake Winnipeg on the Nelson river route to Hudson Bay, was subdivided into districts so as to facilitate administration. The area of what is now the Province of Saskatchewan was divided among several districts, the largest portion, including the grassy plains between the Saskatchewan River and 49th parallel, being in the Saskatchewan District, which had headquarters at Edmonton House. The remainder of the Saskatchewan area was divided among the Cumberland, English River, and Athabaska districts.

The elimination of rival fur transport brigades and the reduction in the number of fur forts and personnel resulted in the northwest's first unemployment problem. To cope with it, the company settled many former employees, together with their native wives and children, in the Red River valley in the vicinity of St. Boniface and Fort Garry, where, it was hoped, they would engage in agricultural pursuits. Many of the Halfbreeds, unable to adjust to a pastoral life, turned quite naturally to spring and autumn buffalo hunts on the open plains west of the settlement. In this manner they provided themselves with a livelihood plus something of the excitement akin to the bygone days of rival fur trade, and the Métis especially came to regard themselves as a proud race apart from both their Indian and their European progenitors.

Meanwhile the trading posts became centres of an orderly business. Not only were furs procured at strategic points such as Edmonton House and Fort Carlton in the Saskatchewan District, but also preserved buffalo meat in the form of the all-important pemmican was sent from these points east, west, and north by York boat, packhorse, and canoe. In the company's water transport system the finely responsive canoe was the fast, light express, while the bargelike York boat, powered by oar and auxiliary sail, was the freighter.

The new order and stability in the fur trade was enhanced by the company's efforts to reduce the Indians' consumption of liquor. Another factor contributing to the relative orderliness of life in the territory governed by the Hudson's Bay Company was the extension, after the union, of services offered by various church organizations.

The Christian symbol, the Cross

The company had retained Church of England chaplains at its fur forts on Hudson Bay, and lay reading of the Holy Bible was mandatory at inland trading posts. But the first serious attempt to have resident missionaries ministering to the Métis and Indians of the northwest was made in 1818 when two Roman Catholic priests, including Father Provencher, arrived in the Red River settlement. After 1821, the company assisted missionaries of various faiths and beliefs to establish missions in the hope that the natives in particular, and the people generally, would be guided to peaceable and orderly behaviour. The first resident Anglican missionary at the Red River, Reverend J. West, included the prairie area in his territory. A practice was adopted whereby natives were trained for missionary work. These would, it was hoped, become fitted to promulgate the Word of God in conformity with Anglican doctrine. In 1845, an Anglican mission established at Lac la Ronge was tended by a layman, James Beardy. In 1852, Reverend Henry Budd, the first ordained native, who as a catechist had served in 1840 at Cumberland, started a mission at Nipawin. In 1857, a permanent Anglican mission was set up at Qu'Appelle. Church missionary work in the rough and forbidding northland, or in the prairie area to the south, required men of confirmed conviction, faithful patience, and enduring physique. The Roman Catholic Church assigned this onerous task to its Oblate Fathers (Oblates of Mary Immaculate), the first of whom arrived in 1845. An early arrival was a dedicated young novice, Alexander Taché, who, some eight years later was to succeed Provencher as Bishop of St. Boniface. His task of disseminating the Catholic faith in the northwest took him, early in his career, to the mission of Ile à la Crosse. A year before the Oblate priests reached the Red River, the first Grey Nuns had been welcomed to the colony.

The initial group of Wesleyan missionaries began their activities in 1840. The leader of this group was Reverend James Evans, who performed the laborious task of creating a system of syllabic symbols for the Cree language so as to enable natives of that linguistic group to read the Scriptures for themselves. Best known of Evans' associates were the McDougall brothers, John and George, pioneer Methodist missionaries in the upper Saskatchewan river valleys. The Presbyterians of Kildonan on the Red River were served by the Anglican clergy there until a minister of their own faith, Rev. John Black, arrived in 1851 to satisfy a long-standing demand. The first Presbyterian mission west of the Red River was begun by Rev. James Nisbet at Prince Albert in 1866.

The combined missionary and educational policy of the Hudson's Bay Company was initiated in London. Ile à la Crosse, Buffalo Narrows, and Lake Athabaska trading posts early received the benefit of Roman Catholic instruction, while Lac la Ronge and Cumberland House were served by Anglicans. The Roman Catholic Church eventually established missions throughout most of northern Saskatchewan. The Hudson's Bay Company made financial grants to various religious denominations for the construction of church and school buildings and toward the salaries of the missionaries. These, in most instances, became the school teachers, from whom

Métis and Indians were to learn reading and writing, together with something of the rudiments of arithmetic and farmstead practice.

The combined missionary and educational policy, as laid down by the London Committee of the Hudson's Bay Company, did not always meet with favour from the company officials resident in the northwest. Sir George Simpson, in private letters, expressed a view that the type of education offered to the Indian and the Halfbreed meant rearing the natives in habits of indolence and "will be attended with little other good than filling the pockets and bellies of some hungry missionaries and school-masters". Yet Sir George Simpson, together with the lesser commissioned gentlemen and company servants, loyally put into effect the new policy, though they considered the missionaries meddlesome, particularly when Sunday travel was banned "when the voyageurs were engaged in a race against bad weather".

While the influence of the missionaries was considerable, the word of the chief factor in charge of several trading posts was, within the terms of the company's policy, law in the area. But the chief factor's primary function was to enhance the profits of an orderly fur trade, and his attitude was that of the disciplined and dignified merchant. His first duty being to his company, he was seldom eager to govern for the sake of governing. To help maintain his dignity and prestige, he wore a high black beaver hat, black or dark blue trousers, white shirt with collar to his ears, velvet stock, and frock coat. But there were occasions of winter travel when the penetrating cold of the country forced him to resort to the frontier apparel of wind-resistant, soft-tanned leather and ear-protecting fur cap. Proud was the Indian chief who received a chief factor's cast-off London-made beaver high hat, an article to be reserved for special occasions of summer wear and for indoor ceremonial purposes during winter.

During the early 1800's the hitherto fashionable hard and high beaver hat was giving way to the silk hat of similar proportions. By 1840 the change in fashion had diminished the hatters' demand for beaver fur to such an extent that the Hudson's Bay Company reduced the trading value of beaver pelts and encouraged the Indians to bring in the pelts of smaller furbearing animals.

Attempts to utilize buffalo wool in manufactures comparable to cloth woven from sheep wool were not successful, because of the difficulty of readily separating the short, thick wool close to the hide from the longer, coarse hairs. Though the trading value of buffalo hides was not great, the vast buffalo herds on the open plains provided mounted Indians and Métis with an ample supply of food for themselves and a surplus for trade.

The Indians of the Canadian plains had discarded the dog for the exciting mobility of the horse. This significant change began about 1730. Not indigenous to the Americas, the horses, of Asiatic-Arabian-Moorish-Spanish ancestry, on which Indians were mounted when the first Europeans explored the far western Canadian plains, had strayed or were stolen, or sometimes traded, from as far south as the Rio Grande.

Subsequently the lively Métis settlement in the Red River valley depended on the horse, both to run down and kill the buffalo and to pull their two-wheeled Red River carts loaded with hides and pemmican obtained by the spring and autumn forays westward into buffalo country. By 1840 as many as 1,200 carts were assembled for the spring hunt, in which several thousand buffalo might be killed. As the number of buffalo diminished in the vicinity of the Red River, the hunting parties pushed farther westward, reaching eventually the plains of Saskatchewan. Such large hunting assemblies necessitated organization, and consequently the Métis on their hunts devised their own form of government. No one was to run buffalo before the elected president gave the general order. No rider was permitted to break formation, to ride ahead, or to lag behind unless instructed to do so. For the first breach of regulations, the offender's bridle and saddle were cut up and rendered useless; a second offence meant that his leather coat was ripped from his back and cut up; a third offence drew the penalty of public flogging. Any man or woman convicted of theft of an article, no matter how petty, was made to stand in the midst of the encampment while the camp crier thrice called out his or her name, each time adding the word "thief".

Following a mass slaughter of buffalo, the women and children cut up the meat and began the laborious process of making pemmican to replenish the stores in the settlement. The greatest delicacy of buffalo meat was the tongue, and the number of slain buffalo was reckoned by the number of tongues counted.

While Métis and Indians ran buffalo on Saskatchewan's open plains, the Hudson's Bay Company, under the watchful eye of the omnipresent Governor Simpson, carried on an orderly fur trade in the Forest and Pre-Cambrian regions. The elimination, as a result of union, of costly competition enabled the company to limit the take of beaver furs, thus renewing a policy of fur conservation that had been suspended during the period of severe competition.

Nevertheless, Canadian critics of the company, disliking its monopolistic attitude, challenged the validity of its charter and caused the company sufficient concern to induce the owners to apply for a renewal of their licence in 1838, four years before it was to expire. As requested, the British Government renewed the licence until 1859.

This precaution of the Hudson's Bay Company resulted merely in delaying the inevitable. The orderly giant of the western fur trade could not halt indefinitely at the bounds of his domain the tide of political and economic progress. Caught in the cross currents of Canadian political aspirations and American expansionist policies, the ruling company was to be confined, in the 1850's and 1860's, to the function of merchant-trader.

Prior to the formation of the Dominion of Canada, a French-speaking Lower Canada along the lower St. Lawrence River and an English-speaking Upper Canada along the upper St. Lawrence and the northern shore of Lake Ontario were recognized. No geographical barrier separated Lower and Upper Canada, but social and economic differences were accentuated by language and religion. These differences were reflected in the midcentury Canadian political life, which became increasingly stormy. Personal and group animosities sharpened. Some politicians proposed that legislative union, once considered as a solution, be replaced by a federal union. Others, regarded by many as impractical enthusiasts and visionaries, favoured a federal union to include the colonial settlements of the Maritimes and eventually the northwestern territory of the Hudson's Bay Company.

Canadian advocates of such confederation included, by the late 1850's, Scottish-born John A. Macdonald, the bold, witty, but patient political genius who eventually succeeded in uniting elements of both political parties who were willing to compromise, under the banner of the Liberal-Conservative Party. Such men were undaunted by the physical difficulties involved in uniting the northwest territory with Canada. Realizing a lengthy delay at this stage might forever frustrate their plan for transcontinental federation, they urged upon the initially unenthusiastic United Kingdom Government the necessity of forestalling possible action by American expansionists, who were turning bold eyes to the virtually empty British northwest.

When, in the fulfilment of her "manifest destiny", the United States pushed westward to the Pacific coast through the Oregon territory, controlled jointly by that nation and Great Britain, enthusiasm for republicanism and anti-British sentiment were expressed by Americans with whom the Métis of the Red River settlement were in contact in the course of carrying on an illicit and profitable fur trade across the border. This contact deepened the discontent of the French Halfbreeds who already felt that their rights as native-born northwesterners had been usurped by the Hudson's Bay Company. However, the peaceful settlement of the Oregon boundary dispute and the presence of British troops on the Red River in 1846 caused the Métis to discard their ideas of direct action and to turn to constitutional means of attack on the Hudson's Bay Company. Exaggerated charges of maladministration in the Red River settlement and mistreatment of the Indians elsewhere were laid against the company in petitions to the Crown.

These petitions, together with continuing agitation of Canadians for union of the northwest with Canada, led in 1857 to consideration, by a select committee of the British House of Commons, of the Hudson's Bay Company's eligibility for a renewal of its licence in 1859, and of the possibility of colonization in the area under charter to the company.

Great Britain at this time was more interested in extending freer trade than in maintaining traditional colonial controls. The committee's findings contributed, in 1858, to the establishment of the colony of British Columbia and led to the lapsing, in 1859, of the Hudson's Bay Company's licence for a monopoly of trade outside the Hudson Bay watershed. Of more lasting importance to Saskatchewan was an examination of the region with regard to agricultural possibilities.

In 1857, two separate expeditions, one from Britain under Captain John Palliser and one from Canada under S. J. Dawson and Professor H. Y. Hind, were sent to the northwest to make a general examination of the area. In their reports they were to include opinions concerning the suitability of the Plains and Parkland regions for colonization. Both reports roughly indicated a fertile parkland belt suitable for agriculture and a semi-arid area of open plains considered not suitable for agriculture. Palliser included in his semi-arid area more of the general prairie area than did Professor Hind. The optimistic Hind, probably because he reflected the desires of the Canadian expansionists, in his report described a larger area as potentially agricultural.

Both expeditions recognized problems of setting up lines of communication and transportation over the rough and forbidding thousand miles of bush, rock, lake, and muskeg separating Upper Canada from the prairie west, but arrived at different conclusions. Palliser considered the only practical plan was to link up with railway lines of the United States. Dawson proposed a road-water route from Lake Superior to Lake Winnipeg, while Hind, whose optimism tended to override physical obstacles, considered practicable a diversion of the South Saskatchewan River into the Qu'Appelle so as to provide water transportation across the southern prairie land. Both parties considered the Hudson's Bay Company, preoccupied with the fur trade, incapable of governing well any extensive settled colony. Canadians therefore sought a transfer of the territory, but no agreement had been reached when, in 1863, ownership of the Hudson's Bay Company changed hands. While the new management was more receptive to British and Canadian proposals for railway and telegraph lines and for colonization of the prairie, it made difficult the actual transfer of the area (in 1869-70) by its failure to consult either its employees in Rupert's Land or the settlers on the Red River concerning the negotiations with the British Government.

While these negotiations were in progress, plans for federal union of all the colonies of British North America were being drawn up at Quebec. These plans allowed sufficient local control to allay the fears of the French-Canadians and sufficient cash inducement to win Nova Scotia and New Brunswick. The Quebec Resolutions allowed for future admission of other colonies into the federation but failed to mention the Red River settlement. These resolutions, given the form of a bill at the London Conference of 1866 and passed by the British Parliament as the British North America Act, became effective on July 1, 1867, when the federation of the two Canadas, Nova Scotia, and New Brunswick became a political entity as the Dominion of Canada.

Simultaneously, the enterprising and expansive nation to the south, the United States of America, accelerated its push westward across the great central plains to the mountains and the Pacific coast. There was apprehension in Canada that land-eager settlers of frontier Minnesota might occupy arable land in the territory still nominally governed by the Hudson's Bay Company. The United States had purchased Alaska from the Russian Government, and, it was thought, might persuade the colony of British Columbia to throw in its lot, for economic advantage, with the United States. Therefore the new Canadian Government, led by its first prime minister, Sir John A. Macdonald, who visualized a Canada from the Atlantic to the Pacific, sent two of its ministers to London to negotiate with the owners of the Hudson's Bay Company. On the recommendation of the Imperial Government, an agreement was reached whereby the Hudson's Bay Company was to receive £300,000 (approximately $1,500,000) and retain a block of land surrounding each trading post, and in addition one-twentieth part of each township in the "fertile belt" yet to be surveyed. The company was to surrender claim to all other territory and abandon its exclusive trading privileges. The British Parliament passed an act in 1868 empowering the Imperial Government to accept surrender of the territory on the terms agreed upon, and the Canadian Parliament made temporary provision for administration of the area, which it named the Northwest Territories. Thus the centre of control was transferred from London to Ottawa.

The "Act for the Temporary Government of Rupert's Land and the North West Territory when united with Canada", passed by the Canadian Parliament, offered no specific guarantee of land titles to settlers already established in the northwest, an omission that, together with the apparent lapse of authority in the northwest between the time of the signing of the Deed of Surrender and the transfer of the land to Canada by order-in-council, was in some measure responsible for the aggravated discontent in the Red River settlement. While an order-in-council subsequent to the Act for Temporary Government did indicate that established settlers' rights, including squatters', would be respected, the intent of the order-in-council was not made clear to the settlers, who had little or no previous experience with mathematical surveys and legal titles. The intention of the Macdonald government seems to have been fair. In practice the government failed to clarify its intention and policy to a people uninformed concerning either. Thus the resultant Red River disturbance largely arose from misunderstanding. Roman Catholic priests of French origin, who sought to guide the affairs of the Métis, regarded this portion of the Red River settlement as a frontier duplication of the eastern St. Lawrence River settlements, and these clerics cherished an ambition to nourish a type of society similar to that prevailing in rural Quebec. The Métis regarded themselves as a distinct though native group, neither Indian nor French-Canadian. The Métis, contented with their successful buffalo-hunting economy and free way of life, feared the rumoured prospect of an agricultural expansion from an English-speaking Ontario said to be intolerant of the Métis way of life. In dark-eyed, nervous Louis Riel, a miller's son with an indubitable but not readily disciplined imagination combined with an acknowledged oratorical prowess and a brooding sense of mission, the Métis found both spokesman and leader for their "nation". While leading his own people, Riel succeeded in neutralizing opposition of local English-speaking settlers to the Métis movement. He proceeded to set up a "Provisional Government" and took over Fort Garry, where he flew an improvised Métis flag at the masthead. His "Bill of Rights" was to influence the eventual drawing of the Act for the establishment of the Province of Manitoba.

During the Red River disturbance Thomas Scott, an ardent Orangeman whose abusive language and threats toward the "Provisional Government" disturbed Riel and his group, was jailed, condemned, and executed by order of Riel's "Provisional Government". Although Scott had acquired no organized local following, his death at the hands of French-Indian Halfbreeds of Roman Catholic persuasion became, largely through the Ontario press, a sensation which resulted in Canada's sending a military force, under Lieutenant Colonel Garnet Wolseley, to the gateway of the Canadian northwest. The purpose of Colonel Wolseley's mission was not primarily to put down an armed rebellion of doubtful existence, but to ensure a peaceful assumption of administrative power by Lieutenant Governor Archibald when he would arrive to begin his duties as the first chief executive of the newly formed Province of Manitoba (1870) and the Northwest Territories, and to serve notice to the United States that Canada was prepared to defend its new possessions in the west. Although Riel decamped to the States, some militiamen from Ontario encouraged, and in several instances actively assisted, settlers who had opposed Louis Riel and his "Provisional Government", to demonstrate their ardent loyalty to the Queen by persecuting the Métis. To escape this bullying and to be closer to the buffalo country, many Halfbreeds trekked westward to settle in wooded valleys of the North and South Saskatchewan rivers, while a few families made new homes in the valley of the Qu'Appelle River and the Willowbunch area.

The area of the Northwest Territories eventually to become the Province of Saskatchewan was now governed by a lieutenant governor. The 200 year-old rule of the northwest, "the great lone land", by the Gentlemen Adventurers of England trading into Hudson Bay thus came to a close, while the function of the Hudson's Bay Company became restricted to that of a trading concern unprotected by legal provisions upholding a monopoly.

In Europe, Spain and Portugal previously had lost their initial advantage in the continuing drive for far-flung exploration, exploitation, and world commerce. France had failed to maintain its early foothold on the North American continent, but French culture would long be felt in an expanding Canada.

Great Britain, leading the industrial revolution and controlling the sea lanes of world commerce, was achieving, in these 200 years, its zenith of power and influence. Within the United Kingdom of Queen Victoria an expansive urban population, heartened by a wider franchise, was reaching toward a higher standard of living. Parallel with the surge toward popular government were new and revolutionary inventions, the railway locomotive, the steel-hulled ships, the telegraph, and the tempered ploughshare; these and related developments were soon to have an irresistible impact on the great grasslands of Saskatchewan.

4

Survey, Steel, and Settlers

CONFEDERATION meant little initial change in the Pre-Cambrian northland of primal forest, rock, and lake, where the Indians continued to barter their fur catch in orderly trade at Hudson's Bay Company posts.

To the south, over the greater extent of the Parklands and Plains regions, wandering bands of Indians and Métis continued to follow the yet plentiful buffalo herds. In wooded river valleys, at widely scattered points, the Hudson's Bay Company maintained trading posts loosely linked by horse and ox-drawn Red River cart trains in summer, and sleighdog teams in winter. Most travelled overland route was the Carlton Trail linking the Red River settlements of Manitoba with Edmonton House via Fort Ellice and Fort Carlton. West of Fort Ellice, where the main cart trail angled northward toward the Touchwood Hills, a subsidiary trail continued west to Fort Qu'Appelle. From the main route west of Fort Ellice, a branch reached northward to Fort Pelly. Squealing, wooden-axled, two-wheeled carts, carrying trading goods, and occasional passengers, were owned and operated mainly by Halfbreeds to whom life on the open trail was a lure of economic importance second only to the buffalo hunt.

In the Duck Lake, St. Laurent, and Batoche area, where wood for shelter and fuel was plentiful on the northern edge of the great buffalo range, there wintered growing numbers of French Halfbreeds, that is, Métis, who had trekked northwestward from the Red River valley where encroaching agricultural settlement and an embryo, but expanding, civilization of the European pattern were not to their liking. By the banks of the South Saskatchewan River the Métis built their log huts for warmth and shelter from winter's icy winds. But when the snows melted and the prairie crocus bloomed with spring, the men, women, and children again prepared for the nomadic way of the buffalo hunt on the open plains to the south. Numerically smaller groups wintered in the Qu'Appelle River Valley, Touchwood Hills, and in the Wood Mountain—Willow Bunch area. Roman Catholic missionaries, who ministered to the Métis of French-Indian background, had little initial success in attempts to persuade them to adopt permanent settlement and pastoral ways. As early as 1869 the redoubtable Father André visited the wintering place at Duck Lake, and subsequently a mission was established at nearby St. Laurent.

On the south bank of the North Saskatchewan River were the Prince Albert settlement and, nearby, an English-speaking settlement started by James Isbister in 1862. These English-speaking Halfbreeds were ministered to by Reverend James Nisbet, who established a Presbyterian mission there in 1866. Like the Métis, the English-speaking Halfbreeds, whose fathers and grandfathers were mainly Scottish, staked out their holdings on narrow strips of river frontage. They too hunted the buffalo, but supplemented their diet with potatoes and other hardy vegetables grown in their garden plots. Less nomadic and more inclined to permanent settlement were these Halfbreeds of Scottish and English origin.

At this time, when neither police nor courts had been established, the Hudson's Bay Company, though no longer responsible for governing the Northwest Territories, continued its influence in the direction of orderly behaviour in the immediate vicinity of company posts.

This influence, together with the moral persuasion of the missionaries and a less clearly defined inclination of the shifting population itself, was the sole support for law and order. In areas remote from the settlements, the improvised government of the buffalo hunt prevailed among the Métis, while the Indians remained free to deal with theft and murder in accordance with ancient tribal custom.

In the Cypress Hills down in Saskatchewan's southwest corner, there was neither Hudson's Bay Company trading post, church mission, nor attempt at agricultural settlement. A hunter's paradise, the coveted hills with their lush grass carpet and sky-aspiring timber were a social no-man's land where Indian war parties ambushed people of other Indian bands and itinerant Métis horsemen unable to resist the lure of this "good country and bad medicine". In this geologically unique and socially fabulous place adjacent to the 49th parallel, Indians and Halfbreeds were in turn the victims of itinerant, Montana-based traders of doubtful but violent character who crossed the then unsurveyed international border to barter raw whiskey, sometimes spiked with tobacco juice, for buffalo hides. Here lawless abandon was the order of the day. Murder, rape, arson, and horse-theft at gunpoint were the more spectacular manifestations of generally accepted brigandage. For freebooting traders of European origin there was ready profit in trading firewater to the Indians in exchange for buffalo hides, then in steady demand by the eastern manufacturers of fashionable sleigh robes. For the aborigine, the trade resulted in demoralization and the accelerated disintegration of the native culture.

The mounting slaughter of the buffalo in the Saskatchewan area was temporarily retarded when, in the summer of 1870, another epidemic of smallpox broke out among the Indians. In this emergency Lieutenant Governor Archibald appointed a council of three—an Englishman, a French Halfbreed, and a Hudson's Bay Company representative (a Scot)—to try somehow to cope with the rampant disease rapidly decimating the Indian population. The council in turn appointed a Saskatchewan board of health, composed mainly of missionaries. In an effort to stop the spread of smallpox, the sending of furs out of the area was temporarily prohibited. Native consumption of liquor, brought in by independent traders, was considered to have added to the ravages of the smallpox plague by lowering the natives' resistance to disease. Hudson's Bay Company officials together with the missionaries advocated legislation and enforcement to prevent the sale of spirituous liquors in the Northwest Territories.

In the United States the axe-conditioned pioneer had long hesitated on the treeless threshold of the windswept open plain where wood for fuel and shelter was scarce, or non-existent. Steel in new forms was an essential to westward expansion and settlement: the steel-barrelled six-shooter to deal ruthlessly with hostile bands of mounted Indians reluctant to relinquish their buffalo country; the steel-axled, four-wheeled covered wagon for transporting settlers and their supplies; the steel plough for turning over the tough prairie sod; the steel chain of the land surveyor; and finally steel rails for steam trains which brought in barbed wire for fences, the deep well-boring machine and metal-bladed windmill for pumping water from the depths of the earth, equipment for the mechanical grain elevator, lumber for buildings, firewood and coal for the settler's cookstove and for the trains themselves, which were to carry the settlers' livestock and grain eastward to expanding markets in industrial towns. In the United States the great plains adjoined the older settled areas. There a venturesome man and his wife and family could load their belongings in a prairie schooner, hitch up the oxen or horses, and trek northward.

In Canada, a thousand miles of agriculturally non-productive, harsh, and forbidding bush, lake, and rock separated the old settlements from Canada's newly acquired Plains and Parklands regions. This geographical barrier, a southern indentation of the Pre-Cambrian Shield, precluded a westward wagon trek similar to the pre-railway settler's to the south. Thus Canadian Government policies, plans, and their implementation necessarily preceded intensive settlement of Canada's prairie west and resulted in a more orderly and much less violent penetration. In Canada's far west of the early 1870's, frontier gun-play was in evidence only in southern Alberta and the Cypress Hills region of southwestern Saskatchewan, and this lawless condition was an influx from the adjacent state of Montana. Establishment of law and order in the Northwest Territories, confinement of the Indians on reserves to release large tracts of potentially agricultural land for survey, steel, and settlement, the financing and building of telegraph and railway lines into the "great lone land", now concerned the Canadian Government. It was early recognized that venture capital for railway construction would not be readily forthcoming. Not only was the vast expanse of the Canadian west virtually unsettled and therefore non-productive of revenue in return for freight and passenger service, but there was also little immediate hope that the thousand miles of bush, lake, and rock, through which a trans-Canada railway must pass, would become a revenue producing area. The Canadian Government was soon convinced that, if a railway linking Montreal and Toronto with Vancouver on the Pacific coast was to become both a reality and a commercially feasible project, the potentially agricultural land of the Province of Manitoba and the westward area that was to become Saskatchewan and Alberta provinces must eventually bear, in one form or another, much of the financial burden of railway construction and subsequent operation. To pay for the railway, intensive agricultural settlement was essential. Equally essential to agricultural settlement and production was the realization of the railway. Thus the railway must precede the settlers, but land settlement should follow the steel rails as rapidly as they could be laid down.

Ahead of both steel rails and settlers came the government surveyors, rugged and resourceful men, who moved by Red River cart in summer and dogsled in winter. The international boundary itself was marked by American and Canadian surveyors jointly. This 49th parallel became known to the Indians as a "Medicine Line". Some United States Indians, such as Sitting Bull and his band, found they could escape the encroachment of both the gun-toting frontiersmen and the U. S. Cavalry by crossing the line into Canada.

Perhaps the Canadian Government would have awaited the penetration of its projected railway line before sending a police force westward, but reports of a band of Assiniboine Indians massacred in the Cypress Hills hastened the formation of the North West Mounted Police, who travelled overland by horseback and the Red River cart to reach, in 1874, the scene of mass murder committed a year or so before by desperadoes from Montana.

On May 23, 1873, the Canadian Parliament passed an act providing for a council for the Northwest Territories. In April of that year Prime Minister Sir John A. Macdonald had introduced a mounted police bill, which also became an act on May 23. By the terms of this latter act, the force was to be under military discipline, though civil authority. Mounted Police, rather than Mounted Rifles, was the term preferred, so as not to offend U. S. authorities who might be resentful of a military force so close to the international boundary. It was stipulated that the North West Mounted Police were to wear scarlet, especially bright red coats so as to attract recruits and impress the natives. Wolseley's drab-uniformed Canadian militia in the expedition of 1870 had not been popular. Recruits were to be hardy, adaptable, amenable to discipline, and capable of individual initiative. In subsequent practice they were also to know the letter of the law as well as having a shrewd appreciation of the day to day difficulties of the prairie frontier. An inducement to signing on was an offer of land at expiration of service. Organizer of the force was Lieutenant Colonel Frederick White; the first commissioner was Lieutenant Colonel George A. French.

In 1873-74, 150 men, enlisted mainly in central Canada, were in training at the old stone fort in the Winnipeg area. Colonel French, during his first month in the west, was certain that the force must attain its full objective strength of 300, or, better still, exceed that strength, if it was to deal effectively with lawlessness in the vast Northwest Territories. Additional recruiting early in 1874 brought the force to a strength of more than 300.

Lieutenant Colonel J. F. MacLeod was appointed Assistant Commissioner of the force that assembled at the International Boundary Commission quarters at Dufferin in southern Manitoba. From Dufferin the recruits from central and eastern Canada, together with partially trained men from the Winnipeg area, began their long and arduous ride westward. The main contingent was routed through the semi-arid country of the southern open plains to be near minor trouble spots. They wished to reach Cypress Hills as rapidly as possible, to proceed on to the infamous Fort Whoop-Up at the junction of the Belly and St. Mary rivers, and at the same time to maintain contact en route with the boundary commission, which gave assistance in providing feed for the horses and other supplies. En route, oxen strayed from the camps at night; once the horses stampeded. On still days a cloud of mosquitoes hovered over the line of march while good water for man and beast was often difficult to find in a shortgrass land of shallow alkali lake and pothole. A few men deserted and those who remained were conditioned for the frontier rigours to come. When the vanguard reached Fort Whoop-Up of the whisky traders from Benton, Montana, the Stars and Stripes was flying from a mast but the fort was abandoned. The establishment of the mounted police post at Fort Walsh brought an end to the disreputable condition in the Cypress Hills. The initial mounted police outposts looked mainly to Montana for supplies. In Benton, on the Missouri River steamboat route, was located the enterprising and reliable trading firm and general outfitters, the I. G. Baker Company, whose long bullteams brought food and building materials for the police forts and provided pioneer artisans for construction. From Montana came the cheerful and indomitable Jerry Potts, son of a Piegan Indian mother and White trader, whose practical knowledge of frontier trails and ways became indispensable to a police force in the process of becoming conditioned to exacting work in a new environment.

Meanwhile the Canadian Government was clarifying its land and railway policies for the area. The land policy was partly predetermined by agreements made prior to taking over the territory; one-twentieth of the "fertile belt" went to the Hudson's Bay Company. This fraction constituted section 8 and three-quarters of section 26 in each township, and section 8 and all of 26 in townships with numbers divisible by five.

Under the Manitoba Act of 1870, the Canadian Government retained control of public lands in that province. In the other provinces, because of different historical developments, the lands were already under provincial jurisdiction. In the Northwest Territories, the public lands remained under dominion jurisdiction, necessary at that time since the Canadian Government had agreed to compensate the Hudson's Bay Company in part through lands and in part through money raised by sale of lands. Retention of land control by Ottawa involved railway settlement policy as well. To discourage U. S. ambitions, the Canadian Government undertook a rapid and uniform settlement of the prairie west. This required a uniform survey system and the introduction of a free homestead policy, similar to that which had so rapidly attracted land-eager settlers in the midwestern United States.

To bring the land survey system in line with that of the U. S. west, the 640-acre square survey system was adopted. The intention was to have the survey completed prior to agricultural settlement, in order that the survey might be uniform throughout the area. But the riverfront pattern of settlement, previously established by Half-breed squatters in the valley of the South Saskatchewan River and other river valleys, required some local modification of the survey plans. The first Dominion Lands Act of 1872 provided for a free homestead of 160 acres for incoming settlers. There was a three-year residence clause, and a nominal fee of $10. In addition, the government was prepared to make available grazing leases on lands considered

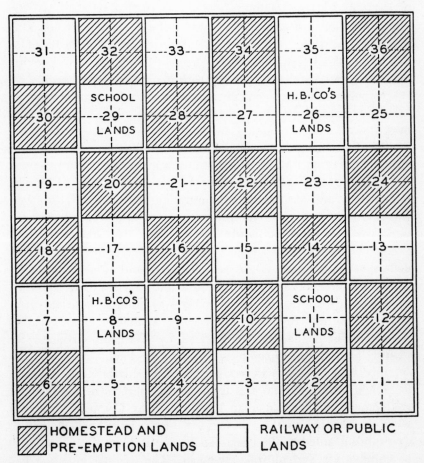

A township survey

unsuitable for cultivation. Also adopted was the practice of pre-emption to enable the settler to purchase an adjoining quarter section of 160 acres.

Important and far-sighted in the land policy was the reservation of sections 11 and 29 in each township as school lands to provide educational funds when the settlers should become established, plus provision for a public road allowance bordering every section surveyed. Although two sections in each township were to provide money for educational facilities, it was not until 1879 that the Consolidated Dominion Lands Act provided for the administration of school lands. Initially, school land administration was in the hands of the Minister of the Interior and sale of lands was to be by public auction after required advertising, but there was also an "upset" price based on fair value of adjacent unoccupied lands. The terms were one-fifth cash, and nine annual instalments with interest at six per cent.

The policy of using potentially agricultural land to gain revenue for railway building led to the railway land grants. In 1872 an act was passed with reference to a Canadian railway to the Pacific coast, limiting the land grant to 50 million acres. There were subsequent changes under the Mackenzie administration when the building of the railway temporarily reverted to the government itself. However, under the second Macdonald administration, beginning in 1878, there was a return to the free enterprise concept and, in 1880, final terms were reached with the newly formed Canadian Pacific Railway Company Limited which provided for a money grant of 25 million dollars, a land grant of 25 million acres, and other concessions, which included certain exemption from property taxation "forever". During a 20-year period the company was granted a virtual monopoly of railway building between its mainline and the 49th parallel. The Canadian Pacific Railway Company acquired the existing line, agreed to complete a line to the Pacific coast within a specified time, and was to receive special consideration with respect to freight rates. Within the terms of the agreement between the government and the Canadian Pacific Railway Company there was what was known as the "fit for settlement clause" which implied that lands granted to the Canadian Pacific Railway Company must be suitable for agricultural settlement. The original intention had been to build the railway through the Parklands Region, but during the early 1880's acceptance of the Macoun survey, authorized by the Canadian Government, was a factor in altering the proposal. Macoun, a naturalist who in the Fleming railway survey of the 1870's had observed that the land of the open plains was not lacking in fertility, reported that rainfall, though limited, occurred mainly in the growing season of June and July. There was the added inducement of less costly and more rapid construction across the southern open plain, plus a position commercially strategic for competition with railway projects south of the 49th parallel. Therefore the Canadian Pacific Railway was rerouted. Regina, Moose Jaw, and Swift Current rapidly appeared on the prairie horizon as mainline centres, while Battleford's metropolitan dreams were shattered. The railway company understandably wanted its grant of lands to be along its right of way where rapid settlement seemed a certainty. Within a 48-mile belt bordering the railway, the C.P.R. was to have every other section while the government was to retain the intervening sections. Thus, the C.P.R. would have an equal number of sections with the government. The government would offer its sections to settlers either on the homestead plan or by direct sale for immediate agricultural development. The C.P.R. would be in a position to hold its sections until the development of the adjacent government sections had enhanced the value of the land held by the railway. This was part of the land grant policy designed to assist the C.P.R. to finance its rail construction and operating costs. However, despite the Macoun survey, the Canadian Pacific Railway insisted it could not find sufficient arable land along its mainline route. Consequently, though much of the railway land grant was located in the 48-mile belt westward approximately as far as Moose Jaw, large blocks of land were reserved elsewhere, particularly in the northern Parklands Region and in the middle Parklands Region in the vicinity of Yorkton.

A typical township, 36 sections, in the 1880's consisted of sections 11 and 29 set aside for schools, and sections 8 and 26 set aside for the Hudson's Bay Company; half of the remaining sections were open to settlement; the other half were held by the Canadian Pacific Railway Company for eventual disposal.

In 1873, the newly formed council of the territories, located at Winnipeg and presided over by Lieutenant Governor Alexander Morris, had enacted the first formal legislation passed by a regularly constituted government of the Northwest Territories. Alexander Morris, who had been an influential member of Prime Minister Macdonald's Liberal-Conservative cabinet, had long been an active publicist for the idea of Canadian westward expansion.

On March 8, 1873, the council prohibited the sale of intoxicating liquors in the territories, as previously recommended in Lieutenant Butler's report which referred specifically to the demoralizing effect of liquor, especially on the natives. Butler, who had been appointed by Lieutenant Governor Archibald to investigate the effects of smallpox and lawlessness in the territories, is credited with the introduction of the phrase "the great lone land".

The North West Mounted Police, working closely with the council, was expanding its far-flung line of forts and finding communication increasingly difficult. The Canadian Government surveyed a route for a telegraph line which would connect Winnipeg with Edmonton. At this time it was thought the proposed railway would follow the same general route as the telegraph line. In the summer of 1874 the linemen reached the beautiful valley of the Battle River and there named their camp Telegraph Flat. Around Telegraph Flat grew a small settlement where the mounted police built a fort. In 1876 the administrative centre of the territories was temporarily established at Livingstone, the first headquarters of the N.W.M. Police in the Swan River valley. In the following year the council moved its headquarters to the settlement of Telegraph Flat, subsequently re-named Battleford, which became, for the time being, capital of the Northwest Territories.

The Canadian Government, aware that it would have to compete for agricultural settlers with the western states and that the potentially agricultural land of the northwest must be cleared of roving Indian bands, nevertheless rejected the western frontiersman's maxim south of the 49th parallel: "The only good Indian is a dead Indian." Canada's Indian policy emerged from a combination of the traditional British attitude of paternalistic non-violence toward the aborigines and an extension of the 200 year-old Hudson's Bay Company policy of fair dealing with the natives. The latter were now to be persuaded to abandon their nomadic ways once helpful to the fur trade, and to adopt instead pastoral ways on reservations of land to be set aside for that purpose. The authorities hoped the Indians would, eventually, prove themselves amenable to the Whiteman's laws and ways. Eventual enfranchisement was visualized, as was the ultimate fusion of the races. In Canada's policy there was no trace of legislative enactment, such as existed in several states of the U. S. A., to make illegal the marriage of Indian and White.

The British policy of the fur trade era had been to recognize the Indians' title to the land over which they roamed. Now, with the new concept of agricultural settlement, Canadian policy was to restrict the Indians' title to specified reservations. This confinement was to be accomplished by negotiation with the various tribes and bands. The reservation idea and practice, evolved in central and eastern Canada, became modified to settlement conditions in the Province of Manitoba, where Indian treaties preceded those to be made in the area that was to become the Province of Saskatchewan. The Indian reserve was officially regarded as transitional between the life of the nomadic hunter and that of the farmer or labourer. The government's Department of the Interior, made responsible for the initiation and completion of negotiations with the Indians, was instructed to deal honestly and with justice and good faith. Yet it seems doubtful whether the officials concerned realized the difficulty confronting a Stone Age people adjusting to a pioneer agricultural society dominated by European culture.

Halfbreeds, who spoke French, or English, and native languages, were employed to spread the word of a place and time of meeting for treaty negotiations, and to act as interpreters. Treaty terms followed a general pattern but variations resulted when, in certain instances, Indian bands held out for a better bargain.

Indian treaties numbers one, two, and three had been concluded previously with natives to the east. The meeting for Treaty Number 4 was called at Fort Qu'Appelle in September of 1874. Government surveyors were already at work in the area, and the Indians were perturbed to find these intent and determined strangers with their steel chains, peering through peepholes mounted on tripods, blocking out the land in squares, and driving iron survey stakes deep into the ground. Indian spokesmen told the government representatives that they, the Indians, owned the land and asked why the government had paid the Hudson's Bay Company much money for it. The money, said the natives, should have been paid to the rightful owners, the

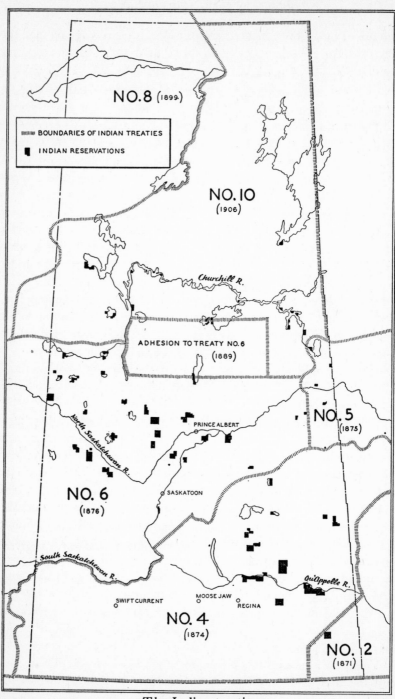

NO. 8 (1899.)

BOUNDARIES OF INDIAN TREATIES
INDIAN RESERVATIONS

NO. 10
(1906)

Churchill R.

ADHESION TO TREATY NO. 6
(1889)

NO. 5
(1875)

PRINCE ALBERT

North Saskatchewan R.

NO. 6
(1876)

SASKATOON

South Saskatchewan R.

Qu'Appelle R.

SWIFT CURRENT

MOOSE JAW

REGINA

NO. 4
(1874)

NO. 2
(1871)

The Indian treaties

Indians. When government representatives tried to explain that the Hudson's Bay Company had not been paid for the land, but for abandoning that company's rights over the land, the fine distinction was a difficult one for the natives to comprehend. Throughout six autumn days of explanation, parley, exhortation, and negotiation, the chiefs and headmen conferred with government representatives in the presence of the assembled bands. And when darkness fell around the camp fires the chiefs and headmen continued to discuss the difficult proposals with the warriors and tribesmen generally. Many were the doubts expressed, especially by the younger men. There were differences of opinion between the Crees and Salteaux, but eventually in the presence of a detachment of militia the treaty received the signatures of Lieutenant Governor Morris, Indian Commissioner David Laird, who was also Minister of the Interior, and numerous witnesses, together with the marks of 12 Indian chiefs.

Treaty Number 4 included a wide variety of items. A reserve of land was set apart for the use of the Indians. It was to be sufficiently large to allow approximately one square mile for each family of five. The land could not be sold or alienated. Each chief present at the parley was to receive immediately $25, a coat, and a Queen's silver medal. Headmen received $15 and a coat. A payment of $12 was made for every man, woman, and child. In addition those present received powder, shot, blankets, and trinkets.

Subsequently an annual payment was to be made of $25 for each chief, $15 for each headman, and for each man, woman, and child $5, payable to the head of the family. Powder and shot to the value of $750 was to be generally distributed. In this way the Indians were to be compensated on behalf of themselves and their descendants.

Other items had to do with encouraging the substitution of agriculture for hunting. Each band agreeing to cultivate the soil was given one plough and two harrows for every 10 families, and for each family, two hoes, one spade, one scythe, and one axe. Seed wheat, oats, barley, and potatoes were supplied for land that would be broken. Each chief with a band engaged in agriculture was supplied with one yoke of oxen, four cows, and one bull. Carpenter tools, such as hand and crosscut saws, augers, files, and grindstones, were also provided.

Education was not to be neglected. The government was to build and maintain schools on the reserve. The sale of intoxicating liquor was prohibited in agreement with the Indian chiefs themselves.

The government retained the right to expropriate the reserve or any part of it, if in its opinion the reserve was not appropriately used. Thus the government stood in the role of guardian, and the Indians receiving its annual payments were its wards. The final adjustment of the Indians to a new way of life could not be clearly seen. The reserve system was adopted as an immediate practical expedient to prepare for a peaceful occupation of the plains by White agricultural settlers, while at the same time it was hoped to induce the Indians eventually to adopt a more stabilized community life.

In Treaty Number 6, signed at Fort Carlton and Fort Pitt in 1876, the Cree Indians there argued for and obtained a famine clause stipulating that in times of dire need the government would provide food for treaty Indians on the reserve. While it was not the intention of the government to include in any treaty the right of the Indian to roam and hunt beyond the boundaries of the reserve, as was his habit during uncounted generations, harder-dealing Indians to the east of Manitoba had secured this privilege written into Treaty Number 3, and subsequently Indians of the plains insisted on, and received on paper, the identical privilege. In several instances government representatives, at the insistence of the natives, also verbally stated that the natives might roam and hunt as before, as well as enjoy other concessions, provided that in so doing they did not impede or disturb the anticipated agricultural settlement of the country. When these verbal assurances were given there were few settlers to disturb, and the rapidly diminishing buffalo herds had not yet disappeared from the plains.

The North-West Territories Act of 1875 provided for a separate lieutenant governor for the Northwest Territories and for elected members to the council; the act provided also for a maximum of three stipendiary magistrates. A stipendiary magistrate associated with the chief justice or a judge of the Manitoba Court of Queen's Bench had authority to try cases in which the penalty did not exceed five years imprisonment. More serious cases involved provision of a jury.

It was on May 8, 1882, that the Canadian Government, by

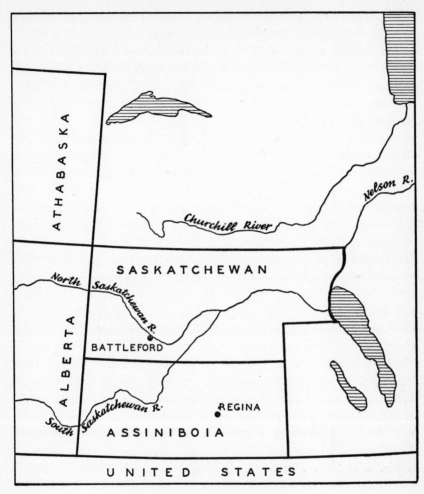

The four provisional districts

order-in-council, divided a southern portion of the Northwest Territories into provisional districts "for the convenience of settlers and for
postal purposes". The order-in-council, subsequently approved by
Parliament, named the four districts Assiniboia, Saskatchewan, Alberta,
and Athabaska; and government members were of the little publicized opinion that the step taken "might result in those divisions
becoming, hereafter, provinces".

In the early 1880's, the few lawyers who had reached the prairies found little demand for legal services in civil litigation, and at times turned to work other than that of their profession.

The earliest doctors were those attached as medical officers to the North West Mounted Police. Practising in Prince Albert was Dr. A. E. Porter, the first registered physician in the Northwest Territories not attached to the mounted police. In addition to his private practice he was attached to the hospital, was medical officer for the jail, and accepted a government appointment in connection with the Indian reserves. In 1885 territorial regulations required a registration fee from medical practitioners and established legal penalties for illegal or unlicensed practice. Some residents in outlying areas complained about these regulations. In their opinion the services of a partly or self-trained medical man were better than none.

Territorial legislation, in 1884, permitted the organization of tax-supported public and separate (either Roman Catholic or Protestant) schools, and the ordinance provided for a board of education to be appointed by the Lieutenant Governor. The first municipal ordinance, passed in 1883, resulted in the formation of municipalities, in 1884, at South Qu'Appelle, Qu'Appelle, Wolseley, and Indian Head.

The Canadian Pacific Railway, in its westward construction across the plains, reached the meagre settlement of Moose Jaw in December, 1882, and declared the site a railway divisional point. With the advent of railway workers and land survey parties, Moose Jaw in the following year had a fluctuating population of between 2,000 and 3,000. That year, 1883, the post office was established, as was the first newspaper, a weekly, *The Moose Jaw News*. In 1884 the first school district in the Northwest Territories was set up: the Moose Jaw School District Number 1. Incorporated as a town in 1884, Moose Jaw that year held its first annual fair under the auspices of the Moose Jaw Agricultural Society.

The older settlements, linked to the C.P.R. by wagon trail northward across the prairie, had advanced considerably during the several years before the advent of the railway to the south. Seed wheat from Russia, where similar climatic conditions prevailed, was brought to the area. In the summer of 1880, two ranchers from the Calgary area came overland with 75 head of cattle to start a ranch near Battleford. At Prince Albert the Hudson's Bay Company grist

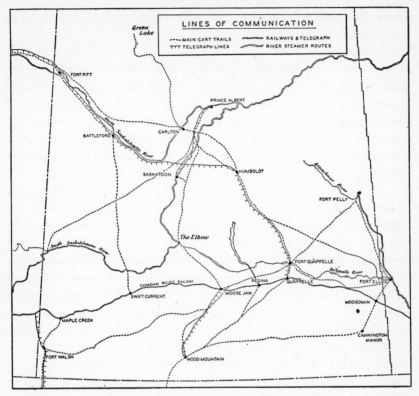

Main lines of communication before 1885

mill went into operation in 1880. That year Thomas McKay built a sawmill by the bank of the North Saskatchewan River, and the Goodfellow Brothers proudly proclaimed the opening of their sash and door factory. The frame lumber house was beginning to replace the log house. *The Prince Albert Times and Saskatchewan Review* began publication in 1882. Most editors of early periodicals were printers also. Incorrigible pioneers, they discussed, in their vigorous and forthright editorials, local, regional, and national affairs.

Individual settlers, arriving on the Saskatchewan scene by way of the newly constructed railway, tended to locate as close as they could to the C.P.R. line. Desire for proximity to the railway plus the prospect of quick money in real estate led to a speculative land boom along the line and contributed to the rapid growth of Regina and

Moose Jaw, two centres that in the first year of their growth were incorporated as towns.

Settlement during the early 1880's was neither confined to individual settlers nor restricted to land adjacent to the railway. Group settlements many miles from the rail line resulted, in part, from a change in the government land policy. The Canadian Government, in 1881, embarrassed by promises made by itself and its predecessor that the projected Pacific railway would not cost the eastern provinces a cent, found it necessary to raise money by means other than taxation. The government, departing from its original land policy of individual or one-family farm settlement, turned to the expedient of selling tracts of land, beyond the 48-mile belt along the railway, to colonization companies. Thus almost 30 colonization contracts were entered into as a means to raise cash for railway construction. Most of the contracts covered land tracts in the area that was to become the Province of Saskatchewan. While many of the colonization companies failed to settle a single family, one of the early and successful ventures was that of the York Farmers Colonization Company in the Yorkton area.

Though most of the colonization companies profited few people other than the company directors, some led to interesting experiments and novel communities and, in certain instances, permanent settlements adapted to prairie life. Names of the British and other European nobility were variously associated with settlements in their early stages, but it was the persistence of men of humbler birth which carried the communities through the first difficult years.

Of a relatively enduring nature was the settlement founded at Saskatoon, on the South Saskatchewan River, by the Temperance Colonization Company. Initiated by a Toronto group of Methodists, the colony in its early stages was guided by John L. Lake, a churchman, who in 1882 selected and named the attractive site of the future city. The name Saskatoon was derived from the Cree Indian name for a distinctive high bush berry prolific in the area and used in the making of pemmican. Prohibition of the sale of spirituous liquors in the Northwest Territories agreed with the Utopian aspirations of the Temperance Colony whose leaders were not averse to settlement isolated from the temptations of the frontier life rampant along the railway to the south. Until 1890, Moose Jaw, 150 miles southward by wagon trail, was Saskatoon's nearest rail centre.

A settlement associated with an aristocratic name was that established south of Wapella in 1883-84 under the sponsorship of Lady Cathcart. The crofters, brought out from the Cathcart and neighbouring estates in Scotland, experienced a difficult period of adjustment, before successfully engaging in mixed farming. Yet more difficult was the degree of adjustment from an urban to a rural life required of those who, in 1884, settled in the East London Artisans' Colony sponsored by Lord de Winton and Baroness Burdett-Coutts in a community south of Moosomin.

Unique was the operation of the Qu'Appelle Farming Company, which purchased an extensive tract of land near Indian Head from the government, the Canadian Pacific Railway Company, and the Hudson's Bay Company. The farming company undertook to prepare the land for the prospective settler and to sell to him a farm complete with basic buildings, machinery, and livestock. The scheme proved not so profitable as anticipated by the originators; adverse climatic and economic conditions made it difficult to recover readily the large capital outlay. But the Bell farm, as it was known from its manager's name, performed a lasting service to western agriculture by its early experiments in dry farming techniques.

A settlement project, coincident with the first land boom period of the Canadian prairies, was Cannington Manor, 40 miles southwest of Moosomin. With other pioneers to this district came the enterprising William Pierce, who set out to create an exclusive community of wealthy young Englishmen whom Pierce, in return for a suitable fee, would train in the arts of farming, thus preparing them for eventual settlement on land of their own.

Most of the young gentlemen, of commercially successful middle class parentage, preferred horse-racing, the hunt, tennis, cricket, shooting, banquets, and balls to the hard work of farming. These did not long flourish on the windswept prairie. But this romantic project put some cash in circulation and left some buildings and various colourful memories.

In the early 1880's the population of the Parklands and Plains regions, apart from Indians and Halfbreeds, was essentially British. Not until 1885 did people of continental European stocks begin to enter the territories in any numbers, and then the first arrivals were

largely from the United States. From south of the 49th parallel
came settlers of Hungarian origin who were established by Count
Paul O. d'Esterhazy north of Whitewood. Also from the U. S. A.
were the adjacent Scandinavian settlers who named their community New Sweden. Both these settlements received assistance from
Sir George Stephen of the Canadian Pacific Railway Company.

The first territorial newspaper in the area that was to become
the Province of Saskatchewan, *The Saskatchewan Herald*, had appeared in 1878 with Patrick Gammie Laurie as editor, printer,
manager, and principal owner. At Winnipeg he had loaded his
press on an oxcart and set out alone over the 600-mile
trail to Battleford, the new territorial capital located on the route
then proposed for the railway. En route Laurie passed another aspiring newspaper publisher who was in transport difficulty with his
heavier press equipment. He was Edmonton-bound Frank Oliver, who,
when he eventually reached his destination, became a temporary
correspondent for Laurie's paper. Laurie, 72 days after his departure from Winnipeg, reached Battleford as a welcome stranger
in a wilderness village where the mail came every two or three weeks.
In Battleford the telegraph line reaching southeast to Winnipeg
and northwest to Edmonton supplied his fortnightly paper with news
from beyond the settlement. The subscription rate was $2 a year in
advance, the aim "to advocate the best interests of the Territories at
large", the masthead motto, "Progress". In the initial issue was a
local composition, the "Herald's Song":

"I will open this mighty region
Till the land shall ring again,
With the tramp of a restless legion,
Garnering its golden grain. . . .
If danger or gloom or sorrow
Should lower their pall today,
I will live, for a sunny tomorrow
Shall glorify my way."

Like most Battleford citizens, the editor was critical when the
territorial capital was moved from Battleford to Regina, March
27, 1883. During five years Battleford had been the capital of
the Northwest Territories, the seat of the territorial government
having nominal jurisdiction over a vast area that extended from the

Yukon-Alaska boundary eastward beyond Hudson Bay to Labrador and from the 49th parallel to the Arctic Sea.

Regina, the new capital, a tent and shack town which mushroomed on the open plain with the coming of the railway, had a population of almost 500. Regina was on the mainline of the C.P.R. Though early settlers in the vicinity had not the advantage of a forest for building logs and fuel, they found a cash crop in buffalo skeletons bleaching white on the grassland. They gathered the bones and took them by wagon to Regina where they were piled like cordwood in the railway yard, to be loaded into boxcars for shipment east to Chicago, where they were in demand for processing.

Simultaneously with the establishment of Regina, irreverently called "Pile-O-Bones", Nicholas Flood Davin installed a power-driven rotary press in a frame building and began publication of his *Regina Leader*. The sometimes erratic, always energetic Davin—no printer—had a flair for journalism, with an editorial finger in politics and a penchant for poetry. Davin's early issues of the *Regina Leader* championed the rights of the new settlers. A circulation of 5,000 was claimed for the first issue, which found a ready sale among the train passengers who bought extra copies of this provocative western newspaper and sent them to friends and relatives in central and eastern Canada. From its inception an ardent, if boastful, champion of Regina and never unfriendly toward Sir John A. Macdonald, the *Regina Leader* under Davin's direction became eventually less a tribune of local discontent and more the defender of Conservative politics.

Suited for a sparse and considerably isolated White population becoming, sometimes painfully, conditioned to the demands of a new and frontier country, at a time when radio and television were unknown, the local newspaper was avidly received. Its editor was inevitably a leading figure in the community and often the most controversial one.

For many a pioneer on the open plains and the parklands fringe where logs for building were scarce or non-existent, the initial task was to hitch his oxen or horses to the single-furrow plough and, after ploughing a fire guard around the homesite, turn over sufficient tough prairie sod for building a sod shack. He built the walls by piling one layer of sod on another, leaving space for a door and

An early settler's home and fire guard

a window-frame or two. If he had no glass, he used canvas or animal hide to keep out the breeze and let in some light. Willow or poplar poles supported the roof sods on which grass, sagebrush, and prairie flowers continued to grow. In winter a sheetmetal or iron stove provided heat for both cooking and warmth.

A sheet-iron stove

Prairie fires were prevalent and, with a wind behind them, at times blackened many square miles before petering out on a river bank, coulee bottom, or other natural barrier. If caught in the path of a raging prairie fire, the traveller's defence was to light a "backfire", that is, to set fire to the grass on his leeward side and move over on to that burned-over piece.

In his first land made ready for cultivation, the settler almost invariably planted potatoes and sometimes turnips, peas, carrots, lettuce, radishes, and beans. Beans, whether brought in from afar, bought at the nearest store, or grown in the farmstead garden plot, were a staple item of diet. Flour for bannock, bread, or flapjacks; oatmeal for porridge; bacon and salted pork; tea or coffee; sugar or corn syrup; dried apples or prunes—these were among the household essentials.

Oats, both for the farmer's own horses and for sale in nearby centres where the horse was the major motive power for everyone, were generally included in the first grain crop sown in the settler's new breaking. Wheat, another member of the grass family, with a root system designed to make the best of both a surface rain shower and a penetrating downpour, was early regarded as the surest cash crop. Aided by constant experimentation by dedicated agricultural scientists with government and railway company support, sun-loving, wind-resistant, early maturing hard wheat was destined to flourish and ripen where the buffalo in their numberless thousands had grazed throughout uncounted centuries. Waving fields of wheat would everywhere meet the prairie horizon; the golden grain would reach the markets of the world and make men rich. Everyone heard it said, and many believed it, even including the struggling grower whose wife bore him babies, tended the children, scrubbed, baked, mended, milked, and so at the end of the day had little time left to hope the great dream would come true.

The hand-sickle and scythe had given way to the mechanical reaper with its glittering steel knife reciprocating with a furious sound like a gigantic, uncertain sewing-machine while the man rode proudly on an iron seat behind his team and the standing grain fell evenly— as if a dozen unseen backs were bending to the swing of as many miraculous scythes.

In 1883 the prairie credo of progress was muted when, on September 7, Arctic air, flowing down from the tundra and Hudson Bay, blighted with frost the ripening crops. A Montreal milling company took advantage of nature's blow, plus general economic depression prevalent over the North American continent and western Europe, to panic the grain traders by publicly offering to purchase the Manitoba and Northwest grain crop at nominal prices. The price of wheat fell to 40 cents a bushel and oats to as low as 15 cents. This decline, following the collapse of the land boom the year before, meant that debt-burdened farmers were unable to meet their obligations to storekeepers, lumber merchants, and livestock and implement dealers, whose credit in turn became curtailed with wholesalers and manufacturers. A few distressed farmers became convinced they should organize, protest, and place their problems, together with remedies, before the Canadian Government at Ottawa. Agitation was most vociferous in the Province of Manitoba where farmers were more numerous and had greater individual investment than in the Northwest Territories. At Winnipeg, in December of 1883, a week before Christmas, more than 100 farmers met for a two-day convention, during which they formed the Manitoba and North-West Farmers Union. They pondered and discussed "the present depression in agricultural and commercial industries", and drew up a "Declaration of Rights", which referred to "oppressive duty on agricultural implements . . . monopoly of the carrying trade enjoyed by the Canadian Pacific Railway . . . [and] vexatious methods employed in the administration of public lands. . . ." Declaring they were denied "the rights of free British subjects", they demanded removal of customs duties on agricultural implements and building materials and asked for decreased duties on consumer goods generally. They asked for construction of a railway to Hudson Bay to lessen the rail distance and freight rates for transportation of grain to European markets, and earnestly requested representation in the cabinet at Ottawa. The three delegates elected to take the petition to Ottawa returned to report that the government's reception was "not of that satisfactory nature which the importance of our mission demands", while one of the farm union spokesmen threatened that "unless remedial measures for relief are at once provided serious results will be inevitable".

The initial adaptation to the prairies was not easy, but a more serious crisis was imminent.

5

Grievances, Guns, and Gallows

In the Electoral District of Lorne, Northwest Territories, which was to become a part of the Province of Saskatchewan, Prince Albert was a centre of economic unrest and political agitation. There the economic depression, general throughout Canada, was aggravated by the abandonment of the proposed northerly railway route and the consequent collapse of the local land boom. This disappointment was followed by frozen crops and fallen grain prices. In Prince Albert there were public meetings of grievance and protest from which arose pressing petitions to Ottawa. Supplications by letter and telegram to the Canadian Government drew attention to the harsh plight of the Indians and the unrest among the Métis.

While farmers, millers, merchants, and land speculators of European heritage were in some instances impoverished, temporarily embarrassed, disconcerted, and disappointed, they, despite their protests, continued in a long term faith in what, for them, was a next year country. But the Indians of the prairies were now rarely free from hunger. Many were on the verge of starvation and some had died. The mixed blood Métis, of Indian and French origin, especially those in the largest settlement extending along the banks of the South Saskatchewan River in the vicinity of St. Laurent, Duck Lake, and Batoche, were always short of fresh meat, often hungry, generally poorly fed, and ill-clad.

The buffalo, their source of food and clothing, diminishing rapidly in the late 1870's, had practically disappeared by 1882. At first the Indians, and even some of the more wishful Métis, preferred to believe that the buffalo had crossed the "Medicine Line" into the United States, or that the big shaggy animals would soon reappear in the once infamous and still fabulous Cypress Hills, where both Indians and Métis were officially discouraged from going. But with the exception of a few lone, straggling survivors, the thundering herds had gone down in the reckless, often feckless, slaughter by shot from steel-barrelled guns in the hands of mounted Indians, Métis, and Whites. The coming of the land surveyor with his steel chain, followed by steel rails and settlers' ploughshares, made inevitable the eventual disappearance of the buffalo. But the buffalo, which might have helped tide the Indian and Métis over another year or two of "the transition", had been almost annihilated while millions of acres of unfenced prairie grassland still remained untouched by the plough.

Added to the privation of the Indian and Métis was a dim but growing awareness that their way of life was gone with the buffalo. For the native, the Whiteman's new west had become a last year country.

The venturesome and visionary policies of the Canadian Government for the development of the Northwest Territories in a Canadian nation to extend "from sea to sea" were in need of adjustment. Of this fact men and women of all races and creeds and all occupations in the territories seemed certain. Sir John A. Macdonald, practical visionary and deft political architect of dominion *A Mari Usque Ad*

Mare, was now at the helm in far-off Ottawa. Various trusted subordinates failed to make the ageing Prime Minister fully aware of problems in desperate need of solution, and his ministers in turn failed, over a period of months accumulating into years, to heed the persistent pleas and petitions of the people directly affected. During the period, Prime Minister Macdonald, who was also Minister of the Interior, the government department directly responsible for administration of the Northwest Territories, had been absorbed in other affairs of state. He did not visit the territories. When, in 1883, he finally relinquished the office, he appointed as Minister of the Interior Sir David Macpherson, an elderly politician possessed of no first-hand knowledge of the northwest and having little interest in the area and less understanding. Policy decision concerning Indian and Métis affairs in the territories was, for practical purposes, left in the hands of a civil servant, Mr. Lawrence Vankoughnet, Deputy Superintendent General of Indian Affairs and later Deputy Minister of the Department of the Interior. An old and trusted friend of Sir John A. Macdonald, Mr. Vankoughnet's lofty but circumscribed concept of duty coupled with lack of imagination, inclined him to opinionated preconception of a situation. From there this deputy proceeded to ignore relevant facts in so far as they failed to fit his book.

The North West Mounted Police, Hudson's Bay Company officials, priests, clergy, church ministers, merchants, newspaper editors, ranchers, farmers, Indian agents, and the natives themselves warned and pleaded while Ottawa continued to consider.

Cattle thieving by hungry or starving Indians was prevalent and the mounted police, who patiently had gained widespread respect and the co-operation of most of the natives, now were faced with the fact that hunger knows no law. No longer could a lone policeman rely on making an arrest in an Indian encampment.

As early as 1878, the Métis of St. Laurent had sent a petition to Lieutenant Governor Laird, requesting grants of scrip and land for those who had not previously received such grants. English and Scottish Halfbreeds of Prince Albert sent a petition containing a similar request to the Governor General at Ottawa. Among various petitions was one in a letter from that forceful missionary to the Métis, Roman Catholic Father André, who in January, 1883, earnestly requested Prime Minister Macdonald to "order a new survey" so that the Métis settlers could be given legal title to their lands which did not fit into the predominant square survey. Father André stressed the need for immediate action. But his petition to Prime Minister Macdonald was apparently passed on to the Minister of the Interior, Macpherson, who in turn referred it to his deputy minister. There seems to be no record, in this instance, of a reply to Father André.

Where squatters were in possession of land before the arrival of the surveyors, their river-frontage lots had been surveyed apart from the square survey system, but the squatters had not received title to their holdings. Newcomers, mainly nomadic Halfbreeds who had arrived to take up holdings after the survey, found the plots they selected for themselves were already included in the square survey system.

Lieutenant Governor Dewdney, who received his appointment from Ottawa in 1881, was a cautious administrator, anxious neither to burden nor to embarrass his friend and chief, Prime Minister Macdonald. Consequently his mild letters of advice to Macdonald— mild in relation to the acuteness of the problems and the trouble brewing—failed to arouse the Prime Minister. Correspondence passed on to Macpherson was, in various instances, in turn referred to his deputy who was engaged in reducing the budget for expenditure in the Northwest Territories in compliance with government policy arising out of the economic depression.

Further aggravating the economic plight of the Métis was the decline in freighting by Red River cart. Since 1881 paddle-wheeling, flat-bottomed, wood-burning steamboats had been carrying freight and passengers on the Saskatchewan river system. The railway in the south, the influx of settlers of European heritage with their steel-axled wagons, heavier teams, and generally greater efficiency—these combined with economic depression to reduce drastically the demand for the Red River cart transport, which, together with buffalo hunting, had been the dual basis of the Métis economy.

Though members of the Northwest Council were usually in agreement concerning the seriousness of the situation, editor Frank Oliver, elected member for Edmonton, vigorous reformer, and vituperative critic of the Conservative Party and administration, aroused in cautious, loyal-to-Macdonald, Dewdney, a reaction opposed to ready acceptance of Oliver's forthright proposals. Moreover, the council demonstrated an accelerated tendency to split along political party (Conservative versus Liberal) lines.

Though Dewdney, as the chief appointee of the Canadian Government, had the advantage of authority, Oliver possessed a forceful voice in *The Bulletin,* the second newspaper to be published in the Northwest Territories. *The Bulletin* had little or no general circulation in that area of the Northwest Territories which would become the Province of Saskatchewan, but newspaper editors in the Saskatchewan area received *The Bulletin* and, from time to time, referred to editorial opinion in the Edmonton paper. Mr. Oliver editorially replied to an Ontario newspaper which had asserted that the pioneers of Ontario overcame difficulties by "persistent perseverance" rather than by petitions to the government or threats of rebellion.

The Bulletin editorial in reply was reprinted in *The Prince Albert Times*:

If it was not by—not threatening, but actual rebellion and appeals to the British Government for justice that the people of Ontario gained the rights they enjoy today and freed themselves from a condition precisely similar to that into which the Northwest is being rapidly forced, how was it? Was it not by armed rebellion coupled with murder, that Manitoba attained the rights she enjoys today from the very men who now hold the reins of power at Ottawa[?] If history is to be taken as a guide, what could be plainer than that without rebellion the people of the Northwest need expect nothing, while with rebellion[,] successful or otherwise[,] they may reasonably expect to get their rights[?]

The Prince Albert Times comment followed: "There is a ring of true metal about it which indicates pretty plainly the temper of the Nor'wester."

Newspaper comment continued to be vigorous, often provocative, and critical of eastern apathy, although there is no indication that prairie editors and their readers would have welcomed a native uprising in their midst.

On May 10, 1884, *The Prince Albert Times* editor commented in part: "Where they [the Canadian Government] get the information which induces them to believe the people [are] likely to submit much longer, we do not know; but we can answer them that they need not look for their friends among the Canadians, Halfbreeds, or Indians, as they are likely soon to be made aware of in a manner at once startling and unpleasant."

That editorial in English was translated into French and distributed among the Métis in the area. Those of the South Saskatchewan River settlements had asked their respected leader of the bygone days of the buffalo hunts, Gabriel Dumont, to head their restless movement of protest. But this thick-chested, keen-eyed plainsman with a shaggy beard reminiscent of the departed buffalo, declined. He was a hunter, a hard-riding horseman; he had headed the "Provisional Government" of the great buffalo hunts. But, he said, he was not capable of leading his people in a paper campaign of pleas and petitions.

Older Métis turned their thoughts to Louis Riel, who had manifested dramatic qualities of leadership in the Red River disturbance of 1870. In May of 1884 at a meeting in Lindsay School House in the Prince Albert vicinity, Whites and English-speaking and French-speaking Halfbreeds passed resolutions similar to those of various meetings of protest. Then discussion turned to the advisability of consulting Louis Riel. Some of the English-speaking Halfbreeds objected. The meeting finally adopted this resolution: ". . . we have thought it advisable that a delegation be sent to said Louis Riel, and have his assistance to bring all matters referred to in the above resolutions in a proper shape and form before the Government of Canada, so that our just demands be granted." A collection of money was taken to help defray the expense of the delegation. According to a report of the meeting in *The Prince Albert Times,* one of the "Canadians from Ontario" took "the lead in opening his purse when subscriptions were called for".

Shortly after this meeting, a delegation of four horsemen set off on their 700-mile ride to Montana where they would find Louis Riel and bring him back to Canada's northwest. Gabriel Dumont, Michael Dumas, Moise Ouellete, descendants of unions between Frenchmen in the fur trade and Indian women, and James Isbister, descendant of an Indian mother and English father once in the employ of the Adventurers of England trading into Hudson Bay, reached Riel in Montana early in June. The expectant delegation found him on an

Gabriel Dumont and delegation depart for Montana to find Riel

Indian reserve in the Sun River country. There at St. Peter's Mission, under the direction of Father Damiani, he taught rudiments of French and English to Indian boys of an impoverished Blackfoot band. With his young and adoring Métis wife and their little son and infant daughter, Riel lived in one end of a cabin owned by another family. Louis Riel's previous efforts to arouse Montana's Indians and Half-breeds to political action had failed, but his dreams for emancipation "of my people" were never less than dormant. He had kept himself informed concerning the agitation in the Northwest Territories and he may have been in touch with Big Bear, a Cree Indian originally from the Carlton district, who became chief of various Indian bands and recalcitrant individuals determined not to settle on a reserve. Within 24 hours of the delegates' arrival Riel had accepted their urgent invitation to return with them to Canada's northwest. With a squealing Red River cart containing his wife, children, some meagre household effects, and a battered trunk crammed with political petitions, religious poems, dissertations and other things, the hopeful caravan, headed by Gabriel Dumont, set out northward across the fenceless grassland.

In July, a month of hot sun and sudden storm over the prairie, restless and uncertain Louis Riel had returned to Canada's north-west of 1884. Within nine months he would attempt to repeat the pattern of the Red River uprising of 15 years before. His inter-vening years of exile south of the 49th parallel, a time of frustration and failure, had not been conducive to stability of character or considered judgement. Fluctuating between painful doubt concerning his capacity to lead, and a millenarian vision of heading a triumphant mission to right the wrongs of his people and lift them out of their despair to a proud, happy, and prosperous way of life, he was to find himself heading a constitutional agitation supported by a cross-section of the population, only to lose the general following and precipitate armed rebellion among a militant minority of hungry and ill-clad Métis in the settlements of Batoche, St. Laurent, and Duck Lake near the banks of the South Saskatchewan River. His personal magnetism, persuasive oratory, fanciful flights of divine mission, and sincere desire to help the Métis were offset by his failure to evaluate Canada's new northwest with its established governmental authority, mounted police force, telegraph line to Ottawa, steam railway, vanguard of eager agricultural settlers, and emerging political partisanship along Canadian party lines.

Louis Riel made his headquarters at Batoche, where, among his own people of French and Indian descent, he felt most at home. But following insistent requests from a group in Prince Albert, the mixed population centre of vociferous discontent, he agreed, after considerable hesitation, to speak at a mass meeting there. A petition pressing him to address a meeting in Prince Albert had been signed by more than 80 persons, of whom only five or six were Halfbreeds. Father André, the Roman Catholic Superior at Prince Albert, had added his word of insistent invitation.

On July 19, 1884, Riel spoke to the well attended meeting in Prince Albert. His nervousness disappearing before a receptive audience, he reiterated with vigour the constitutional nature of the agitation for responsible government in the northwest. White settlers, including feverish spokesmen of the newly formed and effervescent Settlers Union, endorsed the proposals, and toward the end of the meeting, when Riel answered questions, the gathering was impressed with his apparent antipathy toward violence and with his gracious oratory.

William Henry Jackson, a graduate of the University of Toronto, a youthful and unstable visionary, vociferous critic of Sir John A. Macdonald and the Conservative Party, and ardent secretary of the Settlers Union, subsequently toured the area to raise funds and support for the agitation led by Riel, who was looked to as the only man who could rally and still control the French Halfbreeds and Indians.

But petitions to Ottawa brought forth little response and no alleviation for the Métis faced with another hard winter. In the northwest, some Whitemen, in fearful support of Macdonald's Conservative Party, criticized bitterly the movement of protest and castigated Riel, who was inclined to regard criticism as unwarranted personal abuse.

The priests, while aware of the grievances and serious discontent, were anxious to avoid a repetition of the Riel-led uprising of 1870, after which Protestant Ontario had accused the Roman Catholic Church of inciting rebellion on the Red River. The distressed Métis were easily excited, while the priests favoured calm but persistent agitation. Moreover, Riel's deviation to his own version of Roman Catholic doctrine led to a growing estrangement between himself and the church. The break was precipitated when Riel publicly proposed to alter the liturgy and to appoint a Pope of the New World. The priests who met together declared him *non compos mentis* and to be denied the sacraments. On March 1, Father Fourmond preached against Riel, who replied, ". . . the priests are spies of the police." As the winter of 1884-85 dragged on to a spring of little promise, a disappointed and doubtful Riel became increasingly distraught.

His threats of violent action alienated, in the main, his White and his English-speaking Halfbreed following, but his devoted Métis runners kept in touch with Indian bands and recalcitrant chiefs. All were aware that Superintendent Crozier of the North West Mounted Police had concentrated a force at Battleford, where Crozier had asked for volunteers in the event of a Métis or Indian uprising. Riel, after ordering the capture and detention of several Whitemen in the area (including the government Indian agent), whom he intended to hold as hostages, following the pattern of the Red River disturbance, attended a religious feast for the Roman Catholic patron saint of the Métis, St. Joseph, at Batoche on March 19. At the conclusion of the feast the Métis were to fire a volley in favour of St. Joseph. Moreover, William Henry Jackson, secretary of the noisy Settlers Union, was to be baptized in the faith at the conclusion of the Novena. Riel took advantage of the large gathering to exploit with fiery oratory a rumour that a strong force of mounted police was on its way to attack the Métis settlements. Proclaiming a "Provisional

Government of the Saskatchewan", he appointed Gabriel Dumont, the great hunter, his adjutant general. Rousing "l'armée" to horse, rifle, and shotgun for the defence of the settlement, he contrived to close the division in the Métis ranks. Temporarily at least, the majority acquiesced in the action of the militant minority.

On March 11, N.W.M.P. Superintendent Crozier, who had accurately forecast the trouble and pleaded with the authorities to alleviate the mounting distress and discontent among the Indians and Halfbreeds, had telegraphed, from Fort Carlton, to his superior officer:

Halfbreeds greatly excited. Reported they threaten attack on Carlton before sixteenth. Halfbreeds refuse to take freight or employment from government. Will stop all freight coming into the country after sixteenth of this month. Leader will not allow people to leave home as they may be required. Origin of trouble I think because letter received stating Riel not recognized British subject. They expect arms from the States. Have ordered twenty-five men from Battleford and one gun to come here at once. Some Whites I think favourable to movement.

Lieutenant Governor Dewdney, in a communication to Prime Minister Macdonald, urged an immediate increase in the police force, and added, "If the half-breeds mean business the sooner they are put down the better. They are like Indians[:] when they gather and get excited it is difficult to handle them, but if they are taken unawares there is little difficulty in arresting their leader."

To this communication Prime Minister Macdonald replied that the responsibility for maintenance of order in the Northwest Territories rested with the Lieutenant Governor.

Mounted patrols of the Riel and Dumont "armée" cut the telegraph wire and seized stores to obtain food, clothing, tobacco, ammunition. Through Hillyard Mitchell, a trader at Duck Lake, and Thomas McKay, a Scottish Halfbreed, Riel sent a letter to Superintendent Crozier demanding his surrender: ". . . In case of non-acceptance, we intend to attack you, when tomorrow, the Lord's day[,] is over; and to commence without delay a war of extermination upon all those who have shown themselves hostile to our rights . . . . Major, we respect you. Let the cause of humanity be a consolation to you for the reverses which the governmental misconduct has brought upon you."

The threatened attack did not materialize. On March 26, Superintendent Crozier dispatched a few men to Duck Lake to secure a quantity of provisions and ammunition stored at Mitchell's trading post. Stopped by Dumont at the head of a band of mounted Métis and several Indians who endeavoured to provoke the police into firing, the police party turned back to Fort Carlton. Crozier, accused of cowardice by irresponsible gossips, became impatient for action. With half a hundred mounted police and less than 50 Prince Albert Volunteers and a seven-pounder gun, he marched on Duck Lake. Gabriel Dumont and his men met this force a mile and a half from Duck Lake. Which party initially invited the violence remains in doubt, but the clash was probably inevitable. "Gentleman" Joe McKay, an interpreter and scout for the N.W.M.P. at Carlton, claimed he fired the first shot after being threatened by Dumont's brother Isadore. Apprehensive of becoming outflanked and certain his force was outnumbered, Crozier gave the order, "Fire away boys." After half an hour of battle, Crozier realized his untenable position and ordered a retreat to Fort Carlton. Dumont, as the Métis general, saw that Crozier's force could be pursued, taken prisoner, or annihilated; but Riel, who had viewed the battle with crucifix in hand, gazed at the blood-stained snow, spoke of God's wishes, and restrained the Métis from further action.

Fort Carlton was abandoned as indefensible. Prince Albert had become a military centre for police and volunteers, with a stockade erected around the Presbyterian Church. News of the defeat of the mounted police and volunteers spread among the destitute Indians and emboldened the dissident chiefs and more desperate and impatient young braves.

When the news of the rebellion reached central and eastern Canada, the newspapers there overnight made electric the interest in the Northwest Territories. Four days before the Duck Lake encounter, Prime Minister Macdonald, prompted by an urgent telegram from Lieutenant Governor Dewdney, had acted with surprising alacrity, ordering mobilization of troops in every province of Canada and dispatching General Middleton to Winnipeg.

At the end of March some 200 Indian warriors in war-paint, adherents of the bands led by Poundmaker and Little Pine, broke into and pillaged the Hudson's Bay store at Battleford. A few days later Big Bear, whose ragged Indian band was hungry and starving through the winter, found his dwindling authority insufficient to restrain the impulsive young men. At Frog Lake, a Hudson's Bay Company trading post, centre of a Roman Catholic mission and residence of a sub-agent of Indian affairs, the war chief, Wandering Spirit, led his warriors in an inflamed foray of pillage, murder, capture, and arson. The government agent, the farm instructor for the Indian reserve, two priests, and five other persons (including a French Halfbreed) were shot down by the Indians. The Hudson's Bay Company trader and two women were taken prisoners. A lone Whiteman escaped to Fort Pitt where he gave news of the tragedy. The massacre at Frog Lake, about 10 miles west of what was to become the boundary between the provinces of Alberta and Saskatchewan, received sensational publicity in the press of central Canada and gave impetus to recruiting for the militia.

There were further and scattered Indian outbreaks, but the natives organized no co-ordinated warfare. Many of the Indians, especially older men, were doubtful of the success of an armed uprising, and there was an inclination to cease hostilities once a sporadic foray had resulted in the acquisition of sufficient food to provide a temporary feast. Indians raided the Hudson's Bay Company post on Green Lake where they allowed the trader to escape and made no effort to overtake the Whites who a few minutes before had abandoned the post and were on the first lap of their journey to refuge at Ile à la Crosse.

Meanwhile the Canadian Government was in the process of mobilizing a force of some 8,000; in addition to rifles, armament included two machine guns and nine mounted guns. The Halfbreeds who took up arms numbered less than 500, but there was fear of a general native uprising together with rumours of Fenian and republican intervention from the United States. Extra rations, which an alarmed government distributed hastily to hungry and wavering Indian bands, included two railway carloads of flour and 15,000 pounds of bacon ordered to Indian Head on the Canadian Pacific Railway mainline. Longstanding Indian requests for tobacco, tea, oxen, and cattle were rapidly complied with. Earlier in the month the government had announced by telegram the appointment of a commission to investigate the 10-year-old claims of the Métis for land patents and scrip.

People in Ontario who had been vaguely aware of Canada's Northwest Territories read press reports of the rebellion with avid interest and clamoured for the defeat of the Roman Catholic Halfbreed rebels ungrateful to the government and disloyal to the Crown.

The Canadian Pacific Railway had not yet completed the laying of steel on the rugged rock and muskeg north of Lake Superior, but the enterprising company, with added encouragement from the government, improvised horse-drawn sleigh trains to bridge the rail gaps for troop transport and also for food to pacify the Indians.

The military result of the campaign was a foregone conclusion, despite the clumsy advance of General Middleton, a British Imperial officer who chose to ignore the advice and readily proffered assistance of the North West Mounted Police and other local combatants conditioned to the country and conversant with Métis tactics based on the organization of the buffalo hunt. On April 6, General Middleton set out from Fort Qu'Appelle to march northward across the snows left by a tardy spring to subdue the Métis rebels of the South Saskatchewan River. The Métis, through their Halfbreed scouts and Indian runners, kept themselves informed of the movements of Middleton's force moving mainly by horse transport and on foot with a few men mounted on horseback. On April 17, Middleton's force of 800 men was at Clark's Crossing on the South Saskatchewan River.

Gabriel Dumont, with his mounted and mobile Métis, was eager to take the offensive by harassing the Middleton force under cover of darkness. Riel, fearful for "my Uncle Gabriel" who was still suffering from a head wound received in the clash with Crozier, insisted that the Halfbreed force await Middleton's approach to the rebel headquarters at Batoche. Riel, who had taken the lead in a declaration of war, was inclined to vacillation in the face of actual bloodshed.

On April 23, Dumont with a force of 200 Métis, Crees, Sioux, and Salteaux, left Batoche to intercept Middleton. The next day they encountered the Canadian militia and, taking advantage of their knowledge of the country while firing from the protection of trees and brush of Fish Creek coulee, delayed Middleton's advance on Batoche by a fortnight.

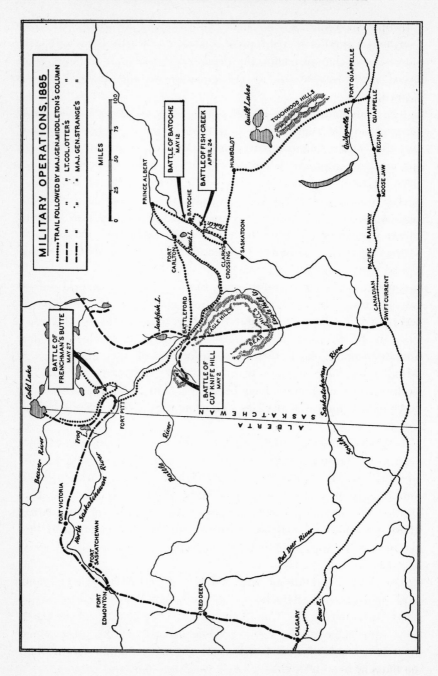

In the meantime the second column of militia, combined with a force of mounted police, under Colonel Otter had marched north from the railway line at Swift Current for the relief of Battleford intermittently harried by Poundmaker's recalcitrant Indian encampment. The Indians pillaged and burned the town, which had already been abandoned except for the stockade, but they did not cross the Battle River. As Colonel Otter's column approached, the Indians departed and the 500 inhabitants of Battleford emerged from their stockade with shouts of welcome.

The third column continued westward to Calgary and from there, leaving the railway, marched to Edmonton, where a part of this force was dispatched down the North Saskatchewan River towards Fort Pitt and the vicinity of Big Bear's Indian band.

After relieving Battleford, Colonel Otter's force proceeded to follow Poundmaker and his band of Crees and Assiniboines who were reportedly camping on Cut Knife Creek. Otter's plan was to march through the night and at sunrise surprise the Indian encampment. But Indian sentries became aware of his approach, and at daybreak Otter found himself engaged in a battle which lasted seven hours before he gave the order to withdraw the troops previously exhausted by the all-night march.

Middleton's plan was to attack the rebel headquarters at Batoche at 8 o'clock in the morning of May 9. His force would be assisted by the river steamer *Northcote,* which had brought reinforcements down the South Saskatchewan River from Swift Current and now, manned by 35 men, was to drift downriver at the appointed hour and open fire on the rebels in their rifle pits. The *Northcote* arrived at the appointed hour and opened fire. But the advantage of joint action was lost, as Middleton did not arrive until an hour later. Meantime the *Northcote,* her mast and funnels carried away by the steel ferry cable the Halfbreeds had lowered, drifted on downstream beyond battle range. Middleton discovered Dumont's force well entrenched along the edge of the river bank; the Métis proved capable of holding off the militia during three successive days of skirmish and attack. On the second day the brigade surgeon reported the rebels were using slugs and duck shot in their smooth-bore, muzzle-loading, single-barrel shotguns. On the third day, ammunition running out, the ill-equipped Métis were loading with iron nails and pebbles.

Many of the militiamen under Middleton's command were irked by constant rumours that British regulars would have to be called in to end the campaign. On the fourth day of battle, when Middleton was determined to effect an elaborate manoeuvre of surround, two Canadian colonels, A. T. H. Williams and H. J. Grassett, their patience exhausted, led their eager men in a charge straight at the rifle pits, driving the Métis defenders out. General Middleton hastily abandoned his manoeuvre and rushed forward supporting troops.

Most of the Métis men fled to the woods, where Gabriel Dumont pleaded with Riel and the discouraged remnants of the rebel army to re-form and make a final stand against the militia. But Riel had decided that the outcome of the rebellion was God's will and that he personally should surrender. On May 15, after receiving an ultimatum from Middleton, Riel allowed himself to be taken prisoner by two scouts. Dumont, accompanied by Michael Dumas, rode southwestward across the plains to seek refuge in Montana, where less than a year before he had gone to persuade Riel to return to lead the Métis in their struggle.

Poundmaker, once a proud chief with lithe and stately bearing, responded to Middleton's note to surrender. Bent and dejected, with his pathetic though picturesque followers he entered Battleford, as directed. General Middleton, brusque with victory and resplendent in a fresh uniform of the Queen, the Great White Mother, refused to take Poundmaker's proffered hand, lectured him severely, and unceremoniously ordered his imprisonment.

The dour and wily Big Bear with his mixed band of Plains and Forest Crees continued on the move, though Big Bear knew of the Métis defeat and Poundmaker's withdrawal from the rebellion. Eventually Big Bear was compelled to yield, less through direct military action than by the logic of the situation. He finally made his way to the place of his youth, Fort Carlton, and gave himself up to Sergeant Smart of the North West Mounted Police. Thus ended the Northwest Rebellion, but not its repercussions.

The campaign had cost the Canadian Government five million dollars and resulted in the formation of 14 Canadian regiments. In Regina Riel, tried for high treason, declined to plead insanity as advised by his counsel financed by voluntary contributions from Quebec. A six-man jury, all of whom were Protestants of Anglo-Saxon stock, found him guilty; Stipendiary Magistrate Hugh Richardson sentenced him to death by hanging. Eighteen of his Métis associates received from one to seven years imprisonment for treason-felony. Of 11 Indians condemned to hang for murder, three were reprieved. Big Bear and Poundmaker served prison terms of two years or less and both died shortly after their liberation. Two Whitemen were tried for complicity in the rebellion. They were William Henry Jackson, erstwhile secretary of the collapsed Settlers Union, and his one-time associate, Thomas Scott. Both were acquitted, Jackson because he was declared insane, though he refused to deny responsibility for his actions while secretary of the short-lived Settlers Union and during his brief trial indicated that he wished to be treated like Riel "whose fate, whatever it may be, I wish to share".

Gabriel Dumont, granted political refuge in the United States by President Cleveland, established a base in Lewistown, Montana, from where he planned a series of secret relay stations of mounted men and remounts stretching northward over the plains to Regina. In Regina a daring party of Montana Métis, led by himself, would overcome the jail guards, whisk Riel from prison, and pass him rapidly across the border to safety. Though Dumont hastily collected money, provisions, horses, and men, and though some relay stations to the south were made ready, the attempt to overcome the prison guard and release Riel failed to materialize.

In prison, Riel retracted his unorthodox pronouncements concerning Roman Catholic dogma and received absolution from Father André, of Prince Albert, and Father McWilliams, of Toronto, who accompanied the condemned man to the gallows on a frosty mid-November morning. Requiem mass was celebrated on December 12, at St. Boniface, Manitoba, where the body of Riel was buried in the cathedral yard in the vicinity of his birthplace, and where, 15 years before, he had led the Red River uprising. On the granite gravestone provided by sympathizers in Montreal, where as a youth he had studied for the priesthood in the Sulpician College, is inscribed: "RIEL, 16 novembre, 1885".

Some of the defeated Métis trekked northwestward to the Peace River country, dejectedly in search of their vanished frontier. Those who had not joined the rebels were granted scrip and land patents which, for the most part, they sold at ridiculous prices to settlers and

Red River cart

speculators. Unable to adapt themselves to the economic and social ways of the dominant Whiteman, they were to become a dispirited, rejected people.

The Indians had appeared in war-paint for the last time, except at fairs and on occasions when visiting White dignitaries were to be made honorary Indian chiefs. They quietly retired to their reserves to stagnate, while around them grew an agricultural and commercial economy in which they were unable to participate.

Repercussions of the rebellion shook the framework of confederation. Many French-Canadians of Quebec, where money had been contributed for Riel's defence and mass meetings of protest concerning his sentence had been conducted, eulogized Riel as a patriot and finally a martyr in the cause of French Catholic resistance to English Protestant domination. Legal minds argued that Riel could not have been legally condemned to death for high treason, as he was not at the time of his sentence a British subject, but a citizen of the United States of America.

English-speaking Canadians of Protestant Ontario reviled Riel as a French-Canadian Roman Catholic traitor to the Crown in 1885, and murderer, in 1870, of a loyal Orangeman.

The Northwest Rebellion cost the Conservative Party its support in Quebec and gave the Liberal Party an opportunity to emerge from its Ontario confines, to restrain its radical reformism, and to gain in

Quebec a growing following later to be consolidated by the selection of a rising young French-Canadian, with an understanding of Anglo-Saxon ways, Wilfrid Laurier, as its leader.

In the Northwest Territories, where the agitation for responsible government continued, a developing Liberal Party faction harassed Conservative adherents by asking them to explain why the Conservative administration had failed, in the face of constant advice and persistent agitation, to take steps to avert the rebellion.

Broadening the Base

THOUGH the Northwest Rebellion had focussed outside attention on the area, the wave of sensational publicity resulted in no immediate inrush of settlers. In the years 1886-87, the trickle of newcomers was almost offset by those who, simultaneously, were abandoning this frontier country. Land speculators lost their enthusiasm when their dreams of quick money failed to materialize, while a number of *bona fide* settlers became discouraged by summer drouth punctuated by occasional, violent hailstorms that beat down growing crops, followed sometimes by late summer or early autumn frost damage to unripened grain. These and other bewilderments of a strange land caused many of the disconcerted to sell out for what they could get, or simply to abandon their equity and leave the country.

Adaptation to this semi-arid, midcontinental area with its climatic extremes was not easy for those who came from climes less harsh and more humid. Among pioneers who "stuck it out" and stayed on to broaden the base of agricultural settlement was Alexander Kindred of Moffat, south of Wolseley. Mr. Kindred described his experience:

[In 1885] we had only ten bushels [per acre] of very badly frosted wheat. I took some to Indian Head and traded it for flour, shorts, and bran. I had no money to pay expenses. . . . In 1886 we had 80 acres under crop. Not a drop of rain fell from the time it went in until it was harvested. I sowed 124 bushels and threshed 54. In 1888, we began to think we could not grow wheat in this country. I had now 120 to 125 acres under cultivation. We put in 25 acres of wheat, 10 to 15 acres of oats, and let the rest go back into prairie. That year we got 35 bushels [of wheat] to the acre! So we went to work and ploughed up again. The next year wheat headed out two inches high. Not a drop of rain fell that whole season until fall. We summer-fallowed that year [1889] for the first time, and, to show the optimism, we put in in 1890 every acre we could. We had wheat standing to the chin but on the 8th of July a hailstorm destroyed absolutely everything. My hair turned grey that night.

Devastation of a promising crop by ice pellets released from an ominous thunderhead was the result of a natural phenomenon beyond the control of man. Equally uncontrollable were excessive aridity and early frost, but the risk of loss from them could be reduced. Men of the prairie learned to plant deeper than was customary in humid lands: to drill the seed into the soil where germination was less hampered by the relentless, moisture-sucking winds of a dry spring. They learned to summer-fallow, that is, to leave some of their cultivated land unseeded each year, and to keep it free from weeds so that moisture would be conserved for next year's planting. With the help of scientists and agricultural experimenters financially aided by the Canadian Pacific Railway Company and the Canadian Government, farmers came into possession of seed wheat certain to ripen sooner than the older varieties of the Red River settlement and thus bound to have "a better chance to beat an early frost".

Red Fife wheat, brought to Canada by David Fife, matured from 10 to 15 days earlier than the old Red River variety. In 1885 Red Fife was the seed most in demand. In that year the Canadian Government adopted its policy of experimental farms under the able guidance of William Saunders, who introduced Ladoga wheat from Russia, where soil and climate were similar to that of prairie Canada. In 1887 the Canadian Government established an experimental farm on the northern edge of the open plain at Indian Head, a Canadian Pacific Railway point. In 1889, a year of extreme drouth, Ladoga wheat ripened four days ahead of Red Fife. From the frost-exposed slopes of India's Himalayas, Saunders sought other varieties of seed wheat. Subsequently Hard Red Calcutta wheat planted at the Indian Head Experimental Farm matured ahead of Ladoga. In a search for improved milling and baking qualities, together with increased yields, the three varieties were crossed, and thus was initiated a process of experimentation which became continuous.

While farmers adjacent to the Canadian Pacific Railway mainline turned mainly to grain-growing as their hope for economic salvation, there were at least three areas where stock-raising predominated. Canada's Plains Region contained the northernmost tip of the great North American cattle-ranging country which once extended northward from the Rio Grande and the Gulf of Mexico. Forty miles

north of Swift Current was the Matador Ranch, a government grazing lease operated by a group of Texan cattlemen who had been accustomed to moving cattle northward on the hoof, while keeping in mind fluctuating markets and grass growth. In the vicinity of Maple Creek and southward to the Cypress Hills, stock-raising prevailed where rainfall was scant and evaporation rapid. High on the slopes of the Cypress Hills more rainfall meant greener grass during a long period, but the altitude resulted also in late spring and early autumn frosts not conducive to grain-growing. Throughout most of the Parklands Region the stockman could move his cattle on the hoof and graze them southward to a railway point linked by steel and steam to world markets.

A few farmers specialized in raising horses for sale to new settlers in a financial position to avoid an onerous beginning with the less expensive but unresponsive ox. Many Scotsmen, and others, preferred Clydesdale horses; there was a ready market for Percherons but less demand for Shires. Farmers were to find that horses with an added Bronco strain resulted in a sometimes difficult to handle, but hardier, breed than any in the strictly European classifications. Few farmers were without a pig or two on the place, and most kept a flock of hens. Sheep were raised successfully where they received the special attention required by their kind, but prospered little when unprotected from the cunning and predatory coyote or the hazards of winter blizzard.

As there were few villages at this time, farmers, to obtain supplies and services, were forced to drive many miles across country to village or town. The centre of the village was the general store, which usually included the post office. The local merchant, when he could obtain credit readily from the wholesaler, in turn extended credit to his customers looking to "next year's crop". Important was the leather-aproned blacksmith with his fiery forge and ringing anvil. Rarely without spectators, he fashioned and fitted hot iron shoes to the smoking hooves of horses excited by the smells and sounds of his shop, tempered the sizzling ploughshares, set iron tires on wagons and buggies or improvised a repair for a breaking plough or a binder. In the larger village, and always in the town, was at least one livery stable, which provided feed and shelter for the horses of visitors and hay bunks for the visitors themselves. Here the doctor could hire a team for transportation to the homes of his rural patients, or have his own team well cared for and made readily available for a trip during day or night. At the sidewalk end of the livery stable was the office furnished with several wooden chairs and benches, occasionally a rolltop desk, and invariably a cast-iron stove of formidable proportions. In winter the office served as an informal meeting place and lounge for fur-coated men before their sleigh journeys home. On the walls hung at least one calendar advertising the business of a local merchant or a distant manufacturer, a garish print of a famous trotting horse, and various public notices. These last called attention to such things as an auction sale, a description of an animal lost or strayed, the services of a purebred stallion or registered bull, a pair of mitts or other articles found on the trail and awaiting their rightful owner, and a coloured poster announcing a travelling show to come, or one that had locally appeared the year before and had long since departed. Within the four walls of the livery barn office was the all-pervasive smell of horse, man, buffalo robe, tobacco (both smoking and chewing), snack leftovers, whiffs of hay dust, and liquor blended and circulated by the heat of the generous stove.

At the fairs and field-days of summer, horse racing, both running and harness, was a popular sport. Football had become a feature and lacrosse was played, while baseball was then only beginning. Englishmen who in their old country had played cricket, lawn-tennis, and croquet brought with them these games, while, in one area at least, top-booted, red-coated horsemen, riding to hounds, galloped over the prairie after the rare and elusive fox. In winter, curling competitions were well attended, while ice hockey was yet to become popular. Dancing, both square and round, was enthusiastically enjoyed in most communities and there was considerable participation in amateur theatricals.

In the towns were various fraternal and social associations. Debates, when between well known participants concerning controversial issues or humorous subjects, were well attended. In this regard, in several communities along the C.P.R. mainline the lead was taken by the "mechanics' institutes", for whose formation as clubs or associations territorial legislation was provided. Among such institutes was the Grenfell Mechanics and Literary Institute, a community project that sponsored meetings of open forum and debate on a variety of topics, and established a reading and lending library. Discussion groups were instrumental primarily in the initiation of what became a Saskatchewan tradition whereby people met together in search of solutions to common problems, and initially provided the atmosphere and training essential to men and women who would emerge on various levels of public life.

School and church buildings were among the first non-private structures to appear on the prairie landscape. In many new communities, church and school preceded the coming of the railway, and were therefore early landmarks of the scattered rural settlements. On the plains more than one church building was built of sods by volunteer labour until the community became able to donate the money for a frame building. Where standing timber was available, local axemen prepared logs for the church or school. In a neighbourhood predominantly Presbyterian, a Presbyterian church would be built; where a Methodist, Baptist, or comparable denomination was predominant, the church would be of that denomination. For people of similar, though not identical, religious affiliation, the tendency was to attend the church initially established in the community. This practice in turn led to less doctrinaire church services and toward an eventual blending of several religious groups. Often the minister rode horseback or drove with horse and buggy, holding services in several church or school buildings during a Sunday. Roman Catholics were exclusive in attending their own services.

Influential in cultural affairs of the community was the school teacher who, more often than not, had selected the vocation because of aptitude and conviction and was imbued not infrequently with the intellectual counterpart of the flexible spirit characterizing the frontier. The advantage of elementary public school and higher learning was eagerly sought for the children. A few pioneers came to the prairie equipped with considerable formal education, while many others, who in their youth had been denied the opportunity, greatly wanted the advantage for their children. The money granted by the territorial government for education was comparable in amount to that allotted for public works (the other principal governmental financial commitment), which included the construction of roads and bridges. Both educational grants and scholastic aims in the Northwest Territories were considered high in comparison with those prevailing elsewhere in Canada. This situation was disconcerting to Canadian Government circles, where an investigation was set in motion concerning "the high salaries" paid to school teachers in the Northwest Territories.

Opportunity-seeking, land-eager, restless, underprivileged, and idealistic people came to the Canadian prairies from many lands and for a variety of reasons. Regardless of where they came from or why, those who stayed were unavoidably conditioned by the intractable geography, uncertain economy, and emergent social consciousness of a frontier sparsely populated by men and women who brought with them various and numerous predilections and customs, while all in common were faced with the need to learn rapidly new ways for survival and success in a new and untried land. The pioneers were for the most part an alert, outspoken, and neighbourly people.

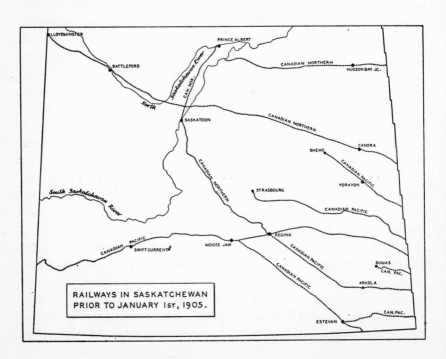

RAILWAYS IN SASKATCHEWAN
PRIOR TO JANUARY 1st, 1905.

In 1886 the Manitoba and North Western Railway, the second railway line to enter the area which was to become the Province of Saskatchewan, reached Langenburg. This railway line was begun at Winnipeg with financial assistance from the Province of Manitoba and without the blessing of the Sir John A. Macdonald administration. The new line eventually passed through Yorkton and was, in 1900, leased to the C.P.R. for 999 years. On the line near Langenburg, in 1886, men of a pioneer German colony worked at railway construction and used their wages to help equip themselves for farming in the following spring. Also in 1886 about 100 Icelanders settled close by the new railway. The German colony was known as Hohenlohe, and the Icelandic as Thingvalla. In both colonies a few settlers in need of financial assistance received small loans from the railway company. To the Qu'Appelle Valley about 30 miles west of the Manitoba boundary, came another settlement of Icelanders; their nearest town, Tantallon, was eventually served by a C.P.R. branchline in 1902. In 1885 German and Rumanian settlers came to the vicinity north of Balgonie. German and Austrian immigrants settled near Ebenezer, and Danes arrived near Yorkton to call their community New Denmark. The Icelanders, together with most immigrants from the European continent, had farming experience of some sort or were conditioned to rigorous living.

Less equipped for agricultural success was a group recruited from the towns and cities of England by the Church Colonization Land Company, whose colony south of Saltcoats, initiated in 1888, failed mainly from lack of elementary agricultural knowledge and of adaptability. Moreover the colonists received impractical though well intentioned advice from some of the sponsors. A member of the directorate, an Anglican cleric, wrote to the colonists that they should have oxen rather than horses because the oxen not only would be appropriate for ploughing but also would at the same time provide a suitable quantity of milk for the families.

While many Englishmen proved themselves less adaptable than newcomers from other lands, among successful settlers were individuals of English birth who gave impetus and virile leadership to social, economic, and political developments. The Qu'Appelle, Long Lake, and Saskatchewan Railway from Regina via Saskatoon to Prince Albert was completed in 1890. On this line in 1891 in the vicinity of

Rosthern, between Saskatoon and Prince Albert, German-speaking Mennonites from Russia began what was to become an expansive settlement. Two years later a few French families came from France to settle near Duck Lake. The Soo line running southeast from Moose Jaw through Weyburn and Estevan, Saskatchewan, to Portal, North Dakota, linked pioneer communities of Canada's prairie west with Minneapolis, St. Paul, and Chicago. In 1897 Ukrainians detrained at Saskatoon, from where they trekked to Fish Creek on the east side of the South Saskatchewan River. Two years later some 7,000 Doukhobors from Russia arrived to settle in three colonies, near Swan River, Yorkton, and Prince Albert.

The determination of both the government and the railways to settle the prairie west rapidly was reflected in an inducement made to pacifist and sectarian peasants from other lands. Written into the Militia Act was a provision exempting from military service members of denominations, such as Mennonites, who because of religious belief were averse to bearing arms. This exemption from military service was made initially to induce German-speaking Mennonites, hard-working and frugal-living farmers, to abandon the southern frontier of European Russia for settlement on the Canadian prairies. Subsequently the Canadian Government by order-in-council included Doukhobors in the exemption from military service.

During the territorial period, Ontario contributed more settlers than any other province of Canada. Though French-Canadians had penetrated the northwest many years before and though the Catholic Church had early become established in the area, comparatively few French-speaking communities were established in the expansive prairie west. The isolation of the prairie farmstead, plus the tempo of this agricultural frontier with its developing technology and men and women of varied faiths, held little appeal for the Quebec habitant or village priest. South of the C.P.R. mainline settlers were coming in from the United States, a vanguard of American settlement which was to increase after 1900.

Developing concepts of parliamentary government that had emerged in England during the previous three centuries had been further adapted to the westward-moving frontier of North America, and were used as weapons in the struggle against political and economic domination by successive centres of government. The principles of representation and executive responsibility were the means by which a free and flexible administration on the frontier was to be attained, in spite of the measure of economic and military dependence on the older centres, a dependence inherent in the kind of expansion taking place. This political vitality was evident in Canada's prairie west.

The importance of representation in the dominion Parliament was early recognized by English-speaking settlers, who were particularly aware of the impact of Canadian Government policy and legislation on the affairs of the Northwest Territories. The lively demand, by a vociferous but persistent minority, for representation in Parliament was recognized in 1886 when the Macdonald administration passed an act providing for two members of Parliament to represent the District of Assiniboia and one each from the districts of Saskatchewan and Alberta. The following year Parliament granted the Northwest Territories two members in the Senate.

In the federal election of 1887, when the Macdonald administration was returned to power, all the successful candidates in the territories were Conservatives. In that year the Canadian Government, in response to the growing agitation for a system of local representation in the northwest, accepted in principle the recommendations for extended autonomy, and in 1888 Parliament granted the Northwest Territories a legislative assembly of 22 elected members, plus three advisory members from the legal profession. The act also provided for an advisory council to be selected by the Lieutenant Governor from the Legislative Assembly. The Advisory Council was to concern itself especially with questions of finance.

Later in that year Prime Minister Macdonald appointed Joseph Royal as Lieutenant Governor, to succeed Dewdney who had been appointed Minister of the Interior in the Canadian Government. Lieutenant Governor Royal had been a member of Parliament elected in Manitoba, where he had practised law and published a periodical, Le Métis. As the Conservative Party had, since the Northwest Rebellion and Riel's execution, continued to lose support in Quebec, the appointment of a French-Canadian as Lieutenant Governor of the Northwest Territories was considered a thoughtful move by Sir John A. Macdonald.

Royal, shrewd politician and diplomat, overcame much of the opposition initially voiced in the northwest concerning the appointment of a French-Canadian. His task was not an easy one, since the Legislative Assembly had a tendency to assume powers of a provincial legislature, and the council those of a provincial cabinet, whereas the money which maintained the administration was mainly a direct grant from the Canadian Government, to which the Lieutenant Governor was himself responsible.

When in 1889 Royal refused to allow the Legislative Assembly to decide how it would spend the money grant, the Advisory Council resigned, indicating that it considered itself responsible to the Legislative Assembly elected by the people of the northwest rather than to the Lieutenant Governor appointed by the Canadian Government in Ottawa. In his refusal Royal, whatever his personal sympathies, was acting strictly in accordance with the act.

After the resignation of the first council, Royal appointed another which agreed to comply with the act. The new council resigned when it failed to obtain the support of the Legislative Assembly. Comparable difficulties continued until 1891, when Parliament extended the powers of the Legislative Assembly and the Advisory Council was declared an executive committee with the provision that one member should reside in Regina, capital of the Northwest Territories, where he would maintain constant supervision over the public business of the area. The first member to assume this responsibility was Frederick W. G. Haultain.

Though Haultain's position as the resident and chief representative of the Executive Committee was in accord with the extension of the act, his title remained obscure and subject to interpretation. Popularly referred to as "Premier" and "Prime Minister" by members of the Legislative Assembly and Executive Committee, and by various newspapers together with the public generally, the meticulous Haultain refused to acknowledge either of these titles for the office he held, his contention being that neither would be applicable prior to the attainment of a larger measure of self-government. The son of an Englishman who had emigrated to Ontario during the midcentury, Haultain, a young lawyer, went west to practise law at MacLeod, Alberta. A dapper man with a cultivated mind, he developed a sense of political strategy. A master of ideas and their expression, somewhat impatient of stupidity, he was considered aloof in various of his political relationships and inclined to ignore popular prejudice when it failed to coincide with his intellectual concepts, but his personal competence and integrity commanded respect in the frontier community.

"Jim" Ross of Moose Jaw, a virile member of the Legislative Assembly who regarded himself as a reformer leaning towards the Liberal Party, became the Conservative-inclined Haultain's team-mate in the continuing struggle for increased responsible government leading to provincial status. Ross, a pioneer farmer, had "come west" from Ontario. Unhampered by intellectual pretensions, a straightforward, sometimes blunt speaker, he knew where he wanted to go and was not devoid of political sagacity.

Later in the 1890's the Legislative Assembly was enlivened by the vigorous debating of a self-possessed young lawyer from Calgary, New Brunswick-born Richard Bedford Bennett, who subsequently became a foremost proponent of the two-province concept as opposed to Haultain's one-province proposal.

In 1892 Haultain gained from the Canadian Government the concession that the money grant from Ottawa was to be turned over to the Legislative Assembly for disbursement as the assembly saw fit. But the Legislative Assembly was not empowered to borrow money. Haultain and his supporters wanted the Canadian Government to provide the money grant in the form of a subsidy similar to that received by the provinces. Subsequently, it became the hope that provincial status would result in the Canadian Government's handing over control of lands to a duly constituted provincial government, or governments, whose area would be carved out of the Northwest Territories. In 1891 the Legislative Assembly, finally empowered by Parliament to control the liquor business in the provisional districts, passed the Liquor License Ordinance which resulted in a marked decrease of both smuggling and bootlegging, and simultaneously gave impetus to an expanding hotel business. Under the ordinance hotels were licensed to sell liquor by the glass over the bar, and by the bottle for removal from the premises. Meanwhile the efforts of temperance and prohibitionist forces increased. Active advocates of prohibition were most prevalent in rural communities, where a very considerable majority of farm women continued to favour prohibition, or temperance as it was called. Prohibition could be attained locally by a majority vote opposed to the granting of a government licence to hotels within the district. Where hotels were licensed, the bars remained open to men 21 years of age and over, other than treaty Indians. In the bar-room, patrons were customarily served so long as they could stand up to the bar and pay for a drink. Some of the profit from the operation of the bar usually went for improvement of the dining-room and hotel service generally. While the trade proved profitable to licensed hotel keepers, sometimes an astute bartender enabled himself—after several years behind the owner's bar—to "get a hotel of my own".

Beyond the boundaries of the provisional districts, that is in the Pre-Cambrian Region and most of the Forest Region, prohibition remained in force.

The 1893 session of the Legislative Assembly, the last during Lieutenant Governor Royal's term of office, produced little constitutional change, a minimum of partisan conflict, and no challenge to Haultain's leadership. Royal, his five-year term of office completed, made a parting attempt to establish the reputation for local liberalism which, at the beginning of his term, he had hoped to build despite Canadian Government restrictions. In a final message to the Legislative Assembly he referred to the power of the Privy Council of Canada and to his being placed "in a somewhat invidious position in appearing to oppose the popular interests".

Royal's successor, Lieutenant Governor Charles Herbert Mackintosh, was selected primarily because of his proved loyal adherence to Prime Minister Sir John A. Macdonald and the Conservative Party. The ebullient Mackintosh had, in Ontario, been attached to various newspapers. Not without literary pretensions, he had written a book on Chicago's great fire. He had been city editor of Ottawa's *Citizen* and then mayor of Ottawa, and in 1890 he had been elected Member of Parliament for Ottawa City. While in the House of Commons, he had been a ready and vociferous defender of government policies, but had paid scant attention to the laborious processes required in the passage of practical legislation. In 1893 Mackintosh resigned his seat in the House of Commons to accept the appointment of Lieutenant Governor of the Northwest Territories, an area in which he had previously shown little if any interest. Not long after his arrival in Regina, he was writing hastily conceived and lofty letters to his political superiors in Ottawa in which he said, ". . .our young friend Haultain . . . is rather inclined to pigheadedness. I fear power was yielded and privileges granted [to the territories] before the proper time." Concerned over the agitation by an aggressive minority including the Patrons of Industry, a small, militant prairie farmers' group, he was critical of the forthright opinion expressed in territorial newspapers. Patronizing in his attitude toward prairie pioneers generally, he sent confidential reports to Ottawa that influenced the Conservative administration in solidifying its opposition to a ready granting of further responsible government. Mackintosh was the last Lieutenant Governor in the prairie west to officiate, either in manner or in fact, as the governor of an outpost colony of Canada. This vast outpost, whose scant and scattered population was politically and socially led by an alert, vociferous, and persistent minority, was continually demanding further self-government in a huge area of growing importance to governmental and financial circles of central Canada.

The combined concern of the Canadian Government and the Canadian Pacific Railway Company for promotion of prairie agricultural settlement was in further evidence when, in 1895, the government allotted $25,000 for the Territorial Exhibition held in Regina that year, while the railway offered to transport exhibits, free of charge, to and from the exhibition. The Legislative Assembly promised $10,000 and the Regina Town Council a like amount. With a total prize list of $19,000, the directors of the Territorial Exhibition were able to announce the biggest prize list offered by an exhibition west of Toronto. Active in the successful promotion was Lieutenant Governor Mackintosh, who demonstrated considerably more enthusiasm for the big fair of the northwest than he had shown for the struggle for responsible government in the area. The exhibition executive included Angus McKay and Major Bell of Indian Head, Thomas McKay of Prince Albert, Michael Oxarat (who raised thoroughbred horses on his ranch near Maple Creek), and prominent stockmen from the District of Alberta. It was mandatory that all prize-winning saddle-horses be sold for $125 to the North West Mounted Police headquarters at Regina. To encourage mixed farming as opposed to straight grain-growing, there was the composite entry competition in which each entry consisted of two bushels of wheat, oats, barley, and peas respectively; one-half bushel of flax;

and one male and two females of cattle, pigs, and sheep. A prize of $500 was offered for the best prairie (grass) fire extinguisher "drawn by not more than four horses, operated by not more than two men, and [at] a cost not exceeding three dollars a day".

Regina's unpainted frame buildings barely accommodated the town's expanding population of nearly 2,000. When, on July 29, the Territorial Exhibition opened, many exhibitors and their exhibits were housed in tents. To stimulate regional industries between the Red River and the Rocky Mountains, there were prizes for bob-sleighs, cutters, top-buggies, axe-handles, harness, saddles, buffalo coats, moccasins, boots, tents, furniture, brooms, blankets, soap, straw hats, and cigars. Essay contest subjects included these: irrigation, butter and cheese making, ham and bacon curing, gopher destruction, and "The Northwest as a Home for the Immigrant". Among new machinery, farmers saw a disc-drill, a type of mechanical grain seeder that would eventually replace the hoe-type drill, while their wives watched the operation of mechanical cream separators (De Laval), forerunners of separators which would dispense with the cumbersome creamer cans.

There was a grandstand "brilliantly lighted" with electricity. There was much enthusiasm. Practical entertainment included a ploughing match, bronco-busting, musical rides by the mounted police, and the Carnival of Nations, the last sponsored by Knox (Presbyterian) Church with a view to integrating the peoples who came from older lands into the frontier communities of prairie Canada. In the Carnival of Nations 60 girls representing 15 nations participated in a musical pageant with four showings under canvas during each day of the Territorial Exhibition.

In the following year, 1896, there was a federal election, when both Conservatives and Liberals prepared for a lively and what was to be a hard-fought campaign. An attempt by the agrarian Patrons of Industry to form in the northwest a third political force was largely a failure, but when the ballots were counted and the Liberal Party, led by Wilfrid Laurier, had been declared elected by a large majority, at least one candidate who had worked closely with the Patrons of Industry was to have a seat in the House of Commons. He was the Reverend James M. Douglas of Moosomin, elected as an Independent-Liberal to represent the constituency of East Assiniboia.

The crusading Mr. Douglas, a farmer impatient of pulpit restrictions, could thus more independently voice and work for his economic ideals and social aspirations. The Patrons of Industry, a minority farmers' educational and agitational association originating in Michigan state, had found advocates in Manitoba and the Northwest Territories, with the result that in mid-1890's a number of local lodges were organized, most of them between Moose Jaw and Grenfell and nearby points on the C.P.R. mainline.

A grain elevator and loading platform

The Patrons of Industry, and farmers generally, had voiced discontent and objection to a C.P.R. directive of 1897 to the effect that the railway company would allow grain to be loaded in its cars in no manner other than by a mechanical grain elevator when such was available. The C.P.R. claimed that the directive was necessary because individual farmers, or groups of farmers, loading railway cars directly from their wagon-boxes or from flat warehouses, unduly detained the cars which could be loaded by means of the grain elevator with great rapidity. The Patrons of Industry, together with the Reverend Mr. Douglas as their spokesman in Parliament, claimed that the railway company and the grain elevator companies had combined to form a monopoly for forcing the prairie farmer to sell his grain exclusively through the elevator companies. Douglas's persistent efforts in Parliament led to the Royal Grain Commission of Enquiry of 1899, which in turn led to the Manitoba Grain Act of 1900, which applied also to the Northwest Territories. Among other concessions to the prairie grain-grower, the act required the railway company to provide loading platforms at shipping points so that the grower could drive his wagon on to the platform and load his grain directly into a boxcar.

On the larger Canadian scene, the Liberal Party, after 18 years out of office, had, with the able leadership of Wilfrid Laurier, regained power at an opportune time. In 1896 the economic depression was receding. Among factors that combined for the emergence of a cycle of relative prosperity were these: A further surge of the industrial revolution in western Europe increased employment in urban centres there and consequently increased purchasing power for food, clothing, and shelter. Two gold rushes, one in the Klondike and another in South Africa, put some hitherto idle money into circulation as a result of the costly search for gold, while further discovery and production of gold increased the economic buoyancy. The Spanish-American War of 1898 and the South African War, which began the following year, were factors in maintaining the circulation of money, always a requisite of general prosperity. After 1896, immigration to the northwest, aided by government and railway policies and practices, gained momentum, and the end of a drouth cycle gave way to a higher average rainfall in the growing season.

Into the Laurier administration went Clifford Sifton as Minister of the Interior. This ambitious young lawyer from Brandon with his intimate knowledge of the west, enhanced when a former member of the Manitoba Legislature, soon was to demonstrate a vigour, vision, and organizing ability which gave decided impetus to the settlement of the prairie region.

In 1896 Nicholas Flood Davin was re-elected to Parliament as a Conservative member by a majority of one vote, which was cast by the returning officer. Davin had sold the *Regina Leader* to Walter Scott, an aspiring young newspaperman with liberal leanings.

The following year, 1897, the year of Queen Victoria's Diamond Jubilee, the Canadian Government granted to the Northwest Territories a further extension of responsible government. The Executive Committee became an executive council (cabinet) with ministers who headed regularly constituted departments, but certain legislative powers still were lacking, the most important of which was the power to borrow money. And a second distinction was that the Government of the Northwest Territories was not entitled to share in the regular system of federal subsidies, but continued to be dependent on the year to year decision of the Canadian Government as to the amount of money granted for the bulk of working expenses. These two principal factors, rendering incomplete full provincial status, curtailed the territorial government's capacity for long term planning of public works and related projects requiring amortization over a period of years.

It was in 1897 that the office of Lieutenant Governor, once paramount, was to become restricted to a colourful and dignified symbol of the Crown. A. E. Forget, who had served as the Clerk of the Northwest Council, was in 1898 appointed Lieutenant Governor by the Liberal administration at Ottawa. Though Forget's previous official designation had been that of Clerk, he had been in fact secretary of the Council, an important and exacting position which he had filled conscientiously. Thirteen years prior to his appointment as Lieutenant Governor, Forget, a prominent French-Canadian of the northwest, had journeyed from Regina to Winnipeg, there to consult with Roman Catholic Archbishop Taché in the hope that Sir John A. Macdonald in Ottawa might be persuaded finally to have Louis Riel's death sentence set aside.

By 1901 the Council of Public Instruction, which had replaced the previously established Board of Education in 1891, was disbanded and replaced by the Department of Education under a member of the Executive Council who was known as the Commissioner of the Department of Education.

While the territorial government and the scattered electorate were concerned with furthering the growth of formal education, plus coping with the pressing need for more roads, ferries, and bridges in a sparsely settled land where railway lines were as yet few and far between, nothing in the mind and mood of the settler exceeded in importance the ever-present question of "What's the weather going to do?" Sudden variability and shifting extremes of midcontinental climate, at a time when scientific weather forecasting was unknown, caused all men, and their women also, to scan the prairie skies, for signs to become their own, or their neighbour's, weather prophet. The mysterious individual who, by some inexplicable quality of sciatica, bunions, chilblains, or intuition—or just plain good luck—could "hit it right a lot of the time" acquired a local prestige not too far removed from that of the school teacher, clergyman, or banker. Observed and evaluated as portents of a late spring or an early winter were the seasonal migrations of Canada geese, "wild turkeys", and ducks. For hour to hour or overnight prognostications the stance of a cow's tail, house-flies' alacrity or drowsiness, the timbre of a coyote's howl, and subtle variations in the optimistic wail of a far-off locomotive's steam whistle were regarded by some people as having significance. Selected Indians, sought out on their cheerless reserves, were consulted concerning the probabilities of a "hard winter to come" or a "dry summer ahead". The opinion of no individual, no matter how inexperienced, was completely ignored in advance of the fact. He might be right. After the turn of the century *Dr. A. W. Chase's Calendar Almanac,* with its patent medicine testimonials and, free of charge, Canada-wide weather forecast for 52 weeks in the year, was furtively lifted from its accustomed nail on the outhouse wall and consulted in a contemplative attitude of wary hopefulness. While everyone talked about it, weather, both predicted and unpredicted, continued to arrive on the prairie scene, it being the one factor of universal consequence for which no one blamed governments, railway companies, the grain trade, or financial interests in Montreal, London, New York, or Toronto.

Rain came at the right time during the growing season of 1901, and frost came little if at all. Farmers along the C.P.R. mainline harvested the best crop since the prairie sod had first been turned there. The price of wheat was fair, the farmers thought. But, as usual, they anticipated a seasonal price decline as quantities of wheat were put on the market. Consequently there was a rush to haul the crop to the local shipping points along the railway. The railway company did not, probably could not, provide sufficient boxcars to move the bumper crop, and soon the elevators were filled at Grenfell, Sintaluta, Summerberry, Indian Head, Regina, Moosomin, and the other shipping points. Early in November it became apparent that a large part of the grain harvest would not be shipped that season. Farm granaries were full, and there were straw-covered piles of wheat in the fields. Farmers had been in sight of paying their debts and having a fair handful of ready cash; the vision ended abruptly in what they called the "wheat blockade".

John A. Millar, secretary of the Indian Head Farmers Association (conceived originally for the improvement of agricultural practice), called a meeting which overflowed into an indignation meeting.

W. R. Motherwell and Peter Dayman, of Abernethy, "were sore along with the rest of them", and they spread the word of a subsequent meeting to be held December 18, at Indian Head, where a committee was appointed to draft a constitution "for some kind of a farmers' organization that will get this wheat moving and get some results". The railway company had built the loading platforms in accord with the Manitoba Grain Act, but the farmer's right to order a car was still in doubt. Only a grain elevator company was accorded that privilege. The local agitation assisted Mr. Douglas, M.P., in persuading Parliament to amend the legislation so that a farmer, or group of farmers, would have the right to order a railway car on equal terms with the elevator companies. The territorial government's Department of Agriculture supported the farmers' movement, and on February 12, 1902, the Territorial Grain Growers' Association held its first annual convention, at which conscientious and tenacious W. R. Motherwell was elected president. Territorial authorities had already aided the formation of the Dairymen's Association of 1891 and the Western Stock Growers' Association of 1896. The sudden and unpredictable devastation of standing crops by midsummer hailstorms—those horrific spectacles of ravaging ice pellets falling from a turbulent sky—was taken into account in a legislative enactment when in 1900 the government passed a mutual hail insurance ordinance to enable farmers to group themselves together and insure their crops against hail damage, at cost. This initial legislative attempt to alleviate the hail problem proved inadequate, essentially because the insurance risk should have been spread over a large area.

The territorial government, with assistance from the Canadian Pacific Railway, brought in purebred stallions and bulls for the improvement of livestock. The government encouraged farmers to start creameries and cheese factories, while the C.P.R. provided free transportation for farmers who would go to the experimental farms to see for themselves what had been done and what might yet be done toward agricultural improvement.

The territorial government worked closely with the Laurier administration. The Canadian Government embarked on a policy of railway expansion which resulted in the formation of the Grand Trunk Pacific and the Canadian Northern railways. Driving, innovating, and flexible Clifford Sifton, Minister of the Interior, encouraged settlers from the United States and central Europe as well as from the United Kingdom. Both the Canadian Pacific Railway and the Canadian Government carried on publicity campaigns for luring settlers to the prairie west. Among promoters who responded was an Anglican cleric, the Reverend I. M. Barr, a vocal gentleman whose grandiosity was not equalled by a capacity for organization. Barr's glowing accounts of the prairie scene attracted hundreds of men and women from the towns and cities of England. On April 17, 1903, the first three trainloads of Barr Colonists arrived in Saskatoon. The 1,500 men, women, and children encamped in tents during two weeks beside the Canadian Pacific Railway track in Saskatoon; then most of them, by ox and horsedrawn wagons, trekked to Battleford and westward to the vicinity of what was to become Lloydminster. Lloydminster was named for the Reverend G. E. Lloyd (later Bishop Lloyd), a vigorous, very British, and determined ecclesiastic to whom the colonists looked for guidance. Despite Barr's acknowledged mismanagement of the much publicized venture, the individual initiative of the colonists themselves resulted in successful settlement on the frontier.

Clifford Sifton, a driving administrator, found time to look after his own growing business interests. No theorist, he was receptive to the theories of other men in various walks of life, and sought on the spot information in personal visits to the settlements. He applied vigorously the ideas of the thoughtful and imaginative immigration authority, Alexander Begg, and subsequent immigration officers of both the railway company and the government. Immigrants from the British Isles and continental Europe were not arriving in numbers sufficient to suit Sifton's determination to populate the prairie west rapidly, to plough up the grassland, to plant wheat, to make the railways pay, and to build the new empire of the northwest. He revived and intensified the policy of encouragement to experienced dry land settlers from the midwestern United States. In 1898, in conjunction with the railways, he instituted free tours for western United States editors, so that they could see for themselves the Canadian west and thus return to their desks to publicize a vision of hope and opportunity for land-eager Americans who knew that in their own country the best homestead land had already been taken up. By 1902 Sifton had placed inviting advertisements in 7,000 American periodicals with a combined circulation of some seven million. Land settlement companies of the 1900's operated under more favourable conditions than those of the 1800's, when both experience and facilities had been considerably less. Various land companies of the early 1900's, backed by American capital, had special appeal to prospective immigrants from Minnesota, Wisconsin, Iowa, Illinois, Missouri, the Dakotas, and other states. The success of the Saskatchewan Valley Land Company, which settled a large tract between Regina and Saskatoon, encouraged subsequent ventures. American dry land farming skill and ready improvisation had an impact on settlement methods generally.

Along with the appointment of immigration officers beyond the boundaries of Canada, the Canadian Government and the Canadian Pacific Railway distributed free pamphlets and booklets, printed in several languages, extolling the promise of the prairie west where a man with willing hands, determination, improvisation, and a next year attitude could, with scant capital, break new land and build a home of his own. Such a man with no material possessions other than the clothes on his body could hire his labour to an established settler, or a railway construction contractor, save his wages, learn the ways of the country, and with payment of a $10 fee to the Canadian Government obtain the right to 160 acres of virgin soil. Often the homesteader's initial "drag" and "drawbar" power did not exceed a team of oxen, while his first outfit of implements was restricted to a wagon and one-bottom breaking plough. Hard work was imperative; some luck in weather, markets, and prices, desirable and often essential. And rarely would he find a better equipped or more fortunate neighbour unwilling to help him "get a start". Usually he began as a bachelor and, when he married, his wife became a welcome partner in the hard work of a harsh land of high sky, luring horizon, and vivid sunrise. On the pioneer farm the children, de-

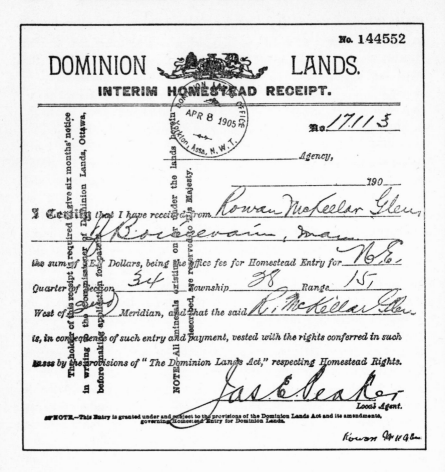

veloping self-reliance at an early age, were soon helping with the family chores both indoors and out.

As word of the promise of Canada's prairie west, both actual and conjured, spread through much of the area of European civilization, the immigrant flow increased. Augmenting official publicity accompanied by accounts in a variety of periodicals, were letters from successful or hopeful settlers to relatives and friends. A description of opportunity in the Canadian northwest reached the Patagonian region of South America and there stirred two hundred Welsh settlers to sell their holdings and cross the equator to Canada. They had left

Wales 30 years before and they found the land of Patagonia largely to their liking, but they had, like the Mennonites and Doukhobors in Russia, objected to compulsory military service. Financially assisted by a group of prominent Welsh compatriots in England, they left Argentina in 1902 and arrived in the Saltcoats vicinity in June of that year.

Throughout the following three years there occurred an accelerated technological advance. The flail a thing of the past, the horse-powered treadmill thresher was replaced by the steam-powered, belt-driven mechanical grain separator into whose humming maws sheaves were fed by men with steel-pronged pitchforks. Revolving knives cut the twine tied by a mechanical knotter attached to the horse-drawn binder which had replaced the mechanical reaper.

At Prince Albert and elsewhere on the southern edge of the Forest Region, steam sawmills were converting logs into boards for frame buildings, while expert axemen turned timber into railway ties and telegraph poles.

In Ottawa some 2,000 railway miles distant from this scene of fast-flowing immigration and expanding settlement, Prime Minister Sir Wilfrid Laurier was doubtful whether the northwest's heterogeneous and scattered population was ready for a final extension of responsible government. But by their prolonged efforts Haultain, Oliver, Ross, Bulyea, and others had finally impressed Ottawa.

Prime Minister Laurier supported a policy of autonomy and the two-province proposal. On September 1, 1905, legislation was proclaimed whereby the provinces of Alberta and Saskatchewan were pencilled out of the Northwest Territories. Though the new provinces were not granted control of public lands, and though they did not receive control of mineral resources, in other respects they did become political entities on an equality with the older provinces of Canada.

7

Turning the Sod

By the trainload came more and more settlers to turn the prairie sod
for grain land. Along extending railway lines, villages and towns
rapidly emerged, while on the luring horizon of the plains the tall, red
grain elevator became landmark and symbol of community and civilization.

Many settlers from the midwestern United States, seeking large and
low-priced tracts of virgin soil, arrived on the scene with extensive
dry farming experience plus mechanical equipment and cash, to begin,
in a spirit of bold enterprise, large scale farming operations. Less
expansive in both attitude and application—tenacious in their desire
to hold with the old yet learn of the new—were newcomers from
central and eastern Canadian provinces, Scotland, and Scandinavian

countries. Most men and women who came from mid-Europe brought with them little else than hope and a readiness to adapt, together with a capacity for the arduous work essential to frontier settlement success without benefit of capital. Thankful for their seemingly miraculous escape from the confining conditions of semi-serfdom in the old land, they became bewildered but eager participants in the new.

So engrossed were the inflowing immigrants in their all-absorbing task of establishing themselves in Canada's prairie west, that many of them—apart from advising relatives and friends in "the old country" of the required change of address from "Northwest Territories" to "Saskatchewan"—paid scant attention to the political fact that Saskatchewan, on September 1, 1905, attained the status of a province of Canada. The newcomers, for the most part unaware of the protracted and persistent struggle for responsible government, did not sense the historical significance of the event as did, for instance, A. E. Forget, the central figure in the inaugural ceremonies of September 4. The Honourable Amédée Emmanuel Forget's extended participation in territorial affairs had begun in 1876 when he gave up his law practice in Montreal and moved westward to make his home in the Northwest Territories where he served as Clerk of the Council and private secretary to Lieutenant Governor Dewdney, and, subsequently, as Clerk of the Legislative Assembly.

Forget, on being sworn in as the first Lieutenant Governor of the Province of Saskatchewan, recalled "a small gathering at Fort Pelly on the 26th of November, 1876, when I witnessed the swearing-in of my esteemed, distinguished, and venerable friend, Commissioner Laird, as the first Lieutenant-Governor of the Northwest Territories".

Yet the people generally were not concerned that the act of the Canadian Parliament, which created the new province as a legal entity, allowed for a distinctive political, economic, and social development. Though the neighbouring Province of Alberta was pencilled out of the Northwest Territories simultaneously with the Province of Saskatchewan, the two provinces were to evolve as individual entities whose respective characteristics would emerge beyond the fact of almost identical constitutional beginnings.

In constitutional essence, the effect of The Saskatchewan Act was to establish a new relationship between the government of the Saskatchewan area and the Canadian Government. This new relationship, as the act specified, was to be based upon appropriate sections of the British North America Acts of 1867 to 1885. While the British North America Act of 1867 left no doubt about the Canadian Government's overruling authority, especially in time of national crisis, Section 92 of the act gave the new provinces exclusive power to make laws relating to municipal institutions, solemnization of marriage within the province, incorporation of provincial companies, administration of justice in the province, erection of hospitals, asylums, and jails, provision of local works and facilities, and property and civil rights— the last a general clause which could be broadly interpreted. Section 92 also gave the provinces the right to raise revenue by direct taxation and by borrowing on the "sole credit of the province", a right which enabled a provincial government to spread the cost of new projects over a period of years. One power specified in Section 92 was withheld from the Province of Saskatchewan. Except for road allowances, Saskatchewan was not given control of public lands. However, Saskatchewan's right in this regard was acknowledged by provision for annual monetary compensation, based on population, to be paid in addition to the normal federal subsidy granted by the B.N.A. Act. A further limitation was placed upon the legislative powers of the new province by a clause in The Saskatchewan Act designed to safeguard the rights of minorities with respect to education. But, despite these disabilities, described by critics as extremely irksome, the autonomy in local affairs, plus the new sources of revenue provided by The Saskatchewan Act, gave to the first administration of this pioneer and fast-filling province opportunity for resourceful statesmanship.

Among a number of older inhabitants of British background, and more especially amidst the expanding and relatively politically vociferous population of the city of Regina, jubilation over the fact of provincial status was marred by controversy concerning the selection of the first premier of the province. On September 5, 1905, Lieutenant Governor Forget chose Walter Scott as Premier and instructed him to form a government to hold office until the first provincial election could be held. Scott, who resigned his seat in the House of Commons to lead the Liberal Party in the province, was a relative newcomer to the local legislative scene, while Haultain had headed the Legislative Assembly and had given capable administration during several years prior to the formation of the province.

Only the day before, Forget had been sworn in as Lieutenant Governor of the new province. At the ensuing luncheon in Regina, Prime Minister Sir Wilfrid Laurier welcomed Saskatchewan as the most recent and promising province of Canada. Other speakers on that official occasion included Earl Grey, Governor General of Canada, the Honourable David Laird, and Sir Gilbert Parker, M.P., Canadian author—sometimes termed "the Kipling of Canada". Among honoured guests was Major General Sir George A. French, the first commissioner of the North West Mounted Police. The omission of Mr. Haultain from the list of speakers caused much comment and some acrimony. Liberal Party supporters in Saskatchewan and elsewhere claimed that Mr. Haultain had injured his chance of being called upon to form the first government of the new province as a result of his participation in the Conservative Convention of 1903 at Moose Jaw, when he accepted high office in that party, and had subsequently destroyed his chances for provincial leadership by taking a violently partisan position in the Ontario by-elections of Oxford and London. Liberal partisans further urged that his attitude toward the new provincial constitution, especially with regard to the provision for separate schools, was dangerous to the peace and good government of the province; and that his choice as premier would have resulted in a long period of political disturbance, constitutional litigation, and sectarian controversy. The Conservative Party adherents, together with independent supporters of Haultain, protested vigorously against the slight to this figure so prominent and able in recent territorial affairs, the man responsible, more than any other, for the constitutional development toward, and final attainment of, self-government. They claimed, moreover, that he was the most capable man available for the position of Premier and deprecated the selection of Mr. Walter Scott, whom they described as a Liberal politician under the control of the Laurier administration in Ottawa.

The 38-year-old Scott, of lean frame and thoughtful brow, was a prominent western Liberal who, since 1900, had been member of Parliament for Assiniboia West. An enterprising journalist and publisher, he was president of a company owning the *Regina Leader* and the *Moose Jaw Times*. As Premier he chose to take in addition the offices of Commissioner of Public Works and Railway Commissioner. For Provincial Treasurer and Commissioner of Education he selected J. A. Calder, who had gained considerable administrative experience as Deputy Commissioner of Education in the territorial government. Calder, astute, discreet, and cautious, proved himself a capable party organizer. W. R. Motherwell, a successful farmer and president of the Territorial Grain Growers' Association, accepted the cabinet positions of Commissioner of Agriculture and Provincial Secretary. J. H. Lamont, who had been elected to the House of Commons in 1904, resigned his seat to become Attorney General in the Scott administration. None of the cabinet members appointed had served in the territorial government.

During the ensuing election campaign, the first in the Province of Saskatchewan, intense party feeling was more in evidence than during the initial election in the neighbouring Province of Alberta. The Liberal Party led by Scott had the advantage of being in office at a time when the people were busy, relatively prosperous or reasonably hopeful of prosperity, and therefore not anxious for a change of administration. The Liberals had the unofficial support of the Territorial Grain Growers' Association plus the benefit of Calder's unobtrusive organizing ability and the effective campaigning of the energetic and forthright Minister of the Interior, Frank Oliver, with his long and intimate experience of prairie affairs. There was, too, a not ungenerous distribution of political patronage emanating from the Canadian Government, which at the same time was pushing western construction of the much desired Grand Trunk Pacific Railway.

Haultain, respected for his integrity and previous governmental service, contested the election not as leader of the Conservative Party but as head of his Provincial Rights Party. He argued that the separate school clause should not have been included in the constitution of the newly created province, but that the people of the province should have been left free to decide the school question. This clause, plus the fact that the Canadian Government had not turned the federally controlled lands over to the Province of Saskatchewan, was a clear indication that the Liberal Party, both federally and provincially, had no intention of granting complete provincial autonomy, Mr. Haultain told the electorate.

The Liberals reiterated that Haultain and his Provincial Rights Party were a thinly disguised Conservative Party and would, if elected to office, involve the new province in lengthy and expensive litigation which might result in disruption of the constitution and the general retarding of provincial progress now well under way.

During the hard-fought and sometimes bitter campaign, W. R. Motherwell accidentally broke his leg. Scott's private response to the accident was that it would gain a sympathy vote and insure Motherwell's otherwise doubtful election. Scott wanted honest and hard-working Motherwell as an administrator but recognized his dubious value on the hustings. Somewhat stiff-necked and disdainful of both liquor and backroom sessions, Motherwell—not a fluent speaker—had twice before stood as a candidate in territorial elections, and on both occasions had lost his deposit.

When the ballots were counted, Scott and his three cabinet ministers were returned to office together with 12 other Liberal candidates, a total of 16 members for the Liberals. The Provincial Rights Party elected nine candidates.

Jim Ross, the energetic reformer and crusader for autonomy during territorial times, was effective in the Liberal organization, but since he had been appointed to the Senate the previous year he was not a candidate in the election. A power on both the prairie and national political scene was the alert and able John W. Dafoe, vigorous editor of the *Winnipeg Free Press,* whose resounding editorials and confidential guidance to men of Liberal persuasion from Sir Wilfrid Laurier down had much to do with western Liberal success.

Premier Scott and his cabinet members worked in harmony both among themselves and with the Laurier administration. Scott had gained in popularity during the campaign, and as Premier he proved himself a capable leader and thoughtful administrator despite a nervous temperament and somewhat frail physical health. Haultain as leader of the Opposition was a competent and not ungenerous critic. Scott relinquished his position as publisher and editor of *The Leader,* but the Regina newspaper continued to be regarded as the organ of the Liberal Party in Saskatchewan.

In a period of fast-flowing immigration and settlement, plus railway and business expansion, the hard-working provincial administration was fortunate in its harmonious relations with Laurier's

A Land Office rush

far-sighted and vigorous administration at Ottawa. For the 12 months ending June 30, 1906, 66 per cent of Canadian homestead entries were in Saskatchewan—a total of 27,692 entries in the province. In this way, along with outright purchase of Canadian Government, railway, and Hudson's Bay Company acreage, thousands and thousands of land seekers—who came from diverse areas of European civilization on two continents, spoke different languages, and adhered to various religious beliefs—rapidly acquired land for themselves. For their share in this unique and wholesale land distribution they had to plead with neither government nor landlord; instead the new settlers were urged by governmental authorities and privileged corporations alike to take the potentially agricultural acreage off their hands and make it pay. Government and financial circles, not sure of the enduring value of the land itself, believed it to be productive, but preferred to have willing individuals assume the initial risk and make the practical test. Some of those who filed on homesteads of 160 acres were unable to cope with the rigorous demands of frontier settlement, while others were speculators; both were weeded out in the process of time. The rapid growth in population is indicated by the figure of 257,000 in 1906, compared with almost half a million in 1911.

In railway construction camps and shack towns without benefit of sanitary sewage disposal, polluted streams and wells resulted in isolated but severe epidemics of typhoid fever, which generally occurred during the accumulated heat of late summer and autumn. These outbreaks were a factor in the establishment of hospitals and more stringent provincial health regulations. Among hospitals opened in 1907 were the Grey Nuns in Regina and St. Paul's in Saskatoon, both institutions initiated by the Roman Catholic Church. By this time no fewer than 12 hospitals were receiving provincial grants.

During the extremely severe winter of 1906-07, when temperatures during January 1907 dropped to 50 degrees below zero and prolonged blizzard conditions prevailed, stockmen lost many cattle and sheep. On farms and ranches insufficient fodder had been put up during the previous summer and harvest; it had been expected that the animals would as usual be able to winter out and forage for themselves. But the extreme midseason cold of that infamous winter, plus the accompanying depth of drifted snow, sapped the energy of the herds and made foraging difficult or impossible. Cattle, unable to get at grass buried deep beneath the snowdrifts, turned tail to the chilling wind and moved aimlessly with the blizzard. Sheep huddled together for warmth; the snow drifting over them formed a hard crust and many smothered to death before they could be located and dug out alive.

On the treeless open plain, people in the vicinity of Estevan burned the lignite coal from the Estevan mines, but the majority in the Plains Region depended on bituminous coal from the mines in Alberta. The additional consumption of coal required for warmth in the severe winter, plus the immobilizing of railway freight trains by snow, and a strike in Alberta pits, resulted initially in a coal shortage and eventually in a coal famine at various points. Some settlers, after driving with horses and sleigh over snow-encrusted trails to a village or town as far as 40 miles away, returned with sleigh-box empty of coal and resumed the unpleasant and frustrating task of cutting down their fenceposts for fuel. Meanwhile a 33-year-old student of political economy, William Lyon Mackenzie King, then Deputy Minister of Labour in the Canadian Government, was negotiating with coal miners and companies for a settlement of the strike. That winter the people who lived in the Parklands and Forest regions were thankful for the native trees which meant shelter from windchill and firewood for their stoves.

With spring came warm, dry winds to lick up the snow and carry away the moisture. Compared to the more humid and milder areas of central and eastern Canada, there was relatively little agricultural benefit from the snow of winter. Much of the moisture from the melting snow was carried away by the winds while most of the remaining percentage ran off before some five or six feet of frost thawed from an impervious ground. Some of the spring runoff found its way to the Saskatchewan river system to be carried away to the salt water sea of Hudson Bay. In early summer the South Saskatchewan River rose rapidly, the current swirling faster over its bed of shifting sandbars.

In June of 1908 the stern-wheel steamer *City of Medicine Hat*, with the Union Jack flying astern, came down the South Saskatchewan River bound for Saskatoon. Captain Ross, anticipating difficulty, put his three passengers ashore by the Grand Trunk Pacific Railway bridge on the outskirts of Saskatoon. Then for the captain and his crew the completion of the final lap of their hazardous journey became a hair-raising episode. At Saskatoon the belching smokestack cleared the Canadian Northern Railway bridge by inches, and the grateful captain steered for shore with the intention of tying up before he reached the next bridge—Saskatoon's one and only pedestrian and vehicle bridge. But the steamboat caught the telephone wires strung across the raging river: they in turn fouled the rudder and jammed the wheel. The captain realized his ship could not clear the next bridge. He rang for full speed astern: the paddle wheel churned in reverse, but the current was too swift. The steamer swept on toward the bridge and struck a concrete pier, there to lie half submerged. This ill-fated voyage was the last serious attempt at steamboat navigation on the South Saskatchewan River. While the Saskatchewan river system had been the great highway of the exploration and fur trade era, the settlers of the agricultural period came to regard "the river" as a barrier and a villain; additional ferries and bridges were being constructed, but they remained hazardous in times of flood and were costly to maintain. During a brief period steamboat navigation was tenaciously continued on the North Saskatchewan River.

But the age of steam continued to advance. While horses and oxen remained the principal motive power on the expanding farm lands, steam was no longer restricted to rail and stream. Like primordial monsters of cretaceous time, the vanguard of huge steam tractors began to move over the prairie scene, their rear wheels six feet high with iron-cleated track three, four, and even five feet wide. Boiler filled with water and bunkers stacked with coal, the traction engines, weighing from 12 to 20 tons, pulled multi-furrowed, sod-breaking ploughs turning 8 to 14 furrows that rolled from the curving mouldboards to glisten like steel ribbons in the sun. Among the various makes of steam tractors on the market was the American-made Reeves tractor. An owner of one of these popular giants would boast he could turn over 100 acres of prairie sod in 24 hours. Somewhat smaller and most in demand was the J. I. Case steamer, rated at 25 horsepower on the drawbar and 75 horsepower on the belt. There was the

Sawyer-Massey, a Canadian-built engine, the Waterloo, and American Abell. Where three horses customarily pulled a 14-inch, one-furrow breaking plough during a maximum 10-hour day, the steamer, operating on two shifts and accompanied by a blacksmith with mobile shop to sharpen shares, could plough day and night, thus in 24 hours doing the work of dozens of good horses.

At harvest time on the plains a steam tractor could pull a string of binders, and for threshing line up to belt-drive a grain separator. The threshing outfit then required a crew of 20 to 25 men, from 30 to 40 head of horses for hauling sheaves and threshed grain, water for the boiler, and straw fuel for the firebox.

While steam was in general use for threshing, the motive power more often in use for ploughing land, including new breaking, was still provided by the horse and the ox. Prolonged were the friendly and humourous arguments of struggling homesteaders concerning the relative merits of oxen and horses. While it was generally agreed horses were preferable, it was admitted they were more expensive to acquire. The ox, much slower, was in some ways more reliable and steady; however, he could not work through the extreme mid-day heat, and the biting flies of summer sometimes stung him to madness. Thus many a homesteader, turning new sod or keeping black his summer-fallow, set the raucous alarm clock for 3 in the morning, rounded up his oxen, ate his own breakfast, and then worked the animals in the field until 10 o'clock or so. During the mid-day heat the oxen were turned loose to graze or seek shelter from the searing sun; about 5 o'clock they were hitched again to plod late until the long evening twilight slowly faded into darkness.

A threshing rig on the move

Few farmers owned a threshing machine; those who did, threshed for many neighbours. In 1908, according to Saskatchewan Government records, there were 3,468 threshing outfits in the province, an increase of 3,100 over the number of machines for the entire Northwest Territories in 1898. The Department of Agriculture supplied thresher's account books so that operators could more readily keep track of charges to the farmer and wages due the threshing crew. Threshing charges to the farmer were by the hour or by the bushel, while the men were paid by the quarter-day. For the threshing crew it was a long day. About 5 o'clock in the morning or before, the tractor's steam whistle blew to rouse the sleeping men from their bunks. The teamsters fed, curried, and harnessed their horses. Breakfast was around 6 o'clock or sooner, and by 7 the crew was in the field. Threshing continued until dark and sometimes several hours after sundown when the strawstack was set afire to

Unwanted strawstacks burning in the night

light the continued operation. For the hard-working threshermen it was often a 16-hour day, but when rain came and the work stopped, the men rested, having free and plentiful meals in the portable cook-house, free bunks in the bunk-car with its straw-filled, blanket-covered mattresses, but no wages. For harvest there were not enough men available on the farms; therefore the annual harvest excursions. The railway companies offered and advertised reduced fares from as far east as the Maritimes for men who would go west for the annual harvest. In the autumn of 1908 more than 14,000 men took advantage of harvest excursions, and a number of them stayed on in the prairie west. That year for stooking and binder work the wages were $1.75 to $2.25 a day; for threshing, $2 to $3.25 a day.

There was about harvesting, whether cutting and stooking the crop or forking sheaves into the humming maws of a separator, a sweat of urgency, a contagious impulsion to garner the grain before it could be overtaken by early frost, autumn rain, or snow; and to haul it to a railway shipping point before a fluctuating price took the anticipated seasonal drop (which did not always materialize) on the Winnipeg Grain Exchange, or the ice of winter closed shipping on the Great Lakes.

Sometimes the tail-end of a late harvest, overtaken by a freezing rain or early winter snow, was not completed that season, and so was resumed the following spring just prior to seeding. In the Parklands Region where relatively smaller farms did not so readily attract the services of the large scale, American-style threshing outfit operating mainly on the expansive plains, and especially among cautious farmers conditioned by the frugality of older lands, there was the practice of stacking sheaves so they would remain dry until a threshing machine became available. Sheaves thus stacked were threshed even after the arrival of winter snow. The period between the completion of harvest and Christmas was a time of meetings both social and for economic discussion. While many meetings and gatherings took place in prairie farm homes, the school-house was a central meeting place in the community.

With increased settlement came a demand for further municipal government, the local governmental unit. November 1, 1908, the Saskatchewan Government established a department of municipal affairs. The provinces of Saskatchewan and Manitoba were the first two provinces of Canada to have such a department. The Saskatchewan Government appointed a municipal commission to inquire into

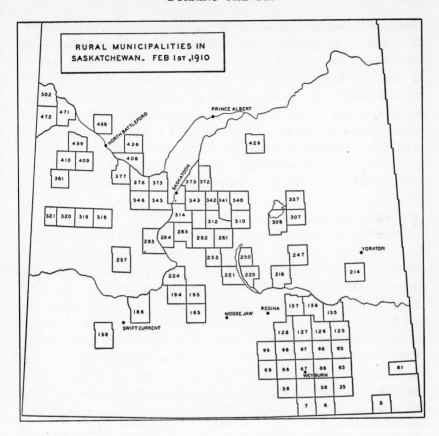

RURAL MUNICIPALITIES IN SASKATCHEWAN. FEB 1ST ,1910

municipal organization and to interview the people. The first departmental report included this statement:

The opinions expressed by the people were crystallized in The City, Town and Village, Rural Municipality[,] and amended Local Improvements Acts, passed in the years 1908 and 1909. . . . Saskatchewan in its laws has taken advantage of the experiences of older provinces, eliminating their mistakes and adopting only their better portions. But, after all, Saskatchewan had no precedent to follow. Conditions were different from what they are even in Manitoba. . . . In dealing with municipal institutions the Department finds it necessary to take the initiative in myriads of cases. . . .

In the Plains Region generally and more especially in its alkali areas, finding good water free from sodium sulphate and other salts remained a problem. Moreover, the water, such as it was, often lay far beneath the surface of the land, thus necessitating deep wells, impractical and hazardous for digging by hand. To assist the settlers in obtaining water for human and animal consumption, Saskatchewan's Department of Public Works provided, at a nominal rental, mechanical well boring machines. The demand for assistance in obtaining water occurred so frequently that it was found impossible to comply with even a small percentage of the applications for the use of drills. Therefore a system of bonus was inaugurated whereby half the cost of approved machines was paid by the government. In 1907 and 1908, 36 machines had earned the bonus and 20 more at work were eligible.

There was a pressing demand for more roads, bridges, and ferries. In 1907 provincial government expenditures for roads amounted to just over $400,000. In 1907-08, bridge and ferry expenditure was more than $450,000. While roads were important for hauling farm products to markets and shipping points, and returning with farm and home supplies from the scattered centres, passable roads were also greatly desired for local visiting and social events. With the exception of religious sects and communal economic settlements, such as those of the Mennonites and Doukhobors who, for the most part, lived in their villages, the prairie farmer built his home and barn in the isolation of his acreage. Though he preferred the individual family farmstead to the gregarious proximity of village life, he and his family were fond of company and much inclined to visiting with neighbours and friends a distance away. Neighbourly visits were a part of community social life, and more: the settler, adjusting to new conditions, was keen to learn of approaches and techniques with which another farmer might be conversant.

The voluntary isolation of the family farmstead was more keenly felt by the womenfolk. In the husband and wife partnership the woman was more confined to the home and she especially found the party-line telephone a blessing; it provided a ready and convenient substitute for the informal and sometimes prolonged chat enjoyed by urban neighbours over the backyard fence. Moreover, the well founded assumption that others besides the two parties directly concerned were most probably listening in on the line, imposed on the principals a calculated restraint which made an art of a seemingly casual and pretendedly private conversation. Here may have been an unpremeditated beginning of the panel discussion technique developed some 20 years later in radio broadcasting. But unlike the radio audience, the unseen audience with ear pressed to a rural telephone receiver sometimes betrayed its identity by the familiar ticking of a clock placed close by the phone, or an exuberant remark of a child at play, or grandfather's snore which had, during a previous Sunday, been unmistakably identified in church. The menfolk "listened in" too, but rarely did anyone "let on" he had acquired valuable information surreptitiously. If, for instance, he had heard that morning, clandestinely, of a neighbour's proposed trip to town, he would, after allowing a decent interval to elapse, phone his neighbour, and say, "I don't suppose you were thinking of going into town today. . . . You are going in? Well, maybe you'd bring our mail out with you. . . . And the wife will phone a list in to the store." Thus was the usefully non-existent privacy of the rural line formally respected.

A general ring—indicated by one prolonged ring—officially summoned all subscribers to lift their telephone receivers and listen. It might be an announcement of an auction sale, a local dance, a farmers' meeting, the postponement of a funeral, or a tragedy such as fire on an isolated farm. Day or night, in good weather or bad, a neighbourhood would respond and neighbours rally to an urgent call for help.

Due mainly to the distance between farm homes and the consequent number of telephone poles and yardage of wire required per telephone installation, venture capital was rarely forthcoming for rural telephone systems considered to be of doubtful value from the standpoint of profitable investment. Thus it was that farmers grouped themselves for installation and operation of their own local rural telephone service. Such a group acquired the poles, placed them, strung the wire, and installed the telephone instruments. In each instrument box was a hand-cranked generator, which provided electric current to ring the bells, and two dry cell batteries to carry the voice over the party-line circuit. In 1908 the voluntary improvisation of local and scattered rural telephone service, together with the need for increased facilities, was recognized in legislation enacted by the Saskatchewan Legislature. The legislature passed The Railway and Telephone Department Act, which repealed the Railway Commissioner's Act of 1906 and established the Department of Railways, Telegraphs, and Telephones. The new act provided for public construction, acquisition, control, and management of telephone systems, but not for taking over all existing systems or effecting a monopoly of construction or operation. An important feature of the act was its authorization of telephone companies, under provincial charter, to issue debentures and borrow money. Under the act, telephone companies were required to submit annual statements of cost, receipts, operation, and management, while the commissioner of the government department concerned was empowered to adjust rates, rentals, tariffs, tolls, schedules, and charges, and to set standards of construction, equipment, and operation. In the same year the legislature passed the Municipal Telephone Act, empowering municipalities to finance and operate telephone systems within a municipality; also passed was the Rural Telephone Act authorizing five or more persons to construct, maintain, and operate a rural telephone system under the Companies Ordinance,

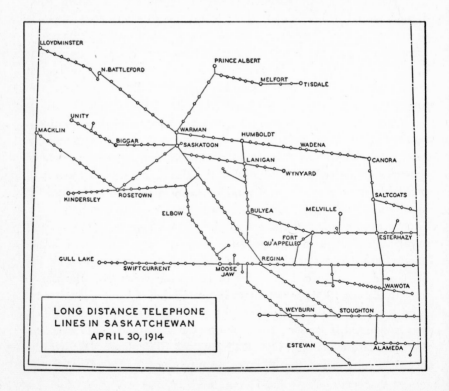

LONG DISTANCE TELEPHONE
LINES IN SASKATCHEWAN
APRIL 30, 1914

which required a capital of $150 per pole mile and allowed for sale of shares at $25 each. A departmental report indicated that 31 rural telephone companies had been organized and incorporated by February 28, 1909. The government remained responsible for long distance telephone service, and arranged for co-ordination of the various local telephone services, both rural and urban.

Where telephone service was available, a phone was invariably installed in the rural school-house. Thus parents were enabled to phone the teacher and learn whether their children, sometimes driving by horse and sleigh a distance of three miles or more, had safely arrived at the school. The school-house door was customarily left unlocked, for two reasons: so a passer-by could use the phone in an emergency any time of the day or night, and to provide shelter for persons who might be caught out in a winter blizzard or a summer storm. Not only did the rural school-house become a community centre for dances, socials, and meetings; church services also were usually held in the school until a church building was constructed.

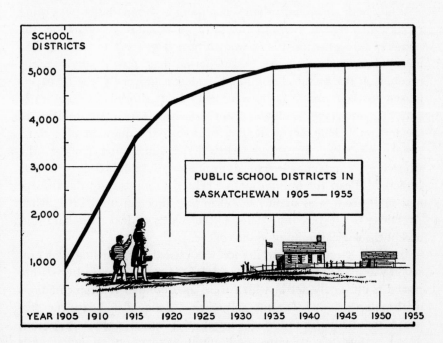

PUBLIC SCHOOL DISTRICTS IN
SASKATCHEWAN 1905 — 1955

In schoolrooms were held rehearsals for the annual musical festival initiated in 1908 by the Saskatchewan Provincial Musical Association, whose aim was "to promote music as an art and unite all musical societies in the Province of Saskatchewan into one organization for the purpose of holding annual festivals". Thus Saskatchewan people, far from metropolitan centres where opera companies and symphony orchestras were established, organized themselves to give expression to musical talent in their own communities. The concept of the musical festival arose neither from the rural square dance fiddler nor the town brass bandsman, but rather from a British choral and pianoforte tradition brought to Saskatchewan by devotees from the old land. Saskatchewan church and school choirs were often the basis of choral groups developed by devoted men and women, those voluntary and mainly unpaid pioneers of the musical festivals which brought together in annual competition musical aspirants from many parts of the province. Moreover the formation of a choir with piano accompaniment required a minimum of musical equipment and so could be organized at considerably less expense than an orchestral group.

While both rural and urban schoolroom accommodation was being rapidly increased to meet the needs of an expanding population, the minds of far-sighted men and women turned seriously to the establishment of a university. As Saskatchewan had few if any wealthy residents in the financial position to endow a university, the taxpayers looked to their provincial government. In territorial times, as early as 1891, university graduates from elsewhere who were residents in the territories had met in Regina to discuss the question of a territorial university. In Prince Albert, the Emmanuel College, the Church of England theological institution, established in 1879 by Bishop McLean for training native helpers to minister to the Indians and Halfbreeds, was mainly useful in this direction until 1907, when Archdeacon Lloyd arranged for 60 catechists to leave England and accept theological training in the college.

In 1903 a university ordinance was passed, but no financial provision was made for its support. In 1907 the Saskatchewan Legislature passed a university act in which were incorporated recommendations of the University of Toronto commission, designed to place the proposed university beyond the control of political parties in power, guard against sectarianism, and admit women on an equal basis with men. Early in the following year a board of governors was appointed, and during the next year an embryo faculty began teaching the arts and sciences. Among centres such as Regina, Saskatoon, and Prince Albert there was keen competition for the permanent site of the university. Two strong arguments advanced by the Saskatoon Board of Trade and the Saskatoon *Phoenix* were that Regina should not have both the provincial capital and the university, while Saskatoon was more centrally located than either Prince Albert, Battleford, Moose Jaw, or Indian Head. At a meeting of the Board of Governors, August 20, 1908, Dr. Walter C. Murray of Dalhousie University was appointed president of the University of Saskatchewan. One day, early in April, 1909, the Board of Governors, meeting in Regina, selected Saskatoon as the most desirable location for the university. That night Saskatoon citizens gathered at their fire hall and the screeching of the fire alarm siren was the signal for an impromptu and boisterous celebration in which a number of gleeful and calculating citizens, not unaware of enhanced real estate values, participated until sunrise the following morning.

A few weeks later the Board of Governors of the University of Saskatchewan was looking for a campus site. With the ready concurrence of the new university's self-effacing, practical, and far-sighted president from the Maritimes, Walter Murray, the board selected a site high on the east bank of the South Saskatchewan River, and acquired 1,176 acres—and later another 160 acres—for a campus and an experimental farm. Murray, a firm and kindly man, alert but unobtrusive pioneer in the academic field, set the tone of the university in these words:

"We should have a university that will leave no calling, no sphere of life untouched; a university that is as broad in sympathy as these wide plains, as deep in richness as this marvellous soil, and as stimulating in spirit as the breezes which sweep over our fields."

Unique among Canadian universities, and notable among universities anywhere, was the initial recognition accorded to agriculture and the encouragement of the farming population to participate in a university of the people, financed by the taxpayers. Along with the arts, sciences, and professional schools, the faculty of agriculture was placed under the same board and supported from the same funds; through its Extension Department the institution was to reach out to

all rural areas of the province. In the words of its first president:
". . . In a province where agriculture will be paramount for generations, where the problems are not limited by provincial or dominion
boundaries, and where the farmers are strongly organized, it is of
very great importance that men engaged in farming should be prepared for the highest public positions. The problems involved in
the export of wheat and other food products, problems of transportation, of finance, of tariff, and of international relations, are so intricate
that safe guidance can be secured only by the use of the best expert
advice. This the university should be prepared to provide, and this the
future leaders of the farmers should get while at the university."

From its original home in Prince Albert, Emmanuel College was
transferred to Saskatoon after the opening of the university there.
While the university's first buildings of collegiate Gothic architecture
were being erected from local limestone left by the glaciers of
half a million years before, plans were progressing for an extensive
legislative building in the capital city, Regina. The Liberal administration, led by Premier Scott and returned to office in the election of
1908, announced a competition for plans for the new building. The
plan accepted was presented by E. & W. S. Maxwell, of Montreal.
The building was to be architecturally imposing with a high dome
visible far out on the flat open plain surrounding Regina. Between
the new building and the town would be an artificial lake created by
damming the trickle of Wascana Creek, all to be surrounded by a
park of planted trees.

The day of the ceremony for laying the corner-stone, Monday,
October 4, 1909, was described in a report issued by the Department
of Public Works:

The spirit of welcome and rejoicing made itself felt in a dozen ways
as the public poured out to do honour on the greatest day in the history
of the province. . . .

In the far distance could be seen the first contingent of school children
marching across the Albert street bridge. The sun, which had hidden its
face, glared down in splendour upon the scene and threw out its beams,
which being caught by the rippling waters of Wascana Lake, were
reflected back a hundred-fold, adding additional beauty to an already
animated scene. . . .

By this time the greater number of visitors had arrived and the stands were filled to the utmost capacities. . . .

Governor General Earl Grey, in his speech, remarked on the tremendous increase in the province's grain output and referred to the excellent crops of 1909. He spoke a warning: ". . . It would be wise of you to treat the big profits of this year as capital and not as income. Nature has a way of averaging her favours and is apt to follow her sunniest smiles with the blackest of her frowns."

Among items "placed in the stone" of the building, over which His Excellency the Governor General spread the mortar to the accompaniment of a massed 100-piece band, were these: a Union Jack, the Holy Bible, a map of Saskatchewan dated 1908, the most recent report of the Department of Public Works, copies of various newspapers including *The Morning Leader,* the "Public Accounts for the Province", and a collection of chartered bank notes varying in denomination from $5 to $100 and representing the Bank of Montreal, Northern Crown Bank, Traders' Bank, and the Canadian Bank of Commerce.

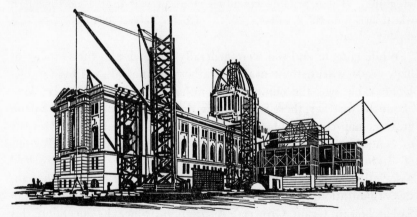

On completion of the ceremony, the Governor General accepted the trowel, to be kept "in the archives of my family", and said: "I understand the handle is made from the horn of the buffalo—the ancient inhabitant of the province—while the whole represents the industry of your city."

The building, to cost an estimated $1,250,000 exclusive of interior furnishings, was scheduled for completion by July 1, 1910. In January, 1911, the Legislative Assembly held its annual session in the stock and reading rooms, while the artisans continued with the work of completing the Legislative Chamber.

Wheat continued to be the principal concern of the Saskatchewan Legislature and a population directly or indirectly affected by the annual wheat yield and the fluctuating price of wheat. Saskatchewan had become recognized as the major hard wheat producing province of Canada, with a yet greater production potential. Milling and baking tests proved the superiority of wheat grown in the prairie west, and the generally favourable climate was summed up by F. T. Shutt, Dominion Chemist:

Climatic conditions influence the quality of the wheat through the vegetative processes by shortening or lengthening the time which elapses between the formation of the kernel and its maturity—the shorter the period, the higher the protein content within certain limits. High temperature, long days, and absence of excessive moisture during the ripening process, hasten the maturation of the grain and increase its percentage of gluten. These are the conditions that prevail in the northwestern wheat areas in those seasons which give the largest proportion of first quality wheat.

While climate and soil were generally conducive to the growing of high grade wheat, the variable weather was not always favourable. Unalterable was the climate, but, although nothing could be done about the weather, there were among the several hazards faced by the growers man-contrived factors which a minority of farmers had set out to control through group action. After the decline of the Patrons of Industry there had emerged the Territorial Grain Growers' Association. Following the formation of the Province of Saskatchewan, this organization, at its annual convention of 1906, was renamed the Saskatchewan Grain Growers' Association. Since its inception this farmers' organization had accused the grain elevator companies of, among other things, failure to allow the grower fair grades, weights, and prices. A pioneer and active member of the organization, English-born E. A. Partridge, who farmed near Sintaluta on the C.P.R. mainline, vigorously campaigned for co-operative handling and marketing of grain. When this strong-willed visionary of fiery eye and fluctuating practicality failed to persuade his organization as a whole, he, with a few of his more venturesome neighbours, initiated a farmers' grain elevator company at Sintaluta. Ed Partridge became president of the Grain Growers' Grain Company, formed jointly in 1906 by the organized farmers of Saskatchewan and Manitoba. September 5, 1906, in a two-room office on the top floor of the old Tribune Building, Winnipeg, the Grain Growers' Grain Company opened for business under a Manitoba provincial charter which permitted the company to sell $25 shares. The Canadian Government, in accord with its Companies Act, had refused to grant a charter which would allow the company to sell shares at less than $100 each. Nevertheless the struggling company, with the personal financial backing of a few determined members, bought a seat on the Winnipeg Grain Exchange, but was almost at the outset refused the privilege of marketing grain through the exchange. Exchange members were generally opposed to the farmers' company and more especially to its proposal to pay patronage dividends to the growers in accord with the Rochdale principles of co-operative enterprise. Though the Manitoba Government, at the insistence of the organized farmers, intervened and succeeded in having the Grain Growers' Grain Company reinstated on the exchange (April 15, 1907), the company had to accept defeat in a forced agreement to set aside an essential co-operative principle, the payment of patronage dividends. But the company did pay dividends on the $25 shares held by grower members. Personally discriminated against by members of the exchange, the forthright and idealistic Mr. Partridge resigned as president of the farmers' company. The shareholders, at their first annual meeting July 16, 1907, in Winnipeg, elected to the directorate an astute young manager of a country elevator, with a capacity for organization and a flair for diplomacy, T. A. Crerar of Russell, Manitoba. At the subsequent board meeting, Crerar was elected president. In 1909 increased support from Alberta farmers led to the establishment of a branch office in Calgary. In the same year the company opened a seed division for provision of improved seed grain, and established its own inspection department to check grading of all grain consigned to the company.

That year, during the grain harvest, the Winnipeg Grain Exchange suddenly suspended its commission rule that had compelled all grain handling firms to charge a commission of one cent per bushel.

Immediately the line elevator companies began handling railway carlots of grain at a commission of one-half cent per bushel, and where there was strong competition from the farmers' company, the line elevators charged no commission. The line, or non-farmer-owned companies, closely linked with the grain trade speculators and large milling concerns, could afford to abandon the commission. The fate of the non-speculative, farmer-owned company, whose sole source of operating revenue was the one-cent commission, now depended on the continued loyalty of its shareholder shippers. Farm leaders, both interprovincial and local, speaking at meetings at many shipping points throughout the prairie provinces, warned the growers that if they deserted their company they would be at the complete mercy of the line elevator companies and the speculators and brokers on the Winnipeg Grain Exchange. In a subsequent referendum vote of shareholders concerning the amount of commission the farmers' company should charge, 98 per cent of those replying were in favour of continuing the former rate of one cent per bushel. Moreover, farmers who had not previously sold their grain through the farmers' company became shareholders in the company, largely as a result of the much publicized battle between the exchange and the company. Impressed with the power of the press in support of the line elevator companies, the grain exchange, and the large millers, the farmers' company began publication of a probing and prodding magazine of fact and propaganda to extol the success of the organized farmers so far, to exhort them to yet greater efforts, and to warn of the dire consequences to follow should they forsake their cause and company. *The Grain Growers' Guide,* published by the farmer-owned Public Press under the able editorship of a Winnipeg newspaperman, George F. Chipman, with its weekly quota of eye-catching and clamorous cartoons, came to occupy, in many a farm home, a place of literary importance not far removed from the profusely illustrated mail-order catalogue of the T. Eaton Company, and the Holy Bible. Partridge and lesser millennium-seekers concerned with the price of wheat—speaking in school-houses, in community halls, and at annual conventions—effectively blended idealism with economics and especially favoured quotations from the Sermon on the Mount and Isaiah.

Under the auspices of the Saskatchewan Grain Growers' Association and the Interprovincial Council of Grain Growers' and

Farmers' Associations, linking the Manitoba and Alberta organizations with the Saskatchewan movement, Partridge led a campaign for government-owned and operated elevators. The "Partridge Plan", as it was known, would have had each prairie provincial government lease, buy, or build grain elevators at country points, while the Canadian Government would have had, in the interests of the growers, a monopoly of terminal elevators at Port Arthur, Fort William, Montreal, and at ocean ports on the Atlantic seaboard and Pacific coast. Thus, it was proposed, would the "unfair practices and unreasonable profits" of the "grain interests" be eliminated. To this proposal only the Manitoba Government, led by the Conservative Party Premier R. P. Roblin, responded by purchasing 163 elevators, a number of which were in doubtful condition and readily sold by line companies at what the farmers considered "exorbitantly high prices".

The response of the Saskatchewan Government was to appoint the Elevator Commission of 1910. The government appointed three commissioners: Green, Langley, and Magill. Fred W. Green, a Lincolnshire Englishman with socialist leanings, had in 1882 reached the end of steel (C.P.R.) near Brandon, Manitoba, and from there travelled west by ox-wagon to locate on a homestead near the site of Moose Jaw. Wiry, witty, and a keen debater, Fred Green in 1909 became secretary-treasurer and general organizer of the Saskatchewan Grain Growers' Association. English-born George Langley, M.L.A., a farmer and executive member of the association, was of short, almost stubby, build; he was an informed and dignified speaker and influential in his community. Both men were active supporters, but occasional critics, of the Liberal Party and government in power in Saskatchewan. Chairman of the commission was Robert Magill, formerly professor of political economy at Dalhousie University, Halifax, who was assumed to have technical knowledge and impartial judgement.

The commission had under consideration complaints put forward by farmers: that the line elevator companies gave lower weights, grades, and prices than the farmer was entitled to; that they deducted too much for dockage and shrinkage; that they refused to clean grain before shipping; that they failed to provide special bins; and that they mixed grain so as to receive for themselves higher grades from which the farmer did not benefit.

Outraged farmers also maintained that the chartered banks restricted or refused credit at harvest time and immediately after, and so forced the farmer to sell his grain when prices were lower, but freely gave credit to the line elevator companies so they could move the crop at their own time and advantage.

Referring to terminal elevator companies, the grain-growers alleged that these took too much off in dockage, did not pay the farmer for screenings, unfairly mixed grades of grain for their own excessive profit, and "loaned" grain in storage to themselves when it suited their purpose. It was further charged that the grading system failed to reflect the value of grain for milling purposes, and that mistakes were made in sampling and grading.

The large milling companies also came under fire. They were accused of taking advantage of the grading system to obtain grain cheaply and at the expense of the farmer, and of keeping the best grain for their own use in manufacture while shipping the poor grades. In this way, so it was claimed, prices were lowered on the domestic and export markets to the detriment of the grower. The Winnipeg Grain Exchange came in for special criticism on the grounds that it operated to the advantage of the line elevator companies and the large milling concerns, that it arbitrarily limited membership and encouraged speculation, and that it periodically and artificially depressed grain prices by issuing false reports concerning crop conditions and prospects.

The commission in its report neither upheld nor refuted the specific complaints of the farmers. It pointed to flaws in the Manitoba Government elevator system, advised the Saskatchewan Government to avoid such errors, and recommended that the farmers should receive government assistance, by a loan and a grant for organization expenses, to set up an elevator company of their own. The commission's recommendations were largely accepted by the Saskatchewan Legislature, which in March, 1911, passed "An Act to incorporate the Saskatchewan Co-operative Elevator Company Limited". The Saskatchewan Co-operative Elevator Company was incorporated, with the executive of the Saskatchewan Grain Growers' Association as a provisional directorate. The first general manager of the new farmers' company was a homesteader of Beaverdale, near Yorkton, and vice-president of the Saskatchewan Grain Growers'

Association. A shrewd and hard-working farmer, Charles A. Dunning was to prove himself a forceful speaker and an able executive with a cultivated flair for practical finance and political organization. "Charlie" Dunning born at Croft, Leicestershire, England, came to prairie Canada (1902) at the age of 17 and worked as a hired man to gain farming experience and savings before he took up his own homestead. Dunning was an omnivorous reader with a retentive memory and possessed of a practical turn of mind. The new farmers' company began to build country elevators. The older farmers' concern, the Grain Growers' Grain Company (G.G.G.C.) in 1912 established an export subsidiary to facilitate sale of grain directly to central and eastern Canadian millers and United Kingdom buyers. In the same year the G.G.G.C. leased from the C.P.R. a terminal at Fort William, and entered into an agreement with the Manitoba Government to lease and rehabilitate its shaky country elevator system.

During the first year of the operation of the Saskatchewan Co-operative Elevator Company an arrangement was made whereby the Grain Growers' Grain Company, with a seat on the Winnipeg Grain Exchange, became selling agent for the farmers' new company. In 1912 the co-op company acquired its own seat on the exchange. Co-op elevators, at competitive country points, offered prices above those of the line elevator companies, thus raising the price paid to the farmer for his grain. Satisfaction concerning operation of the co-op elevator system was reflected in the rapid increase in locals at country shipping points. In charge of organization of locals was George Langley. In 1911 the company operated 40 elevators; in 1912 the number increased to 137. During the 1912-13 season, the Saskatchewan Co-operative Elevator Company handled more than 12 million bushels of grain.

Not all the farmers supported or patronized their own organizations and companies. A complaint persistently reiterated by the pessimistic organizer was, "Farmers never have stuck together and never will." Nevertheless, because of the economic benefits deriving from the farm organizations, plus the consequent development of individual leadership, the farm movement was a factor in bringing together men and women of varied national backgrounds and many religious beliefs, thus hastening the process of assimilation.

In the villages and towns, businessmen were generally not unaware of the indirect value to themselves of the farmers' marketing co-operatives; as the farmer prospered, so did the local merchant and implement dealer. But the merchants and dealers looked with much disfavour on farmers' attempts at group purchasing of farm and home supplies. When farmers locally grouped themselves together, under the auspices of the Saskatchewan Grain Growers' Association, and successfully purchased railway carload lots of apples, binder twine, fenceposts, barbed wire, flour, lumber and coal at or near wholesale prices, the merchants were both disappointed and annoyed. Some of the more outspoken storekeepers told these farmers in effect, "When you are short of cash and need credit, you come to us for your goods and expect us to carry you until you can pay your bills. Then when you have some cash to spend, you by-pass us by purchasing in carload lots." The merchants, with considerable success, put pressure on wholesalers, some of whom as a result refused to sell directly to the farm locals "that operate without any overhead, while our [retail merchants'] overhead goes on continuously whether business is good or bad". A story that delighted the merchants and brought smiles to the faces of many farmers went the rounds. The story was that a grain-growers' local at a small country point brought in a railway carload of flour. Throughout the day as farmers came with their teams and wagons to the railway siding to unload their sacks of flour and take them home, the secretary of the S.G.G.A. local kept an account of deliveries by writing the amounts of flour delivered and money received on the inside wall of the box car. When darkness came, he continued with the aid of a stable lantern, until the car was unloaded. Tired after the long day, he went home to bed intending to return to the car the following morning and transfer the figures to his account book which inadvertently he had left at home the day before. But he never again saw the inside of that car—or his figures. During the night a freight train had stopped by to pick up the empty car.

Among other worries of the immigrant farmers was an increasing concern over immigrant weeds. Various types of weeds not indigenous to the prairies, but introduced with unclean seed grain, spread rapidly through the cultivated land and flourished. In 1910 the Saskatchewan Department of Agriculture employed 71 weed inspectors in an attempt

French weed

Wild oats

Tumbling mustard

to enforce provincial legislation designed for weed control. But as a considerable number of farmers resented the advice of the government weed inspector and regarded him as an intruder "on my farm", the government revised its legislation so that the onus for weed control rested with the municipalities. Thus, if a municipality decided to enforce a degree of weed control within the municipal boundaries, it was empowered to do so. If a municipality chose to neglect the weed problem, that too was its privilege. The effect was that the municipalities in favour of enforcing weed control became discouraged when adjacent municipalities failed to take similar action. In practice the weed problem never ceased to be a concern of the individual farmer. Failure to clean out a grain separator properly before moving it from one field to another was a factor in weed seed dispersal, but the wind was the principal agent.

Threshing

By 1910 the large internal combustion engine was replacing steam for farm traction and threshing. The Rumley, Hart-Parr, and other gasoline or kerosene tractors were arriving in Saskatchewan by the trainload. "Bad water" (alkali), "scarcity of water", and "the distances we sometimes had to haul it", were major factors in the decline of steam.

While many a threshing outfit included a cook-car with "a full-time cook on the job", some operators looked to the women of the family farm for preparation of three meals a day, supplemented by "a lunch in the field" both morning and afternoon. When the men were fed from the farm kitchen, neighbour women "came over to help" and "many a farm kitchen throbbed with the rush of women's feet as an eager threshing outfit pounded through the wheat". Whether the threshermen were fed in portable cook-car or farm kitchen, the meals included "fresh eggs, lots of good meat and potatoes, plenty of bread [and] all the preserves and pie a man could eat".

And it was considered the woman's responsibility also "to keep an eye on the kids, have the girls help inside, and see to it that the boys do their chores outside". Boys, rushing home from school, were impelled irresistibly to the joyous sights, clamorous sounds, and unforgettable smells of a harvest in full swing. Mostly in a hurry to become men, these boys, if they "stayed on farming", would have access to knowledge of agricultural science far beyond the experience of their fathers, whose hope and energy earned for the prairies the anonymous, ubiquitous, and widely publicized term "Bread Basket of the World".

The expansion and importance of agriculture, the economic basis of the province, was reflected in the establishment of the College of Agriculture, within the University of Saskatchewan, in 1910. The College of Agriculture, from its outset, followed a policy of keeping in close touch with the farmer on the land. The farmer who came to consult the professor of agriculture was welcomed to the campus. The farmer's individual problems, such as weed control, moisture conservation, tillage methods, and seed varieties, were readily discussed. While the farmer learned from the professor, the professor in turn learned from the farmer—there existed no hard and fast line of demarcation between the academic and the practical.

When in 1910 Prime Minister Sir Wilfrid Laurier toured the prairie west, he was met by numerous rural delegations, sponsored mainly by the Saskatchewan Grain Growers' Association, requesting a downward revision of tariffs and advocating reciprocal free trade with the United States. The customs duty on farm machinery and manufactured goods generally was a major factor in the agitation for reciprocity. A pioneer in the Saskatchewan farmers' movement, Welsh-born and fiery John Evans, who in 1892 had homesteaded six miles east of Saskatoon, confronted the Prime Minister in Saskatoon and precipitated an informal debate on the tariff question. Evans, spokesman for a delegation of some 300 farmers, asked: "Sir Wilfrid, in 1896 you said you would skin the Tory bear of protection— now we want to know what you did with the hide?" Laurier, undoubtedly influenced by the organized and vociferous clamour for free trade, made reciprocity an outstanding plank in the political platform of the Liberal Party. During the election campaign the following year, a number of irrepressible United States congressmen, supporting the bill for providing for reciprocity with Canada, linked it with the old American cry of "Manifest Destiny". An extreme example was provided by J. Beauchamp "Champ" Clark, Democratic Speaker Designate of the House of Representatives, who lauded reciprocity and declared for all the world to hear: "I am for it, because I hope to see the day when the American flag will float on every square foot of the British North American possessions clear to the North Pole. . . ."

The Conservative Party, ably led by Robert Laird Borden, gave ample publicity to the loud pronouncements from south of the 49th parallel, and in his election-eve message to the Canadian people, Borden said, "We must decide whether a spirit of Canadianism or of Continentalism is to prevail on the northern half of this continent."

Apprehension concerning the possibility of absorption by the United States had little influence on Saskatchewan voters, and only one Conservative candidate was elected. Nevertheless, the suave and gracious Laurier led his party in Canada as a whole to resounding defeat. On September 25, Robert Borden entered a flag-decked Ottawa where a hundred men drew his carriage through the streets packed with cheering people.

Prime Minister Borden, the deep-voiced, contemplative, and purposeful Maritime politician, gained high office at a time of uninterrupted expansion in the prairie west. The continuous rural and urban development, the extension of railway branchlines, and the rapid growth in population—mainly through immigration—were reflected in the increasing number of villages, the incorporation of towns, and the building construction accompanied by hectic real estate transactions in the cities.

The village with its railway station, at least one general store, a post office, and blacksmith shop, often contained a fuel yard, implement agency, and sometimes a lumber yard, and invariably had one or more grain elevators and a chute for loading livestock into railway cars. In front of the village store was a wooden sidewalk bordered by a hitching rail to which were tied the horses of out of village customers. When weary or impatient with waiting for their drivers, horses gnawed on the wooden rail, which over a period of time took on an emaciated appearance, the more durable knots protruding from the surrounding softer wood like nodules of rock in a dry eroded water course. When privileged to follow the wagon or buggy to the village, the useful farm dog, usually a self-reliant Collie type, experienced a gregarious interlude not ordinarily available on the isolated farmstead. A periodic but important visitor from city to village was the commercial traveller who arrived on the passenger train with his immense iron-bound trunks filled with samples of goods for sale from wholesaler to retailer. Always a salesman, the commercial traveller was often well informed concerning business trends in city, town, and country, and was also in a position to make his employer aware of the kind and quality of merchandise most likely to be in general demand.

To facilitate the local government necessary to the curtailment of fire hazard, unsanitary conditions, and animals running at large, and also necessary to provide for public improvement through taxation and the sale of debentures, most villages were incorporated under the Saskatchewan Village Act of 1908. The act, administered by the Department of Municipal Affairs, came into force in November, 1908, and provided for the election by popular vote of three councillors, who, in turn, were to elect a chairman from their number, who was known as "the overseer". A secretary-treasurer, other than a councillor, was to be appointed by the council. Bylaws passed by the village councillors were required to conform with provincial legislation. The Department of Municipal Affairs, in its report of 1909-10, referred to the department's work, ". . . examining the said bylaws of one hundred and forty-five villages in Saskatchewan . . . [their] documents, as might be expected, are not always what might be desired, and our objections to some bylaws when they are sent back are not very cheerfully received by the village authorities. It is unnecessary to point out, however, that every bylaw should be thoroughly safe and valid." The department prepared a sample set of village bylaws to save expense to the villages of legal fees, and with a view to attaining uniformity in village government. Under the act the area of a village was limited to 640 acres, and the village was required to have a resident population of no fewer than 50. Villages closely followed, and sometimes preceded, railway expansion.

Indicated in the department's report for 1912-13 was an amendment to the act, requiring the population of an incorporated village to be 100 persons, "twenty-five of whom must be male adults". The report expressed "regret that in some villages municipal life is at a low ebb, a condition of affairs not found in any other class of our municipal bodies". There were, at the time, in the province 248 villages, 48 of which had been incorporated within the last 12 months.

The railways located their stations some seven miles apart, with little or no thought for beauty of location. There were utilitarian considerations such as a level strip of right of way for both station platform and sidetrack; and where a water storage tank was specified, a plentiful supply of water, suitable for locomotive boilers, was sought. Adjacent to the station, "wherever it was dumped down", emerged the hamlet, village, or town; frame buildings briskly arising amidst the eager clamour of carpenters' hand-saws, the clatter of claw-hammers, and the fresh and all-pervasive smell of new cement, wood shavings, tarpaper, and plaster.

While both "hamlet" and "village" were useful terms for legal identification, the local residents preferred to consider themselves residents of a town, whether or not their community had attained that status. Thus the villager would refer to "my town", rarely to "the village".

Where a railway established a divisional point with its locomotive roundhouse and switching yards, the consequent number of railway employees, plus the generally increased trade attracted by the railway service and activity, precipitated the centre into the population classification required for incorporation as a town.

Under a previous municipal ordinance, a village having a population of 400 could become incorporated as a town, and, by special legislation, some villages with population less than 400 had the dignity of the title "town" officially bestowed upon them. The Town Act, which subsequently came into force November 1, 1908, required a population of 500 for incorporation as a town. The act provided for the establishment of parks, recreation grounds, and skating and curling rinks. It was stipulated in the act that towns or other municipalities were not empowered to bonus or assist railways, but it became the duty of the town to make provision for the care and medical treatment of any person who had been a resident of the town for three months or more and who, for financial or other reasons, was unable to care for himself or herself. As a result mainly of the coal famine experienced during the unusually harsh winter of 1906-07, a town became empowered, with the consent of the Lieutenant Governor in Council, to establish, and to operate temporarily, a fuel yard.

In 1909 Outlook, Melville, and Watrous, the latter two railway divisional points, were incorporated as towns. They had been organized as villages during the previous year. During 1910 and 1911, five more villages attained a population of 500 or more and were incorporated as towns. These were Saltcoats, Kindersley, Scott, Wilkie, and Canora.

While in the villages there was rarely more than one branch of a chartered bank, and many were without a bank, the town could boast of several branch banks. In 1911, 50 new bank branches were opened in Saskatchewan, bringing the total number to 323. Prominent in the financial development of the prairie west and well represented in the villages and towns was the Union Bank, with its head office in Winnipeg. Though the banks were not noted for paying generous salaries to their junior personnel, it was considered, in some circles, both a privilege and a sign of social distinction to "work in a bank".

In most towns and villages there was at least one restaurant, generally a "Chinaman's café" which provided better tea than coffee and specialized in fried foods and pie, and where a "square meal" was served for about 25 cents. Another institution of the prairie town was the "Chinese laundry", famous equally for removing grease and coal dust from a railwayman's overalls, starching a clerical collar, and expertly stiffening the front of a dress shirt. Although the Chinaman's prestige was different from that of the bank clerk, he was esteemed as a law-abiding citizen in most respects, an individual of exceptional monetary honesty who at times acted as temporary and unofficial banker when an itinerant Whiteman wished to leave for safekeeping a portion of his "roll".

Some of the original proprietors of these cafés and laundries had come to Canada to work for the Canadian Pacific Railway Company on railway construction through the difficult and enduring Rocky Mountains. Despite Canada's decision not to grant Canadian citizenship to these Asians, plus further discouragement in the form of a formidable financial barrier against their bringing in their women and children, many Chinese stayed to integrate themselves uniquely into the life of the prairie communities.

No such restrictions were placed on the entry of Negroes of African ancestry who had entered Canada from the United States of America and the British West Indies, and whose services as pullman porters were readily accepted by both the railway companies and the travelling public. Negroes intent on farming initiated a settlement in the Parklands Region, north of Maidstone, Saskatchewan.

Prominent in the restaurant business in cities such as Regina, Moose Jaw, and Saskatoon were immigrants from Greece who, similarly to other racial and linguistic groups, conducted their specific fraternal and cultural societies in the process of merging inevitably with the developing prairie scene. No imposing Statue of Liberty with resounding poetic welcome inscribed in stone was erected on the prairie threshold, nor did governmental authorities institute a forced draft melting pot of Canadianism. So many and various were the people from older lands who arrived so rapidly to settle in the demanding vastness of the new, where neighbours in name became neighbours in fact regardless of nationality, sect, or ism, that no major group could exert overwhelming force to make impotent the influence of minorities.

Each city had its period, or periods, of rapid expansion, and although Saskatoon, for several years without the benefit of railway connections, was not in the vanguard, "boom fever suddenly hit Saskatoon" in the autumn of 1910. Boundless optimism in business circles, extravagant real estate promotions, exorbitant pronouncements by a multitude of boosters—these were accompanied by rapid and solid construction of commercial buildings, apartment houses, schools, churches, and private dwellings. In 1910, when the population of Saskatoon was about 12,000, the city's chief executive, Mayor Hopkins, "predicted a city of 100,000 within a few years and thought the farm land within a radius of ten miles should be subdivided". Farm land was subdivided as far out as six miles from the centre of the city, and the consequent lots were with great gusto bought and sold by a variety of professional and amateur speculators. In 1912 at the height of the boom there were in Saskatoon 267 real estate firms. Indicative of an uninhibited "spirit of progress" was the *Saskatoonlet,* a pamphlet series published by the Saskatoon Board of Trade. One issue, after listing items of the city's phenomenal expansion, commented: "All this did Enterprise and Public Spirit accomplish in about SEVEN SHORT YEARS!", and continued: "Saskatoon has: NO OLD INHABITANTS to hinder progress. An Honest Farsighted City Council. An active, enterprising Board of Trade. The strongest Strategic Geographical Location in the West—see any Map. An exquisite natural charm. A magnificent swift River of Purest Water. Over 16,000 Population, moved but by One Impulse —the City's Good. Four Bridges over the River. Three Trunk Railways. Nine different Operating Railway Outlets—13 very shortly—controlling 45,000 square miles Wholesale Distributing Territory, stretching far into Alberta—indeed within 98 miles of Edmonton, and. . . ." Steel-ribbed brick and stone buildings, which rapidly appeared in the business section, included those erected by The Royal Bank of Canada, Advance Rumley Thresher Company, Massey-Harris, and the Canadian Pacific Railway Company; also included were the King George Hotel and Cairns' store, which became later a Hudson's Bay Company department store. Absorption of small and locally owned flour mills by the larger milling companies was furthered in 1912 when the Quaker Oats Company purchased the Saskatoon Milling Company and enlarged the plant. By the end of 1912, Saskatoon boasted of 41 miles of sidewalk, 4 miles of pavement,

36.65 miles of sewers, 37.39 miles of water mains, 11 miles of street railway, plus 10 schools and 14 churches, including a Methodist cathedral conceived with financial and architectural daring and capable of seating 1,300 people. In 1912, W. F. Herman and Talmage Lawson, an aggressive editor-publisher team, purchased the *Capital,* a weekly newspaper, and in March of that year began publication of the *Saskatoon Daily Star.*

In 1911 Regina spent a million dollars on municipal construction, and that year new buildings were valued at more than five million dollars. On Sunday afternoon, June 30, 1912, Regina was struck by a cyclone which killed 30 persons, injured some 200, and made 2,500 homeless. During the three minutes of whirling wind, 500 buildings were destroyed, including the Telephone Exchange, Young Men's Christian Association, Young Women's Christian Association, Knox Church, Metropolitan Church, and the C.P.R. freight shed. Plans for new buildings on the old sites were being made while the debris was cleared away.

It was a period of the "biggest and best". Northwest of Swift Current, at Leader, W. T. (Horseshoe) Smith built a barn 400 feet long, 128 feet wide, and 60 feet high. The barn, praised in nearby newspapers as "the world's largest", was said to have required 875,000 board feet of lumber, 30,000 sacks of Portland cement, and 60,000 square feet of galvanized roofing.

In 1910 the price of wheat, Number 1 Northern, was more than $1 a bushel. More people were prosperous, or hopeful of prosperity, than ever before and the majority were not anxious for a change of government. In the provincial election of 1912, the Liberal Party, led by Premier Walter Scott, was returned to office. On December 1, 1913, the cabinet consisted of these men: Premier Walter Scott, Minister of Education; J. A. Calder, Minister of Railways and Highways; W. F. A. Turgeon, Attorney General and Provincial Secretary; W. R. Motherwell, Minister of Agriculture; A. P. McNab, Minister of Public Works; G. A. Bell, Provincial Treasurer and Minister of Telephones; George Langley, Minister of Municipal Affairs.

Railway branchline construction, in some instances subsidized by the Saskatchewan Government, and the extension of telegraph and telephone lines resulted in a steady demand for railway ties and poles.

This, together with the ready market for lumber, gave further impetus to the expanding logging and lumber industry. In the Big River area, northwest of Prince Albert, a 100-horsepower steam crawler tractor equipped with front sleigh-runner could haul a train of a dozen or more giant sleighs, each sleigh carrying a load of logs or lumber equal to the capacity of a railway flatcar. White spruce was the principal tree for lumber manufacture. Throughout the forest area and in the northern lakes, trapping of wild fur and commercial fishing added to the production of the province.

On the agricultural scene the continuing technological advance of farm machinery, necessitating constant purchase of more and newer farm implements, plus the expanding unit of farm land required for competitive and efficient operation, resulted in an agitation by the Saskatchewan Grain Growers' Association for cheaper and more readily available agricultural credit and direct access to European markets. Consequently, in 1913, the Saskatchewan Government appointed a commission of enquiry. The commissioners were George Langley, Minister of Municipal Affairs; J. H. Haslam, retired Regina businessman experienced in financing; C. A. Dunning, manager, Saskatchewan Co-operative Elevator Company; and E. H. Oliver, professor of history and economics, University of Saskatchewan. The first three commissioners named were to "examine into ways and means for bettering the position of Saskatchewan grain on the European markets", while the last three named were to "inquire into ways and means for establishing agricultural credit". In each instance, J. H. Haslam was chairman.

The commissioners having specifically to do with agricultural credit subsequently stated:

The province is at the beginning of a new era. We have come in and possessed a goodly land—that has required enterprise and energy. Other virtues must henceforth be more largely called into play. Individual effort has been its reward and it has been abundant. Henceforth thrift and intelligent co-operation will play a greater role than hitherto. In view of the changing conditions of our economic life, the Commission believe that a solution of our problems must be sought along two lines, which after all do not greatly differ[:] 1. The spread of co-operative effort, especially at present, in the direction of selling and purchasing. 2. The fostering of financial institutions of our own, with sympathies for our own problems and control by our people.

In keeping with the sentiments thus expressed and held widely by interested farmers at the time, the government passed the Agricultural Co-operative Associations Act of 1913. Co-operative associations could incorporate under an act specifically designed to further co-operative enterprise and avoid the restrictions of the joint stock Companies Act. In the same years the Co-operative Organization Branch was established under the Department of Agriculture. On February 2, 1914, the first association under the act was formed at Juniata: the Juniata Co-operative Association Limited. Though this local association, along with several others of the early consumer co-operatives, was eventually dissolved, the legislation opened the way for what was to become a major development in consumer co-operation.

In the nine years since inception, the province had experienced a rapid growth in population together with an unprecedented railway expansion, concomitant with the cultivation of a vast expanse of virgin prairie for the growing of grain for world markets. In the five-year period of 1906 to 1911 alone, the population increased by some 235,000. Between 1905 and 1914 wheat acreage was expanded from 1,130,084 to 6,003,522 as more and more of prairie sod was turned.

To serve the new areas being opened up, railway mileage was increased from 1,551 to 5,980 during the same period. In 1905 there were three cities in Saskatchewan; by 1914 four more centres had advanced to city status.

While urban dwellers, sanguine in their expanding towns and cities, chided the farmers for "always kicking about something . . . asking for another royal commission . . . if it's not the price of wheat they're hollering about, it's the price of binder twine or something else. . .", townsmen and rural folk alike knew that their full bank roll, or its lack, was linked inextricably with wheat production and export, and that their "best customer" was Great Britain.

The steam railways, hauling prairie grain to Great Lakes' terminals and tide-water ports, and bringing farm machinery and other factory goods into what was once the "great lone land", reached a peak of expansion in 1914. In that year the Canadian Pacific Railway western lines surely fulfilled the visionful dreams of Sir John A. Macdonald and the dynamic railway builders of the 1880's

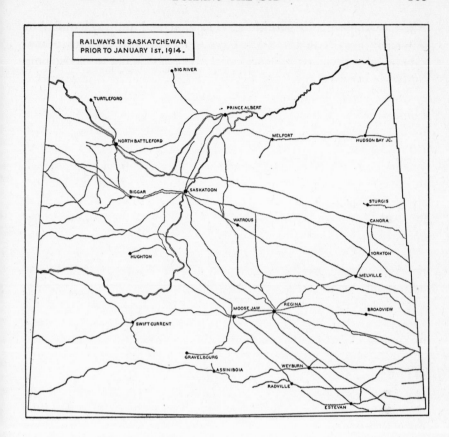

RAILWAYS IN SASKATCHEWAN
PRIOR TO JANUARY 1ST, 1914.

while newer railway systems, the Grand Trunk Pacific and Canadian Northern, assisted and subsidized by the Laurier, and later the Borden, administration, were brought to virtual completion.

Prairie people welcomed, and in fact boasted about, railway construction criss-crossing plains and parklands, while simultaneously they protested against "high freight rates". In summer daylight they were more inclined to accuse the railways of highhanded attitudes, insufficient service, inefficient operation, and "eastern monopoly control", while on frosty winter nights they felt an inexplicable assurance in the pervasive and optimistic moan of the locomotive whistle.

Toward the end of 1913 economic recession and doubt, patently reflecting financial conditions in the world of European civilization, began to replace the flourishing expansion and rampant optimism of the previous decade, but few there were who saw "this temporary setback" as a prelude to a world war in which Canada would become inevitably involved.

8

Patriotism and Production

THE last weeks of July, 1914, hot and dry, were filled with foreboding for anxious Saskatchewan farmers, who saw their crops withering in searing winds beneath a relentless sun. Simultaneously, almost unnoticed by the people of this pioneer province, a violent diplomatic storm, which had been gathering over Europe, came to a head. An obscure fanatic in an obscure town had assassinated an archduke, heir to the throne of the venerable Austro-Hungarian Empire. Largely unheralded in the headlines were economic rivalries together with considerations of prestige, security, and balance of power. The arrangement of alliances between the "Great Powers", designed to maintain peace and balance, extended the area and scope of the subsequent dispute and conflict. By the end of the month Serbia, Austro-Hungary, Russia, Germany, and France were mobilized

and millions of men from the Pyrenees to the Pacific were called
to arms. Great Britain, with interests and honour directly involved,
did not stand aside when Belgium's neutrality was violated. At
midnight, August 4, the British Empire was at war with Germany.
From London to Hong Kong, from Nova Scotia to New Zealand,
millions of men became directly affected by England's declaration
of war. Saskatchewan people, like those elsewhere, were caught
in a swirl of emotion. For them an incredible war, in which they
would be involved, had actually broken out. Instinctively they reacted
to the challenge and the danger, some with elated patriotism,
others with doubt and apprehension.

There was, on that warm night of August 4, 1914, spontaneous
patriotic response in the streets of Regina, Moose Jaw, and other
Saskatchewan centres. Citizens joined in impromptu and sometimes
tumultuous parades. There was cheering from flag-draped automobiles and horse-drawn vehicles decorated with red, white, and blue
bunting.

Anxious for action, veterans of the South African War and former
British regulars joined the self-styled "Legion of Frontiersmen". In
the days that followed, many veterans travelled to Ottawa to join
the Princess Patricia's Canadian Light Infantry, a new regiment whose
initial standards of recruitment required previous experience. Members of local militia formations volunteered for active service at the
first opportunity. Within a week of receiving mobilization orders,
designated units had filled Saskatchewan's first quota of troops for
what became the Canadian Expeditionary Force. On August 23,
more than 1,500 officers and men of Saskatchewan regiments
boarded special trains bound for Valcartier Camp, Quebec; in
November they sailed for England, and less than four months later
entered the line "Somewhere in France".

The Saskatchewan Government officially responded, in November,
1914, with a shipment of 1,500 horses, valued at $300,000, as a gift to
the British Army. Before the end of the year, Saskatchewan people
had contributed nine railway carloads of food to the Belgian Relief
Fund.

By December 31, 1915, 20,000 Saskatchewan men had enlisted.
Increasing casualties caused grief and apprehension in homes where
mothers, wives, widows, sisters, and sweethearts knitted socks, pre-

THE MORNING LEADER

VOL. XI. NO. 184.   PROBS—FAIR AND COOLER.   ● REGINA, SASK., WEDNESDAY, AUGUST 5, 1914.   TODAY'S PAPER 12 PAGES.   PRICE FIVE CENTS

BRITAIN GIVES WORD

GERMANY REJECTED ULTIMATUM OF BRITAIN AS TO BELGIUM AND KING GEORGE DECLARED WAR

ALL EUROPE NOW IN ARMS AUSTRIAN WAR FORGOTTEN IN MOMENTOUS OUTBREAK

KAISER'S REQUEST OF BRITAIN AS TO PRESERVATION OF NEUTRALITY OF BELGIUM AND BEFORE TIME OF ULTIMATUM EXPIRED ORDERS FOR CONFLICT CAME—GERMAN FLEET IN NORTH SEA, AND BRITAIN KNOWS WHERE; GRIM COMMENCEMENT MAY BREAK AT ANY MOMENT.

LONDON, Aug. 4. Great Britain declared war on Germany tonight. The momentous decision of the British Government for which the whole world had been waiting came before the expiration of the time limit set by Great Britain in her ultimatum to Germany demanding a satisfactory reply on the subject of Belgian neutrality.

Germany's reply was the summary rejection of the request that Belgian neutrality be observed.

WILL GIVE HOSPITAL SHIP.

TORONTO, Aug. 4—At a meeting this afternoon of the executive of the Imperial Order, Daughters of the Empire, called to decide what steps the order should take in the event of England being drawn into war, a resolution that the women of Canada should offer a hospital ship was unanimously adopted. The ship will be fully equipped and placed at the disposal of the British Admiralty.

NEWS CRIPPLED BY CENSORSHIP

Newspaper Situation in London Is Most Extraordinary in History

BIG EVENTS LIKELY

May Be Long Ere Real News of Events Proceeding Known To World

LONDON, Aug.—The newspaper situation is an extraordinary one. Everybody feels and knows that events of the most tremendous nature are taking place on the Russo-German frontier, in the Baltic Sea, in Servia, on the Franco-German frontier, and at dozens of other important points, yet the governments concerned have placed an embargo on news.

CENSORSHIP IS AN ACTUAL FACT

CANADA STOPPED PRESS CABLES REGARDING MOBILIZATION PLANS

MONTREAL, Aug. 4—The censorship was established at Canadian cable and wireless stations yesterday having the effect of cutting off connection with the outer world.

FINAL PEACE APPEAL

King George's Wires to Czar Nicholas Make Interesting Note

LONDON, Aug. 4—King George's message to the Emperor of Russia, and a final effort to avoid war and the Emperor's reply were made public.

SAYS BRITISH HAVE BOTTLED UP FLEET OF GERMAN NAVY

New York Paper Says Kaiser's Defenders Are Being Held North of Denmark

HOSTILITIES FLARING

German Cruisers Active in Algiers, and One Is Reported Sunk

NEW YORK, August 4.—A special cable to the American from London says:

"It is said on highest authority that the Admiralty has received a wireless despatch stating that the German fleet had been bottled up by the British fleet north of Denmark.

GERMAN CRUISER SUNK.

PARIS, Aug. 4—A Havas despatch from Algiers says it is reported that French warships have sunk the German cruiser Panther.

ANOTHER GERMAN REPULSE.

BRUSSELS, Aug. 4—It is reported here that following a demand by the Germans for the surrender of the city of Liege, an engagement ensued, in which the German troops were repulsed. The Germans have been repelled from Liege and Namur.

TWO STEAMERS SEIZED.

BORDEAUX, France, Aug. 4—Two German steamers in the port here were seized

IN ALGIERS TOO.

PARIS, Aug. 4—The Governor of Algiers in a telegram received by the French Government, says that the German cruiser Breslau fired eight broadsides—some 60 shells—into the French fortified town of Bona this morning.

KING TO COLONIES

LONDON, Aug. 4—King George today addressed a message to all the British colonies expressing his appreciation of their spontaneous assurances that they will place the fullest support in the Motherland.

"They reach to me," His Majesty says, "the great self-sacrifice and help given by them in the past in the Motherland country. I shall be strengthened in the discharge of the great responsibility which rests on me that in this trial of the Empire, it will be united, calm and resolute, and trusting in God."

KAISER EXPLAINS COMING OF WAR WITH RUSSIANS

Tells Parliament His House Demanded Serbia Against Russian Duplicity

HAS CLEAR CONSCIENCE

Calls on Almighty and Greys Sword with Quite Clear Conscience

BERLIN, Aug. 4—Amid the greatest enthusiasm the German's never demanded that the parties against them depositely, was told the Reichstag today by Kaiser Wilhelm. He caused the session of the German parliament at 1 o'clock. An extraordinary feature was the fact that the entire lower house in its entire roster of the actors instead of the National building. The Kaiser made a speech...

SIGNAL FLASHED FOR MOST TREMENDOUS NAVAL BATTLE EVER FOUGHT IN HISTORY

LONDON, Aug. 4—England's wireless broke loose tonight. Immediately after midnight King George sent a personal message to the entire fleet sailing against the German armada cleared for action:

"I have confidence that the British fleet will revive the old glories of the navy. I am sure that the navy will again shield Britain in this hour of trial. It will prove the bulwark of the Empire."

This was the first message sent to the fleet since it cleared from Plymouth Harbor, and cleared to the secret rendezvous in the North Sea. Ever since the wireless has been silent, no word was permitted to go forth until tonight the signal for the most tremendous naval battle ever fought spattered out through the darkness from the great naval wireless station.

Immediately after the orders to "capture or destroy the enemy" had been flashed to the admiral commanding, it was followed by the King's own words.

DOMINION PARLIAMENT CALLED TO MEET UNTIL PEACE DECLARED

SESSION OPENS ON AUG. 18 TO SANCTION WAR PREPARATIONS, VOTE FUNDS, AND DO ALL THAT MAY UPHOLD FLAG OF EMPIRE—NO DELAY, AND ORDERS IN DRAFT —SOME TALK OF WAR TAX.

OTTAWA, Aug. 4—At the conclusion of tonight's national council meeting the Prime Minister announced that Parliament would be summoned to meet on Tuesday, August 18, two weeks hence. The first business of Parliament will be to vote funds required for defence purposes and to do all that may be necessary to uphold the flag of the Empire.

(Continued on Page Two)

(Continued on Page Two)

pared bandages, and made up parcels of chocolate and delicacies for shipment to men in uniform. In homes, community halls, school-houses, and church basements, women met to co-ordinate their activities in voluntary associations such as the Soldiers' Wives and Mothers League, and the Canadian Red Cross. Financed by organizations and individuals was the Saskatchewan Hospital Unit, for which the College of Physicians and Surgeons contributed $10,000. Men and women joined the Citizens Recruiting Committee dedicated to persuading men of military age to put on the King's uniform.

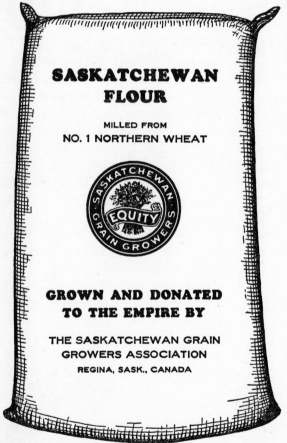

The Saskatchewan Grain Growers' Association sponsored the Patriotic Acre Fund to which individual farmers were encouraged to contribute each year grain harvested from one or more acres. The Saskatchewan Co-operative Elevator Company agreed to accept the contributed grain at carload track price and turn the money over to the trustees of the fund. Robin Hood Flour Mills Limited agreed to mill flour, at cost, from wheat thus contributed or its equivalent, and the flour was put in sacks marked with the S.G.G. emblem, for shipment as a gift to the United Kingdom. From the 1915 crop alone a train of

40 railway cars of flour, each containing 80,000 pounds, was dispatched to the United Kingdom. Wage earners assigned contributions to the Canadian Patriotic Fund. The voluntary contributions were augmented by the Saskatchewan Government in order to make up monthly distribution of payments to soldiers' dependants relying on the fund. "Patriotism and Production" was a slogan prominently displayed in the province. A provincial Boy Scouts Association was formed, in which more than 900 boys were soon enrolled.

The Rural Municipality Act was revised to exempt from taxation farm land of men accepted for overseas service in the war. In this regard, it was stated in the 1916-17 report of the Department of Municipal Affairs: "It is clearly stipulated that the home of each such resident of a municipality to the extent of a quarter-section of land [160 acres], along with an additional 160 acres, shall be exempt from all taxation. Thus the soldier's mind is relieved of anxiety so far as payment of taxes on his farm is concerned."

Similar legislation respecting the towns and cities relieved the soldier from taxation, to the extent of $50, on his urban home.

While many men and women of varied backgrounds, other than British, participated in the war effort, there was a small minority among recent arrivals who covertly or openly expressed sympathy with the enemy countries, for these were the lands of their birth or ancestry. In the spring of 1915 funds were collected from Austrian settlers, in the vicinity of Vonda, as a contribution to the Austro-Hungarian war effort; the scheme exposed, one man was convicted of an offence. German nationals who entered Canada via the United States attempted to recruit funds, manpower, and sympathy for Germany in the German settlements near Rouleau, Wilcox, and Avonlea, not far from the Canadian-U.S. border. Persons were arrested and charged with aiding enemy aliens to escape across the border, and for distributing seditious literature and making seditious utterances in favour of German victory. *Der Courier,* a German language newspaper published in Regina, lauded German culture, urged that German be taught in public schools "where German Canadians are strong enough", and referred to the desirability of educating "[Canadian] German children in the rich treasures of the German mind which are stored in our literature".

Many settlers of German origin had emigrated from the midwestern United States to Saskatchewan, and some German priests of the Roman Catholic Church had arrived on the prairie scene directly from Germany. There were, besides, settlers of British ancestry and American citizenship who came to Saskatchewan from the midwestern states, and who brought with them the attitude of isolationism, or non-participation in European affairs and wars, traditional in that strongly Republican, midcontinental area. The eventual entry of the United States into the war on the side of the British Empire and the Allies, on April 6, 1917, modified the attitude of Saskatchewan's "German-Americans" and even more that of its "Americans", who during three years of war had hitherto held a neutral position.

The disintegration of the Tsarist regime, followed by Russia's withdrawal from the war and the Allied cause, aroused in thousands of settlers of Ukrainian origin a hope for an autonomous and even an independent Ukraine in Europe.

Mounting casualties in the Canadian forces overseas caused, among relatives and friends in Saskatchewan, increasing resentment against those who, for any reason, were not in full accord with participation in the "War to make the World Safe for Democracy". Compulsory military service introduced by the Canadian Government in June, 1917, channelled a mounting resentment toward Mennonite and Doukhobor sectarians who, before the turn of the century, had been exempted from military service by a Canadian Government anxious to settle Canada's prairie west with hard-working agriculturists, whether of pacifist persuasion or not.

Premier Scott, who prior to the war had travelled widely throughout the British Empire and in continental Europe, was by temperament and training admirably equipped to preside over the initial wartime stress and strain in Saskatchewan. While Scott encouraged patriotic endeavour, he urged tolerance among peoples of divergent views. As Minister of Education, he endorsed legislation requiring the Union Jack to be flown in all school-yards, and encouraged patriotic singing in the classroom, provided the songs were not calculated to accentuate disharmony in communities of mixed national backgrounds. A strictly limited teaching of languages other than English and French was allowed by modification of the School Act in May, 1915, despite strenuous opposition by W. B. Willoughby, Conservative Party leader in the legislature. In the midst of the war a German Lutheran college was opened in Saskatoon with a faculty of three professors and an initial registration of 12 students.

Despite the obviously heterogeneous nature of the population, the response of Saskatchewan men and women to the "call to the colours" was both ready and sustained. During the four years of 1914-1918, 20 recruiting centres in the province enrolled 844 commissioned officers, 70 nursing sisters, and more than 40,000 other ranks for service in the Canadian Expeditionary Force.

Regina, "the Queen City" named for Queen Victoria, provincial capital and centre of pioneer Anglo-Saxon settlement, which had grown rapidly around the prairie penetration of the Canadian Pacific Railway, became an outstanding enlistment centre for overseas service. In Regina 323 officers, 43 nursing sisters, and almost 20,000 other ranks "joined up": nearly 50 per cent of Saskatchewan's enlistment. These enlistment figures in the Canadian Expeditionary Force do not include those of British (United Kingdom), Belgian, French, Russian, Serbian, Japanese and other reservists who embarked for their "old lands" to fight in the Allied cause. Nor do these figures include the Saskatchewan men who enlisted elsewhere in Canada, or who joined services other than the Canadian Expeditionary Force (Army).

Prior to the "Great War", which was to become known later as World War I, 11 militia units were based entirely or in part in Saskatchewan. During the war 30 additional units were formed and brought up to strength with recruits mainly from Saskatchewan. In Regina two cavalry squadrons were mobilized by the Royal North West Mounted Police. From Saskatchewan went men to augment non-combatant formations such as the Canadian Railway Troops, the Canadian Forestry Battalion, and the Canadian Army Service Corps.

On the battlefields of France and Belgium, Saskatchewan units participated in major battles involving British Empire troops on the Western Front. From the wearisome mud of vermin-infested trenches they "went over the top" through shell holes, barbed wire entanglements, and withering fire. Men of Saskatchewan experienced,

in 1915, the war's first gas attack at Ypres, and formed part of the spearhead which, in 1918, pierced the "impregnable" Hindenburg Line.

A number of unit battle honours were recorded on badges and regimental colours of Saskatchewan formations. Elements of what in 1936 became the Prince Albert and Battleford Volunteers, whose origin goes back to 1885, added to the earlier honour of "North West Canada, 1885", those of "Ypres, 1915-17"; "Festubert, 1915"; "Mount Sorrel"; "Somme, 1916"; "Flers-Courcelette"; "Ancre Heights"; "Arras, 1917-18"; "Vimy, 1917"; "Hill 70"; "Passchendaele"; "Amiens"; "Scarpe, 1918"; "Drocourt-Queant"; "Hindenburg Line"; "Canal du Nord"; "Cambrai, 1918"; "Valenciennes"; and "France and Flanders, 1915-18". Almost 1,500 members of Saskatchewan units in the Canadian Expeditionary Force received individual honours and awards, from both British and other Allied sources. Six men of Saskatchewan were awarded the Victoria Cross, Britain's highest recognition for valour: they were Hugh Cairns, Arthur George Knight, William Johnstone Milne, George Harry Mullin, Michael O'Leary, and Ralph Louis Zengel. Only the last three lived to receive their awards in person.

While these few were singled out for special recognition on the field of battle, they more prominently represented the exploits of the many. Casualties among Saskatchewan enlistments serving with the Canadian Expeditionary Force, 1914-19, totalled 17,594, of which 4,385 were deaths on the field of battle.

In World War I Canadians generally were recognized for their tenacity and endurance under the trying conditions of trench warfare, plus individual initiative tempered by discipline and a driving determination when "over the top". On both sides of the line of battle it was recognized that Canadians regularly appeared in "the tough spots". Men of the prairies, conditioned to pioneer ways wherein individual initiative and innovation were commonplace necessities, "could readily repair a gun carriage with hay wire" and "carry on when cut off from their command".

On the "home front" the dominant position of wheat in Saskatchewan's economy, dependent in part on uncertain rainfall during the growing season, was, in 1914, further emphasized by below average yields throughout most of the province and a virtual crop failure on the southwestern open plains. Hot, dry days and searing winds, prevalent especially during the latter half of July, were, in the northern agricultural area, followed by a sudden and severe frost on August 9. By the middle of August harvesting of the short crop was general. In the southwest some farmers had ploughed under much of the sparse standing grain. In the area of total crop failure, which extended northward, were recent homesteaders ill-prepared to bear their loss of income. In consequence the Saskatchewan Government and the Canadian Government provided relief food for settlers and fodder for their livestock. When it became evident that men, women, and children faced a winter with insufficient warm clothing, the Homemakers' Clubs of Saskatchewan, a women's voluntary association, collected clothing and began distribution to needy families. Further organization was required, and during November the Bureau of Labour, a branch of the Saskatchewan Government Department of Agriculture, co-operated with the Homemakers and various church and philanthropic organizations to collect and distribute 63 tons of new and used clothing to 879 families. Moreover, the Saskatchewan Government requested large creditors not to press for collections that year. While in the drouth-stricken areas the crop averaged less than two bushels per acre, the average yield for the province was 12.42 bushels per acre, resulting in a total production of less than 75 million bushels.

As a result of persistent complaints concerning sales and collection practices of implement companies and their local agents, the Saskatchewan Government on April 24, 1914, had appointed a royal commission whose subsequent recommendations resulted in The Farm Implements Act and an act respecting homesteads. These acts, passed by the legislature in June, 1915, required the implement companies or their agents to make plain to the purchaser, in a language he could understand, the contents of written contracts. Furthermore the purchaser could not transfer his homestead in payment for farm machinery, nor could he place any encumbrance against the homestead, without the voluntary consent and signature of his wife.

The legislation also required the implement companies to file with the Department of Agriculture lists of implements offered for sale together with the selling price and terms of credit. The vendors were required to file lists of repairs, and to state the cash selling price and the points in the province where repairs were available.

The royal commission in its report had pointed out that many farmers were too readily inclined to buy, on credit, large and expensive machines, equipment their acreage and operations could neither justify nor support. To the commission various witnesses testified they had "gone broke" trying to pay for large threshing units by doing custom work for neighbouring farmers. Yet the farmer wanted his own threshing unit so that he could thresh his crop as soon as it was ready. This was a factor in the development of smaller tractors and grain separators. The Waterloo Boy, Titan, and Fordson internal combustion traction engines came into general use for threshing and to a lesser extent for drawbar work on the land. America's Henry Ford, the genius tinkerer and master of mass production, who put the Fordson tractor on the market, was producing his Model T car in ever-increasing quantities; this durable automobile of simple design and rugged construction was replacing the horse and buggy on the prairie farm.

During the growing season of 1915, rain came "at the right time" and the resultant big crop of high grade grain matured before the advent of autumn frosts. This fact, combined with rising wheat prices and a shortage of farm labour, both attributable to wartime demands, gave impetus to the trend toward self-sufficient units of farm machinery and the ploughing of hitherto uncultivated land for extended grain-growing. Both the raising of beef cattle and an increase in dairy herds

Model T Ford

were encouraged by the wartime economy. Horse-breeders, in response to an expanding market, increased their herds. The general agricultural expansion was accelerated by Canada's chartered banks offering credit to finance increased production to meet the heavy demands of war. But the banks did not loan money on land, and farmers complained that the rates of interest asked by mortgage companies were too high. To provide further credit for agricultural operation and expansion, the Saskatchewan Legislature in 1917 passed the Farm Loans Act. The resultant Farm Loans Board, virtually a government loan company, took first mortgages at 50 per cent of the board's evaluation of the land, on a 30-year repayment plan. Rates of interest were relatively low. Funds for the loan company were raised by sale of bonds guaranteeing interest at five per cent.

In the hot and unusually humid summer of 1916 an unprecedented grain yield was anticipated until severe and widespread hailstorms began to beat down a percentage of the standing crop. Yet more devastating was the appearance of rust. This parasitic fungus disease, favoured by humidity, ate into the standing stem and greatly curtailed the number of kernels in a head, while reducing considerably their size. Adversely affected was Marquis wheat, an early maturing and

Rust

popular variety developed about the turn of the century by the outstanding experimenter, Dr. William Saunders of the Dominion Experimental Farm, Ottawa, and his capable son, Dr. Charles Saunders. While rust had not been unknown prior to 1916, it was in that year the disease reached epidemic proportions on Canada's prairies, and hastened the search for rust-resistant wheat varieties. While research was initiated in the universities of Manitoba, Saskatchewan, and Alberta, individuals engaged in experiments of their own. Among successful individual experimenters was Seager Wheeler, who had previously won awards in national and international competitions for high quality wheat grown on his farm near Rosthern, Saskatchewan. Seager Wheeler, a prairie homesteader of 1888 born on the Isle of Wight and son of a fisherman, had little formal education but possessed a natural aptitude for crossing wheat varieties; by selection he had produced Red Bobs in 1910, and Kitchener in 1911.

Beyond the control of man's experimentation were the ice pellets which periodically fell from ominous skies. Heavy and widespread losses from hail during the growing season of 1916 prompted the Saskatchewan Government to amend the Municipal Hail Insurance Act of 1915, and in 1917 to enact legislation to provide for the Saskatchewan Municipal Hail Insurance Association. Thus the responsibility for hail insurance, other than that offered by commercial companies, reverted to the municipalities.

In addition to hazards of hail, rust, and frost, the gopher was recognized as a crop-reducing pest. In 1917 the Saskatchewan Department of Agriculture estimated "that gophers destroy [in the

Hail

province] on the average a quarter of a million acres of crop each year". The department initiated a campaign for the destruction of the prairie rodents, multiplying as a result of man's reduction of their natural enemies: the coyote, badger, weasel, and hawk. Municipal and farm organization officials together with school teachers were urged to encourage the children to snare, trap, and shoot gophers. Competitions, among schools and children, were stimulated by awards of 37 inscribed shields, 36 medals, and a gold watch. May 1 was Gopher Day when 880 schools accounted for more than half a million gophers.

To encourage high school lads from the towns and cities to help in seed-time and harvest, the Canadian Government issued bronze buttons inscribed "Son of the Soil". While these miniature medallions were favourably received and proudly displayed on lapels of Sunday suits, a major inducement was the folding money for pants pockets and bank accounts. Wage rates for threshing hovered around $5 a day, rising in exceptional instances to $10 per day plus food and shelter before the war ended.

The gopher

The soldier, enlisted in Canada's army, received $1.10 per day.

In May of 1917 the price of Number I Northern wheat climbed to $2.72 per bushel on the Winnipeg Grain Exchange. Early in June the Canadian Government appointed a board of grain supervisors under the chairmanship of Dr. Robert Magill with power "from time to time to fix the price at which grain stored in any elevator may be purchased and the conditions as to price, destination or otherwise under which grain shall be removed from such elevator, and may also prescribe what shall be sold to millers or milling firms in Canada or elsewhere and what grain shall be sent to the United Kingdom and the Allied powers". In September the Board of Grain Commissioners brought the price of first grade wheat down to $2.21 a bushel, fixing it there until August 31, 1918. This price-fixing policy prohibited "trading in futures" on the Winnipeg Grain Exchange.

As a result of the partial crop failure of 1917, seed grain was scarce for planting in the spring of 1918, but the combined efforts of the Canadian Government, the Saskatchewan Government, and mortgage companies made seed grain available for all who could plant it. The wheat acreage in 1918 was almost one million acres greater than that of 1917, though the 1918 yield was only about 10 bushels per acre, owing mainly to insufficient rainfall during the growing season in the western parts of the province and the killing frosts of July 25-26 in northern agricultural areas.

Prior to World War I, Saskatchewan's butter production had, for the most part, been consumed in the province or shipped westward. Wartime scarcity and demand opened markets in eastern Canada and subsequently in the United Kingdom. During 1918 the Saskatchewan Co-operative Creameries Limited, an amalgamation of 16 local co-operative creameries, manufactured nearly three million pounds of butter and handled more than 100,000 pounds of poultry. Saskatchewan shared in Canada's mounting bacon exports to the United Kingdom. In 1914 Canada exported 24 million pounds of bacon to the United Kingdom; in 1918 bacon exports reached 200 million pounds.

Because of the labour shortage in Canadian coal mines, plus United States export restrictions and the wartime strain on the railway systems, coal was often in short supply. In 1917 the Canadian Government partially decentralized the administration of fuel control, with provision for each province to appoint a fuel commissioner who would attempt to equalize the distribution of coal when and where necessary and to encourage increased production in the coal mines. Though

Saskatchewan consumers looked mainly to the superior bituminous coal of Alberta's deep-seam mines, wartime shortages resulted in an expansion of the mining of inferior lignite coal in Saskatchewan.

North American wartime prosperity was reflected in the sale of fur coats for women. Muskrat pelts—clipped, dyed, and made into coats—became seal: Electric Seal, Red River Seal, and Hudson Bay Seal. During the season ending June 30, 1918, the Saskatchewan Government's Department of Agriculture estimated that Saskatchewan trappers received more than two million dollars for furs; and of this amount almost one and three quarter million dollars was for muskrat pelts, averaging $1.25 each.

The Liberal Party's large majority in the legislature was increased by one more member as a result of victory in a by-election of 1914 when a 31-year-old school teacher was elected to represent North Qu'Appelle, a constituency formerly held by a Conservative. The successful young politician, Ontario-born James Garfield Gardiner, had received part of his formal education in Lincoln, Nebraska, prior to graduation from Normal School in Regina, 1905, and the University of Manitoba in 1911. From that year until his election to the legislature Gardiner had been principal of Lemberg Public School.

The Conservative Party leader of the Opposition in the legislature, W. B. Willoughby, declared during the first wartime session that he would not oppose, on a partisan basis, the introduction of legislation to further the war effort. However, he added that his patriotic motives should not be construed as approbation of all government measures.

Harrowing

Early in 1916 when the 49-year-old Walter Scott, whose health had further deteriorated, was on the verge of retiring from public life, a Conservative member of the Legislative Assembly, J. E. Bradshaw, representing Prince Albert, made serious charges of corruption within the administration. The allegations included bribery of government members by the liquor interests, and payment of public funds to individuals for construction of roads which had not been built by them. With reference to the charges of corruption, Premier Scott stated: "In ten years we have expended about $20,000,000 on capital account for various buildings, bridges, telephone, roads, and other construction. If any member of this Assembly is prepared to make a charge that any part of this large sum has been misappropriated or stolen, or that any contractor received improper profits or payments for political or any reasons; or that any member of the Government or any member of the House has participated in a contract or received benefit therefrom—I say that if any such charge is made it shall be my duty to see that the member making the charge is granted fullest and freest opportunity to make the charge good."

To investigate the charges three royal commissions of inquiry were appointed. There was evidence which indicated that the liquor interests had spent some $15,000 to defeat or delay liquor legislation designed for prohibition. Though in this regard the charges of bribery were not substantiated, the Speaker of the legislature resigned.

Concerning corruption in relation to highways, warrants were issued for the arrest of several individuals. Among these were two members of the Legislative Assembly who were found to be involved. Sentences respectively of three years hard labour in Prince Albert Penitentiary and 18 months in jail were given to them. Others were also punished.

To reduce the possibility of further frauds, a new system of departmental accounting was instituted. The Board of Highway Commissioners was discontinued and a department of highways established.

Prior to the completion of the work of the royal commission concerned with highways, Walter Scott resigned as Premier and Minister of Education. When Calder, who had on several occasions been Acting Premier, declined to accept the position of Premier, there arose a lively discussion as to the successor. Prominent Liberals, including Saskatchewan cabinet ministers, were desirous to have as

Premier the 39-year-old William Melville Martin, a member of Parliament who had represented Regina since 1908.

Ontario-born Martin, son of a Presbyterian minister, had come to Regina in 1903 to practise law and had become prominent in prairie political life. When Lieutenant Governor R. S. Lake called upon him to form a government, Martin resigned his seat in the House of Commons to accept the position of Premier of Saskatchewan. Immediately thereafter he contested a by-election in Regina and on November 13 was elected to the Saskatchewan Legislature.

Another successful Liberal candidate in a by-election was Charles Dunning, who joined Martin's cabinet as Provincial Treasurer.

When Premier Martin led his party in the provincial election campaign of 1917, he appealed to the electorate on the record of his predecessor, Walter Scott, and the Liberal administration. Conservative newspapers, formerly hostile to Liberal Party policies, pointed to the high calibre of cabinet ministers, with particular reference to Calder, Motherwell, and Dunning.

The election, with the newly enfranchised women of the province voting for the first time, resulted in a resounding government victory: Liberals, 51; Conservatives, 7; Independent, 1; and 3 soldier candidates elected by overseas members of the armed forces.

Though less imaginative than Scott, and more prosaic in his utterances, Premier Martin proved an able and popular administrator. The Martin government largely continued the policies initiated by the dynamic Scott administration.

Most members of the Legislative Assembly in Saskatchewan favoured Prime Minister Robert Borden's proposal for a Canadian government prepared to introduce military conscription for overseas service and composed of outstanding Conservatives and Liberals. When Borden led the "Union Government" supporters in the election of 1917, his proposals had the support of all 16 successful Saskatchewan candidates, including the nine Conservatives and seven Liberals. On December 16, the vote in all provinces, with the exception of Quebec, was heavily in favour of union government. Among prominent Liberals to join Prime Minister Borden's new administration was James A. Calder, who resigned as Minister of Railways in the Saskatchewan Government. His resignation entailed a reorganization of the Saskatchewan Cabinet. In addition to his portfolio of

Provincial Treasurer, Charles Dunning accepted the appointment as Minister of Railways; and S. J. Latta, first elected to the legislature in 1912, was appointed Minister of Highways.

In the Canadian general election of 1917, Calder stood as a Liberal "Union Government" candidate in Moose Jaw constituency. The Liberal member of Parliament for Moose Jaw, W. E. Knowles, had stepped aside in favour of Calder's election to Ottawa. In the Saskatchewan Legislature, Moose Jaw was represented by W. B. Willoughby, the provincial Conservative Party leader. Prime Minister Borden appointed Willoughby to the Senate, thus necessitating a by-election in Moose Jaw. In that provincial by-election of June 13, 1918, Knowles stood as Liberal candidate. Opposing Knowles was a C.P.R. railway conductor, W. G. Baker, the first political participant in Saskatchewan to stand as a Labour candidate. Knowles, with the support of Moose Jaw Conservatives, received 1,958 votes and was elected by a majority of 447. A month previous to his election, Knowles had been appointed Provincial Secretary, and on February 15, 1919, he became Minister of Telephones.

When Willoughby was appointed to the Senate, Conservative members of the Saskatchewan Legislature selected as their leader Donald Mclean, M.L.A., elected in Saskatoon.

The Canadian Government had, in 1916, appointed a royal commission to inquire into the railway problem, concerning mainly the inefficient operations of the Canadian Northern Railway and the Grand Trunk Railway systems. These companies, along with others conceived at a time of ambitious railway company promotion in the wake of the successful Canadian Pacific Railway and in a period of optimistic expansion, were operating at a deficit. Capital from London and New York for refinancing was no longer forthcoming. As a result of the recommendations of the royal commission, known as the Drayton-Acworth Report, the Canadian Government in 1917 reluctantly acquired the daringly conceived Canadian Northern Railway, with its ill-ballasted roadbeds, leaky boxcars, and insufficient motive power. Subsequently the Canadian Government took over the Grand Trunk Pacific, and the Grand Trunk Railway with all its subsidiaries. The final merger in 1923 under the Canadian National Railways, an unprecedented venture in public ownership contrary to the free enterprise policies of the administration, was initiated by the wartime necessity of maintaining a maximum of rail transportation. U.S.-born Sir Henry Thornton, knighted by the British Government for his wartime railway administration in the United Kingdom and France, was to become the dynamic and integrating head of the amalgamated railway systems. As president of Canadian National Railways, generous, driving, and expansive Henry Thornton, who would stop his private train to talk with a section crew, rapidly became a popular legend to railway workers of the amalgamated lines.

During the "Great War" period the emergence of women in public life continued. Saskatchewan farm women of the Saskatchewan Grain Growers' Association, with the support of women from other groups, continued their agitation for equal franchise for both sexes. The crusade for "votes for women" became almost indistinguishably merged with the prohibition, or temperance, movement.

Besides the organized farm women, other associations, including the Temperance and Moral Reform Association and Protestant church groups, had petitioned the Saskatchewan Government for a drastic reduction of liquor consumption. In addition to the moral virtue of abolishing the bar, it was argued that liquor manufacture and consumption were a waste of labour, money, and time and were therefore unpatriotic. By legislative enactment all bars in the province were closed on June 30, 1915. At 9 o'clock on the morning of July 1, Saskatchewan Government liquor stores opened to operate on a local option basis. Agitation for total prohibition followed, with the result that the government closed its liquor stores on January 1, 1917. On March 10, the Saskatchewan Temperance Act was passed, but the province could not legally prevent the thriving mail-order business in liquor ordered from purveyors in other provinces. Some prohibitionists accused some of the doctors and druggists of abusing their privileges to obtain liquor for medical purposes, and of becoming wealthy in the process.

Although the persistent admonitions of ardent crusaders for prohibition, plus sincere though somewhat doubtful temperance desires of a large section of the populace, had succeeded in having the bar banned in Saskatchewan, less complicated than the legislative enactments was the relatively simple process of producing alcohol from fermented grain. Impartial chemistry, combined with a human demand for liquor plus nefarious business enterprise, would defy the intent of the legislation.

Small but determined was the minority of women initially active in demanding the vote. Many women remained indifferent to the crusade; a few expressed doubt and hostility. Among a variety of arguments advanced by individuals opposed to universal franchise were these: happy homes would be broken up as a result of political squabbles between husband and wife; women did not possess the intelligence required in political affairs; women interested in politics would neglect their homes; women, if allowed to go to the polls with the men, would become contaminated.

A woman advocate

Proponents of female enfranchisement were convinced that participation of women in politics would sweep away evils which, they said, men in public life had long been prone to accept; the women would clean out the political stables of corruption and graft and put an end to dubious deals of political backrooms redolent of tobacco smoke and whisky fumes. It was in the fresh air of rural picnics and field-days, when surreptitious exhalations of alcohol from the breath of furtive males were unostentatiously carried away in the prairie breeze that the resolute crusader for women's rights and persuasive temperance advocate, Nellie McClung, found opportunity to mount wagon-box or improvised platform, from where she urged women, men, and children to see the unfiltered light of her convictions. Mrs. McClung, together with other women ardent in the cause of equal franchise, grateful for the outspoken assistance of a few trail-blazing males, gathered thousands of names on petitions for presentation to "the government". English-born Violet McNaughton, wife of a Saskatchewan homesteader and an enthusiastic votary of vocal farm women, was among those who saw the need for suffrage advocates to unite and consolidate their pleas, petitions, and exhortations. Mrs. McNaughton, at a meeting of the Women's Section of the Saskatchewan Grain Growers' Association in Delisle, June 25, 1914, sponsored a resolution: "That a Women's Suffrage Federation be formed, composed of representatives from the W.C.T.U. [Women's Christian Temperance Union], Political Equality Leagues, W.G.G.A., and any other women's organizations in favour of women's suffrage, and that the said board be empowered to deal with all plans in the campaign for the franchise of women." Subsequent to this resolution was the formation in February, 1915, of the Provincial Equal Franchise Board of Saskatchewan which stimulated local organization in the province.

As the agitation for equal franchise gained increasing support and momentum, Premier Scott became more inclined to endorse the proposal. The Saskatchewan Legislature on March 14, 1916, granted to Saskatchewan women (21 years of age or over) the right to vote in provincial elections on an equal basis with men.

The Women's Christian Temperance Union had assisted the Women's Section of the Saskatchewan Grain Growers' Association to gain the equal franchise, and they in turn had joined with the W.C.T.U in a vociferous campaign to "Ban the Bar".

In the midst of the 1918 harvest, the widespread influenza epidemic struck, resulting eventually in about as many deaths within the province as had occurred among Saskatchewan men on the battlefields of France. This rampant disease, which struck down the apparently healthy in the prime of life, added to the accumulated tension of four years of war.

On November 11, 1918, when confirmation of the Armistice was flashed over telegraph wires, people in cities, towns, and villages began what became for many an all-night victory celebration. At railway divisional points locomotive whistle cords were gleefully "tied down" so that the multiple and prolonged blasts of these wind instruments of railway crossing warnings aroused yet more citizens and sent them into the streets. Railway torpedoes, designed for alerting the locomotive engineer to "proceed with caution" or to make an emergency stop, were generously attached to railway tracks approaching a town—all in a hectic, popular, and temporary disre-

gard of the Canada Railways Act. The resultant detonations set off
by passing trains added to the revelry of citizens burning an effigy
of Germany's Kaiser Wilhelm: there were people who sincerely
felt that, had the German Kaiser been "properly put in his place",
there would not have been the Great War.

Relieved from tension, mothers, wives and sweethearts, fathers
and brothers were then unlikely to recall the words of Charles A.
Dunning, Provincial Treasurer, who a year before, when speaking
for the Victory Loan bond drive, had said:

The economic situation is now such that not one bushel of wheat can
be purchased by Great Britain and her Allies, here, unless Canada
extends the necessary credit. The war has been the economic salvation
of Saskatchewan. At its outbreak men viewed the situation with alarm,
but the Province and its people are more prosperous than ever before.
The war has brought ruin and desolation to all the countries engaged
in the war; it has brought money to you and me.

While in those words Provincial Treasurer Dunning made reference
to an economic consequence financially evident throughout North
America—an economic effect which before the war's end had become
obvious to the population of the province—the spontaneous rejoicing
of the Armistice arose directly from a sense of relief that the far-away,
bloody, and life-consuming hostilities had ceased; and now brave
men spared in the struggle would soon return to their homes and
security. Retrospectively inclined citizens could look back over four
crowded years of activity in their personal and governmental affairs,
of agricultural expansion, and of difficult social adjustment inherent in a populace far from homogeneous. In many a little village,
as well as in the larger towns, citizens erected memorials to "the
boys" from the neighbourhood who did not return.

Though the storm of the Great War was over, its agitated waves
did not immediately subside. They continued to be felt on the
Saskatchewan prairie, where in the aftermath economic problems
centred in wheat. Political problems were to become heightened by
exaggerated hopes and slogans, and social problems, accentuated
by the wash of human desire and frustration, entered a new phase.

9

Progressives, Politics, and Pools

In the spring of 1919 flag-waving and gesticulating crowds cheered Canada's victorious returning troops as they stepped down the gangplanks at Halifax and St. John. Similar exuberance was in evidence at civic receptions and railway stations across Canada.

Amidst Ottawa's humid heat of July, members of Parliament in avidly grateful speeches and solemn resolutions officially recorded the nation's gratitude for the courageous job well done by Canada's armed forces.

Of peacetime reconstruction, Saskatchewan's Premier Martin said: "The provincial government is giving preference to returned men in the Civil Service, provided they are qualified for the work available, and already 150 are in the employ of the government.

Reconstruction in this province simply means the beginning of our development again at the point where we left off when war began. We want more railways, we want more and better roads, we want immigration, and we want better schools."

Of politics, Premier Martin, speaking at Weyburn on June 17, 1919, said: "While I believe that a reorganized Liberal Party with a progressive platform is the best medium of expression for western opinion, I do not intend, nor do the people of Saskatchewan intend, to slavishly follow the Liberal Party or any other party. . . ."

While in Saskatchewan the continuity of personal political leadership remained at war's end relatively stable, the reverse was evident in Ottawa. There Prime Minister Robert Borden, strained by the war years, was in ill health. Opposition Leader Sir Wilfrid Laurier, struck by paralysis, had in February passed on. Despite the consequent uncertainty of future party leadership, Parliament was practically unanimous in legislation to grant pensions to dependants of those killed in the war, pensions for the disabled in war, special military hospitals for the wounded and sick, and loans to assist able-bodied returned men to earn a livelihood. To this end the Canadian Government set up a new department, the Department of Soldiers' Civil Re-establishment. To co-ordinate the work of six departments, variously concerned with problems of the returned soldier and the dependants of those who had not returned, the Canadian Government formed a repatriation committee of the cabinet with J. A. Calder, Minister of Immigration and Colonization, as chairman. The Canadian Government's Land Settlement Board, supervised by T. A. Crerar, Minister of Agriculture, received the requests of veterans who desired to farm. The policy held special interest for the prairie west, where untilled land with an agricultural potential was still available.

While the official task of rehabilitation continued, together with the difficult individual task, in many instances, of the returned soldier settling down to civilian life, His Royal Highness Edward, Prince of Wales, in the autumn of 1919 toured Canada by rail. The young prince, who had visited the front lines under fire in France, received across Canada an enthusiastic reception. In civilian dress and with his engaging smile and youthful, offhand manner, he won the unofficial title of "Prince Charming". In Saskatoon, on September 11, when "farmers poured in to help pay honour to their future King", he was entertained by a specially prepared wild west rodeo show, and "amidst the wildest cheers from 20,000 spectators he rode on a broncho he had requested the length of the course and back again and straight into the hearts of the people". And, according to the *Canadian Annual Review*, ". . . near Viscount there stood on the roof of his little homestead a solitary figure in khaki outlined against the sky, completely equipped, even to his 'tip' helmet, and as the Prince's train passed he brought his rifle to the salute."

But neither "Prince Charming" nor the "solitary figure in khaki" was to become the symbol of the war's aftermath with its unemployment, falling commodity prices, and general unrest. The sudden cessation of destruction of men and materials, concomitant with an end to ravenous wartime consumption, was to result in a painful period of economic adjustment accompanied by Canada-wide deflation and retrenchment in government spending.

In Saskatchewan the condition was aggravated by drouth, excessive hail, and a severe grasshopper infestation. The dry growing season of 1919, which reduced the grain yield throughout the province, resulted in a total crop failure in the southwestern area. Grasshoppers did their greatest damage in the southeastern area, where crops were less affected by drouth. The Saskatchewan Government's Department of Agriculture supplied poison

The grasshopper

bait, which was effective where properly applied, but the department had no authority to compel farmers to poison grasshoppers. The department urged both mortgage and implement companies not to press for immediate payment of debts owed them by "dried-out farmers".

In the face of declining prices for farm products, the Saskatchewan Grain Growers' Association was again leading an agitation for lower tariffs. In the neighbouring provinces of Manitoba and Alberta, the organized farmers were turning to the idea of political action in the federal field, while the United Farmers of Ontario campaigned throughout the summer and autumn of 1919 to elect the astonishing number of 43 members. In October of that year this U.F.O. block, in association with Labour members, formed a provincial government. The Canadian Council of Agriculture, a federation of farm organizations drawing its main strength from the prairie provinces and Ontario, had, in November, 1918, issued an agrarian political platform with the challenging title of "New National Policy", which proclaimed for drastic tariff reduction and urged "an extension of co-operative agencies in agriculture to cover the whole field of marketing".

In Winnipeg on January 6, 1920, a conference, sponsored by the Canadian Council of Agriculture and presided over by doctrinaire, unyielding, but respected Henry Wise Wood, president of the United Farmers of Alberta, launched the National Progressive Party to contest the forthcoming federal election. While the new political party did not then name a leader, T. A. Crerar, former cabinet minister in the Borden administration, emerged as leader, being named by a caucus of farmer members in the House of Commons. In the summer of that year, Robert Borden, ill in health, resigned as Prime Minister, and Arthur Meighen, Minister of the Interior, was called upon to form a government. The 46-year-old austere and incisive Meighen became, for a brief period, Canada's youngest prime minister since Confederation. Comparative youth was coming to the fore in the political arena. A year previously delegates to the national Liberal Party convention, the first held in Canada for the purpose of electing a Liberal Party leader, had rejected the presumably secure but ageing W. S. Fielding's bid for Laurier's mantle, and by a narrow margin had chosen a younger man, William Lyon Mackenzie King, who had served under Laurier as Minister of

Labour. Prime Minister Meighen and Opposition Leader King, who had been contemporary students at the University of Toronto, were men with clashing personalities who carried on an unrelenting political struggle in the House of Commons and out. About their respective political pronouncements was an undefined awareness that the winner of the election would be expected to usher in on the Canadian scene a vaguely predicted and variously conceived "new and better world".

A community hall

In Saskatchewan, the Saskatchewan Grain Growers' Association, now committed to political action on the national level, for the most part continued its close but unofficial relationship with the Liberal government of the province. Thus to the Saskatchewan Grain Growers' Association, provincial Liberals were one thing and federal Liberals quite another. In Saskatchewan's 16 federal constituencies, with the one exception of Humboldt constituency, the S. G. G. A. organized for political action under the banner of the National Progressive Party. Constituency delegates stated in no uncertain terms their lack of faith, on the national level, in both the old political parties, and their conviction that it would be possible to secure implementation of the New National Policy only through the election of a National Progressive Government.

An example of how federal political winds were blowing on the prairies was to be seen in the federal by-election of 1919. Prior to this, J. G. Turriff, M.P. for Assiniboia, Saskatchewan, had been appointed to the Senate. In the resultant campaign O. R. Gould of Manor, president of the farmers' political executive in that constituency, was nominated as the organized farmers' Progressive candidate. The Liberals persuaded W. R. Motherwell to oppose Gould. Among those who supported Gould in the hard-fought campaign were Saskatchewan farm leaders E. A. Partridge and J. A. Maharg, and Alberta's Henry Wise Wood. Motherwell, whose roster of supporting speakers included Saskatchewan's former Premier, Walter Scott, and the redoubtable Frank Oliver of Alberta, lost his deposit when the ballots were counted on October 27. The farmers elected their candidate with 7,712 votes to the Liberal nominee's 2,488.

In the general federal election of December 6, 1921, the Progressives in Saskatchewan elected 15 candidates and the Liberals elected one. Throughout Canada, the Liberals secured 117 seats, the Progressives 65, and the Conservatives 50. There were three other members of Parliament usually denominated as Labour. The only successful Liberal candidate in Saskatchewan, W. R. Motherwell, who stood in Regina constituency, a Liberal stronghold of urban voters, was promptly appointed Minister of Agriculture. King, who became Prime Minister, was kept in office by the day to day support of the Progressives who, with the exception of a minority later to become known as the "Ginger Group", were destined to be absorbed by the Liberals. Promises of a world fit for heroes to live in largely evaporated, together with those concerning reduction of tariffs. The government, hesitant in attitude and act, and faced with a national debt which had risen from about 500 million dollars in 1913 to about three billion dollars by 1921, became concerned with balancing the budget at home and avoiding commitments abroad, especially those which might suggest automatic British Imperial obligations.

In the Saskatchewan provincial election of June, 1921, the Progressives did not oppose the Liberals who, under Premier Martin, were returned with a substantial majority. George Langley was the only member of the Liberal cabinet who suffered defeat. Within a few weeks he stood again in Cumberland constituency, where he was successful. Cumberland, a vast, sparsely populated, and traditionally Liberal constituency, embraced much of Saskatchewan's Pre-Cambrian Region. The Opposition consisted of Conservatives and a scattering of Independents. Outstanding among the opponents of the government was the blind war veteran Harris Turner, a sparkling journalist.

In September Premier Martin obtained George Langley's resignation after Langley had attempted to interfere on behalf of a policeman charged with an offence. In December, Maharg, Minister of Agriculture, resigned apparently because he did not agree with the Premier's varying attitude toward the Progressive movement in provincial, as opposed to federal, affairs. While Progressivism impinged on Saskatchewan politics provincially, it did not dominate their course.

The enforcement of prohibition presented a continuing problem. On June 28, 1920, W. F. A. Turgeon, Attorney General, had introduced in the Saskatchewan Legislature a bill to curtail further the sale and consumption of liquor. Mr. Turgeon's bill, which came into force in December, 1921, was in the main "aimed to forestall possible breaches of the Prohibition Act by druggists and the medical profession".

This legislation was not directed at those Saskatchewan-based liquor export firms that discovered and exploited a lucrative business in the legal export of liquor, much of which, by devious means, found its way to the "dry" United States of America, where high prices were paid by "rum-runners" and bootleggers organized for large scale illegal trade south of the 49th parallel.

Subsequently, liquor export warehouses were abolished. But the illegal manufacture of liquor increased in the Yorkton area and elsewhere in the province. By 1923 it was estimated, in a Royal Canadian Mounted Police report, that there were "more illicit stills in Saskatchewan, with a population of 760,000, than there are in all the rest of Canada with a population of over 8,000,000". In the Parklands Region with its woodland groves, improvised and widely

The still

spaced portable liquor stills could be more effectively concealed. Moreover, in the eastern and central sections of this region, a percentage of farmers of mid-European background had had, in the countries of their origin, prior experience in the comparatively simple process of distilling alcohol from fermented grain and potatoes. Nor had their pre-Canadian conditioning been conducive to respect for inland revenue enforcement officers. The obvious fact that grain converted into liquor brought a greatly enhanced price to the grower, was the dominant factor in the rise of these "local industries" during the brief but hectic period of the noble experiment known as Prohibition, when Saskatchewan suddenly and unofficially came to the fore as "a manufacturing province". The illicit product, when sold on the local market, was colloquially known as "bolshevik", a Russian word meaning "majority". The portion that reached the export market became spuriously labelled as White Horse, Haig and Haig, or with the names of other various and established brands. The sale of illicit liquor in the larger Canadian cities and the illegal "export trade" to the United States required the powerful and unscrupulous organization of gangster cartels, to which Saskatchewan contributed, inadvertently, at least one well known figure who cunningly contrived to evade prosecution in the courts while various of his henchmen, when caught and convicted, silently "took the rap".

Saskatchewan's Provincial Police, hastily instituted in 1917 because of a personnel shortage in the ranks of the Royal North West Mounted

Police as a result of wartime conditions, had an onerous task in its attempts to cope with the contraband liquor trade. While Premier Martin had been adamant that the work of the Provincial Police should not be obstructed by political interference, there were politicians who in this regard were not possessed of Martin's integrity. The Provincial Police were in part discredited, largely because of a demoralizing degree of political interference. The Royal North West Mounted Police headquarters had, in 1921, been moved from Regina to Ottawa when that force became the Royal Canadian Mounted Police. In 1928 the Saskatchewan Government disbanded its Provincial Police and the R.C.M.P. resumed its work in the provincial field, enlisting some of the experienced members of the disbanded force.

During the first six months of 1923 a verbal battle continued between the prohibitionists and the supporters of the Moderation League. Public opinion was swinging toward some form of government liquor control which, it was hoped, would put an end to widespread illicit distilling, rum-running, bootlegging, and "the putting of plentiful money and consequent power into the hands of the least desirable citizens". In a referendum vote on July 16, 1923, Saskatchewan, by a decisive majority of nearly 40,000, discarded prohibition and reverted to a system of government liquor control. An act, passed in the subsequent session of the legislature, provided for the sale of liquor in government stores: "4 gallons of beer, a gallon of wine, and one quart of any other liquor, to a permit holder in one day". The bill for government liquor control was introduced by Attorney General J. A. Cross, the only lawyer in the cabinet at the time, who was also Minister in charge of the Bureau of Child Protection. He said he was reluctant to see the government enter the liquor business, but the voters had indicated their preference.

Premier Martin had resigned in April of 1922, to accept a seat on the Saskatchewan Court of Appeal. Immediately thereafter government supporters meeting in caucus unanimously elected C. A. Dunning as leader of the Liberal Party in Saskatchewan. Asked to form a government, the ambitious but unhurried Dunning, able administrator and astute politician, at the age of 37 became Premier of Saskatchewan, Provincial Treasurer, Minister of Railways, and President of the Council. As his Minister of Highways and Minister in charge of the Bureau of Labour and Industries, he had a tireless young man possessed of a remarkable memory for statistics plus a persistent capacity for political organization, James Garfield Gardiner. The Dunning cabinet included a country doctor who had travelled prairie roads by horse and buggy in summer heat and by cutter or closed sleigh in winter blizzards, J. M. Uhrich, M.D., Provincial Secretary and Minister of Public Health. Minister of Public Works and Telephones was rugged, talkative, and popular A. P. McNab: "Archie" to his friends and, "Nearly everybody is my friend." Both McNab and Uhrich had supported the move to replace prohibition by government liquor stores.

The closed sleigh

Premier Dunning, when he accepted his high office, had said: "Most of the members of the Government and its supporters in the Legislature are members of the Saskatchewan Grain Growers' Association, which they joined as a farmers' organization admitting all on an equal basis, regardless of race, religion, or political belief. . . . it is my sincere hope that this farmers' organization will not set up, either actually or by implication, a political test for membership." The Liberal Party, with its genius for compromise plus absorption, or nullification, of reformist movements and splinter factions, was once more in the ascendancy on the Saskatchewan political scene.

Under pressure from the farmers' organization, Premier Dunning considered the possibility of a moratorium to alleviate the predicament of farmers who found themselves hard pressed by indebtedness to implement concerns, mortgage companies, and banks. Dunning's decision was that a moratorium would be a "practical impossibility" except "as a very last resource".

While the Saskatchewan Grain Growers' Association continued, for the most part, to give unofficial but uneasy support to the Liberal Party on the provincial level, it showed little enthusiasm for the Liberal administration in Ottawa. Moreover, the lack of unity within the Saskatchewan Grain Growers' Association, aggravated by unsolved economic problems, was reflected in the formation of a new Saskatchewan farmers' organization with the far-reaching title of Farmers Union of Canada, which had been formed at Saskatoon in 1921. The impatient and vociferous leadership of this minority organization accused the Saskatchewan Grain Growers' Association and Saskatchewan's Liberal government of failure to persuade the Canadian Government to reinstitute the wheat board and to fix the price of wheat in the farmers' favour.

First secretary of the Farmers Union of Canada was Harry N. Schwarz, a nervous, fiery, and uncompromising idealist. Rugged and dynamic six-footer L. P. McNamee (who in 1923 was elected president of the Farmers Union of Canada) stumped the province, speaking at meetings in school-house, community hall, and open air picnic, and exhorting the wheat producers to organize for the complete control of marketing.

Farm union officials, including Louis C. Brouillette of Landis, heard of a lawyer, with an office in Chicago, who had returned from a survey of co-operatives in Scandinavian countries, and had set about to organize the tobacco growers of Kentucky and the citrus fruit growers of California into giant marketing co-operatives designed to control the price paid to the growers. The name of this growers' magician was 39-year-old, San Francisco-born Aaron Sapiro, who as a lad had been selected from a group of orphans to study for the duties of a rabbi. The Farmers Union of Canada wrote, on April 23, 1923, a letter of invitation to Mr. Sapiro in the hope that he would consent to visit prairie Canada.

Co-operative marketing of farm products was not a new concept on Canada's prairies. The "pooling idea" had been advocated as early as 1906 when E. A. Partridge urged the farmers to establish a system of "orderly marketing". Fred Green, when secretary of the Saskatchewan Grain Growers' Association, had said in 1907, "It would be necessary to bring the whole grain trade under the management of one agency . . . created by the farmers who owned the grain . . . and . . . subject to their control . . . to market the entire product in the best interests of the whole."

It was not until some 10 years later that a basis for orderly marketing of wheat was introduced, and then not by the growers themselves but by the Canadian Government. The Canadian Government, on June 11, 1917, appointed the Board of Grain Commissioners, which in turn fixed the price of wheat for the 1917 crop at $2.21 per bushel basis Number 1 Northern at Fort William. This wartime price control measure, in the face of rising prices for wheat, was not popular with the growers. For the 1918 crop the board set the price at $2.24½. World War I came to an end in November 1918. Early in 1919 the Saskatchewan Grain Growers' Association, apprehensive concerning the possibility of declining prices for the 1919 crop, requested the Canadian Government to fix the price of wheat in line with that guaranteed to U.S. growers by the United States Government. This request was endorsed by the Saskatchewan Legislature. The Canadian Government took no action until it became obvious that the price of wheat on the open market was not declining, but continuing to rise above the price set for the 1918 crop. Then the government suspended trading on the open market and set up the Canadian Wheat Board to take control of marketing the 1919 crop.

When in 1920 the Canadian Government, under the leadership of Prime Minister Arthur Meighen, announced that the Canadian Wheat Board was not to function for the marketing of the 1920 crop, the organized growers, again apprehensive about the stability of the market, clamoured for re-establishment of the board, while the grain traders expressed their satisfaction with the return to the open market. When it became evident that the government was not prepared to re-establish the Canadian Wheat Board, the Saskatchewan Grain Growers' Association in conjunction with the organized farmers of Alberta and Manitoba and with the assistance of the Canadian Council of Agriculture, seriously turned to the concept of orderly marketing, "a centralization of selling" through a grower-controlled organization to become known as a "wheat pool".

When the Canadian Wheat Board had been in operation, the growers had received an initial payment on wheat delivered to the board, followed by subsequent payments until the price set for a specific crop year had been reached.

As initial, interim, and final payments were conceived as an essential part of a farmer-controlled "wheat pool", the farmers, or a considerable number of them, were somewhat conditioned to the pooling idea when ardent votaries of orderly marketing appeared prominently on a receptive prairie scene of the 1920's.

The United Farmers of Alberta, which in 1921 had elected a U.F.A. government in that province, proceeded to organize a co-operative in which, it was hoped, all the growers would pool their grain for collective marketing. The price of Number 1 Northern (top grade) wheat, which in 1922 had descended to less than $1 a bushel, showed little sign of rising to a figure "commensurate with the cost of production".

Aaron Sapiro, the lawyer who combined dedicated brilliance with folksy platform appeal, appeared on the prairie scene during the harvest season of 1923, to fire the imagination of thousands of farmers who set forth on a millenarian crusade to "sign up the neighbours far and wide in a 100 per cent contract pool". First in Alberta, then in Saskatchewan and finally in Manitoba, Sapiro sparked the crusade which resulted in formation of the three prairie wheat pools. The Saskatchewan Co-operative Wheat Producers Limited (popularly known as the Saskatchewan Wheat Pool) was incorporated in August, 1923. In Regina, July 25, 1924, the elected board of directors selected as president a Ladstock farmer, practical, puritanical, and purposeful A. J. McPhail. Enthusiastic, imaginative, and loquacious Louis C. Brouillette, Landis area farmer and auctioneer, became vice-president. Able, astute, and cautious, Scottish-born George Robertson, a farmer and one-time Presbyterian lay reader from Wynyard, was appointed secretary. An enthusiastic majority of Saskatchewan Co-operative Elevator Company shareholders, in the delegates' annual convention on December 17, 1925, voted to amalgamate with the Saskatchewan Wheat Pool, but negotiations failed in an attempt to have the United Grain Growers Limited unite with the pools. Through virtual absorption of the Co-operative Elevator Company, the infant but lusty Saskatchewan Wheat Pool acquired more than 330 grain elevators at widely scattered country points.

In 1926, delegates in the annual conventions of the Saskatchewan Grain Growers' Association and the Farmers Union of Canada, respectively, after many heart-searchings, voted for amalgamation and selected a fresh name, United Farmers of Canada, Saskatchewan Section. The new name implied the existence, or potential existence, of United Farmers of Canada sections in other provinces; but, though this was an intent in the selection of the name, the United Farmers of Canada was to remain a Saskatchewan organization.

The Saskatchewan Wheat Pool concerned itself with an expansive programme of grain elevator construction at numerous country shipping points, and through its field service staff and weekly newspaper *The Western Producer* (formerly *The Progressive*) worked for a gradual increase in contract signers. To co-ordinate their respective selling agencies, the three prairie wheat pools—Alberta, Saskatchewan, and Manitoba—formed the Canadian Co-operative Wheat Producers Limited, which became generally known as the "central selling agency", of which A. J. McPhail was elected president.

Meanwhile, heralded neither by the trumpetings of a millenarian crusade nor by highly publicized ideological differences, local consumer co-operatives were consolidating or expanding at various country points. And despite shareholders' losses suffered in the collapse of the Saskatchewan Grain Growers' Association Trading Department, set up in 1914 and inherited by the United Farmers of Canada, Saskatchewan Section, a small but representative group of individuals intent on the establishment of a co-operative wholesale similar to the co-operative wholesale societies of England and Scotland formed the Saskatchewan Wholesale Society, incorporated under the Companies Act of Saskatchewan, July 30, 1928. On February 2, 1929, the name of the corporation was, as a result of an act passed by the Saskatchewan Legislature, changed to Saskatchewan Co-operative Wholesale Society. The society acquired the undoubted debts and doubtful assets of the "old Trading Department", and was initially managed by a co-operative enthusiast with promotional ability, Harry W. Ketchison, who had resigned as secretary-manager of the flourishing consumers' co-op local at Davidson. Subsequently, in March, 1931, cautiously determined, North of Ireland-born Robert McKay, a Melfort area farmer experienced in local consumer co-operative practice, became the wholesale's secretary-manager, and with the approval of an anxious board of directors, embarked on what was to become a tenacious and extended struggle for the survival and expansion of the fledgling co-op wholesale.

This was an expansive period for co-operative enterprise. The Saskatchewan Livestock Co-operative Marketing Association Limited began operation of what became popularly known as the Saskatchewan Livestock Pool. With the advent of the Saskatchewan Co-operative Poultry Producers Limited, known generally as the Egg and Poultry Pool, the Saskatchewan Department of Agriculture discontinued its poultry marketing efforts. Saskatchewan Co-operative Creameries, one of the oldest marketing co-operatives, absorbed Caulder's Creameries Limited. The Saskatchewan Seed Growers'

Co-operative Association, organized in 1924, continued to extend its marketing of cereal and forage seed. On the community level, grazing associations, community hall construction groups, and local beef rings became increasingly in evidence. While consumer co-operative stores, already established at country points, continued to expand in both membership and business, more local co-ops were initiated.

With farm leaders, on both local and provincial levels, concentrating mainly on marketing and consumer co-operation as a means to agricultural economic salvation, the provincial political field was left largely to the Liberal Party, whose policies included encouragement of co-operative enterprise. In the Saskatchewan provincial election of June 2, 1925, the Liberals were successful in 50 constituencies, while the Progressives elected six members, the Conservatives three, and Independents two. One of the three Conservatives elected was J. T. M. Anderson, Saskatchewan school inspector, who in 1924 had become the new leader of the Conservative Party in the province. Deferred elections in the two constituencies which included the Pre-Cambrian Region, where summer-time travel was principally by canoe, were customarily deferred until July when it was certain the northern lakes would be ice-free.

During the ensuing federal election campaign in Saskatchewan, Prime Minister W. L. Mackenzie King stated his intention to ask Saskatchewan's Premier Dunning to join the federal cabinet should the Liberal government be returned to office. King, personally defeated in the Ontario constituency of North York, subsequently stood in a by-election in Prince Albert, Saskatchewan, where Charles Macdonald, M.P., had provided a vacancy by resigning. In Prince Albert, King won over an Independent candidate, Captain D. L. Burgess, M.C., and the apparently flexible but inwardly tenacious Liberal leader undertook to lead another minority government at Ottawa, with the support of most of the Progressives.

In the House of Commons the Conservatives had 116 members, the Liberals 102, and the Progressives 25, while several Independent and Labour members accounted for the remainder of the seats. On February 22, 1926, Dunning's appointment as Minister of Railways and Canals in the King administration was announced. Dunning, who had been called "the Empire's youngest premier", resigned as Premier of Saskatchewan, stood for election in the Regina constituency vacated for him by F. N. Darke, M.P., and was elected by acclamation.

Saskatchewan's Liberal Party caucus then chose as leader J. G. Gardiner, who thus became Premier and undertook to head the Department of Highways. For Minister of Municipal Affairs and Minister in charge of the Bureau of Labour and Industries, Premier Gardiner selected a 37-year-old Prince Albert-born lawyer, T. C. Davis, who had already proved himself an alert, forthright, and fighting politician. Less voluble than the dynamic "Tommy" Davis, and considerably more cautious in his utterances, was William J. Patterson, whom Premier Gardiner appointed as Provincial Treasurer and Minister of Telephones. The honorary and decorative place of Lieutenant Governor went to H. W. Newlands, who was appointed by the Canadian Government to preside for a second term.

Especially during the latter half of the 1920's political uncertainties, later to be revealed, were obscured by an overlay of urban optimism and actual material expansion, evident mainly in the cities and arising from new or augmented industries. Besides, a number of business men found hopeful satisfaction in speculative ventures in a pyramiding stock-market daily reflected on the tickertapes of North American brokerage houses. In the minds of speculators in corporation and company shares, King Wheat, though still enthroned on his prairie dais, loomed less dominant as a ready source of profit to the middleman. Financial Canada was awakening to the mineral riches of the Pre-Cambrian Shield of northern Ontario and Quebec, and the search for mineral-bearing ore had extended northwestward.

Northeast of Amisk (Beaver) Lake in the area of the Saskatchewan-Manitoba boundary by Flin Flon, Manitoba, copper, gold, zinc, silver, and cadmium were mined by the Hudson Bay Mining and Smelting Company, while mineral-seeking prospectors penetrated to the rugged wilderness of Lake Athabaska's north shore. Another source of wealth in the Pre-Cambrian and Forest regions was commercial fishing. The average annual catch was valued at half a million dollars during the last three years of the 1920's. In the Forest Region the lumber industry was valued at a similar amount during the same period, according to figures publicized later by the

Saskatchewan Government's Department of Industrial Development and Natural Resources.

Southward in growing cities and towns of the Parklands and Plains regions, enterprises were expanded and new services added. In Regina, Saskatchewan's leading wholesale centre, the Imperial Oil Company refinery, the first large scale oil refinery erected on Canada's prairies, was extended to meet a growing demand for automobile and tractor fuels. On May 24, 1927, the Canadian Pacific Railway Company, world famous for its trans-Canada hotel chain, opened the Hotel Saskatchewan in Regina. In the following year, in Regina, General Motors of Canada began operation of its automobile assembly plant. In Saskatoon, the Robin Hood Flour Mills doubled its milling capacity.

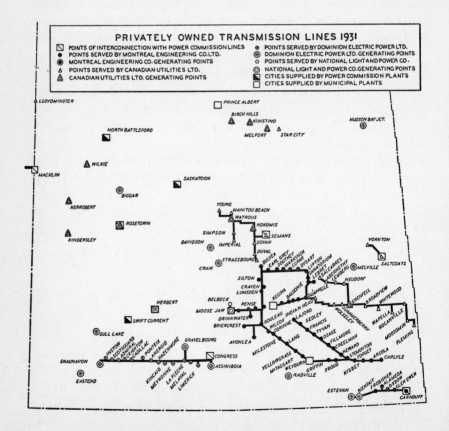

Public and institutional buildings constructed included the Weyburn Mental Hospital, the Saskatoon Normal School, and the tuberculosis sanitarium at Fort Qu'Appelle. The monetary value of buildings constructed in 1929 was estimated at $34,184,300 as compared to $22,127,100 in 1928.

An official report of the Department of Industrial Development and Natural Resources (1930), with particular reference to the year 1929, stated in part:

Agricultural expansion generally is demanding more packing houses, creameries, cold-storage plants, fruit houses, canneries, and other facilities to provide for the expanding production of diversified farm products.

The growth of the light and power industry is another example of an established industry expanding to keep pace with increasing population. . . . In addition to the growth of these established industries, many new minor industries have been established in the province, including the fur farming industry [mainly fox], straw board industry, a new sodium sulphate refining plant at Ormiston, a raw clay export industry, the beginning of a small pottery industry, and industry based on the bentonite deposits of the province having to do with the refining of oil, a new fruit house [concerned with handling bananas and citrus fruits], registering and grading of seed at Moose Jaw, concrete products, a paint and varnish industry, and so on. . . .

In the business and professional listings of thicker telephone directories appeared more names of physicians and surgeons, dentists, lawyers, and accountants, serving a population of over 800,000 which was augmented annually by a renewed stream of immigration from Europe. A second period of expansion and extension of services was in evidence on the campus and in the faculty of the University of Saskatchewan.

Though the population remained largely rural, a trend toward centralization and specialization continued. The village-based country doctor moving his practice to the larger town and city was indicative of increasing automobile traffic on improved roads.

Beyond the city streets there was no pavement, and few roads were gravelled. But the Department of Highways was following a policy of building provincial highways generally higher than the

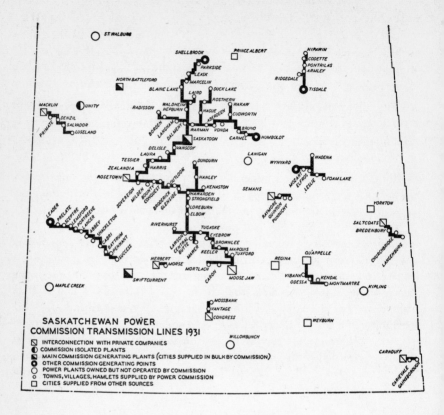

SASKATCHEWAN POWER
COMMISSION TRANSMISSION LINES 1931

▧ INTERCONNECTION WITH PRIVATE COMPANIES
◖ COMMISSION ISOLATED PLANTS
◪ MAIN COMMISSION GENERATING PLANTS (CITIES SUPPLIED IN BULK BY COMMISSION)
◉ OTHER COMMISSION GENERATING POINTS
○ POWER PLANTS OWNED BUT NOT OPERATED BY COMMISSION
○ TOWNS, VILLAGES, HAMLETS SUPPLIED BY POWER COMMISSION
□ CITIES SUPPLIED FROM OTHER SOURCES

surrounding terrain so that snow would blow free from the road, and the sharp square corners of the horse-drawn era were being replaced by inclined curves to accommodate the faster traffic of car and truck. At Dunblane, Saskatchewan's Department of Highways and the Canadian National Railways jointly completed, in November, 1926, a dual traffic and railway bridge across the South Saskatchewan River near Elbow.

Over mosquito and black-fly infested muskeg and hardrock country of northern Manitoba, the Hudson Bay Railway, vociferously agitated for in Saskatchewan, was under construction to the mouth of the Churchill River on Hudson Bay.

While iron bones of the dinosaurian steam tractors and early, cumbersome, internal combustion tractors were sold for scrap metal, or rusted by the edge of farmyards, a new mechanical monster began moving over the harvest scene. The combine-harvester, first developed in Canada by the Massey-Harris Company, cut and threshed an evenly ripened crop in one operation. Again the rapid and continuing technological development in prairie farm machinery was demonstrated by acceptance and demand for "the novelty which became commonplace, the combine-harvester". Combines in operation in Saskatchewan in 1926 numbered 148; in 1927, 382; in 1928, 2,356; in 1929, 2,279. Almost simultaneously was introduced the "one-way" seeder and tiller, which enabled growers to seed grain and discourage weeds in one operation, while "retaining the straw from last year's harvest as a trash-cover to retard soil-drifting".

A combine harvester

Heedless of technology, the vagaries of prairie weather continued as the dominant factor in annual crop production. In 1928 a cool spring, which retarded germination, was followed by rain at the right time during the growing season. Though some of the standing crop was damaged by frosts in August, the wheat yield in Saskatchewan, which amounted to more than 321 million bushels, exceeded that of any previous year. Part of this success was due to persistent research, the results of which were essential to the agricultural future of the province, irrespective of political colour or ingenious marketing arrangements. Dedicated men of science continued their experiments to evolve earlier maturing and rust-resistant wheat varieties of good milling qualities.

While farm organizations were, in the 1920's, far from united in policy and aim, Protestant church groups edged closer to union. Born of the undoctrinaire practicality and neighbourly co-operation of prairie pioneer missions, when duplication of similar church maintenance was recognized as obviously impractical in sparsely settled communities, a minority movement for church union had gradually gained momentum and popular support, which spread eastward to "old Ontario" and westward beyond the Rocky Mountains to the Pacific coast. In 1923 ardent promoters of the church union concept obtained sanction from their respective authorities for creation of a combined church to embrace Methodist and Congregational denominations, together with those Presbyterians (a large

A crystal set radio

proportion) who were favourable to the project. In the spring of
1924 the Saskatchewan Legislature passed an act to facilitate church
union. In July of that year the Union Bill passed through the House
of Commons and the Senate, and the federal legislation became
effective on June 10, 1925. While the name of the new church,
"United Church of Canada", was a misnomer as obvious as the
"United Farmers of Canada", an ardent hope was implied.

In Saskatchewan's larger social sphere the automobile had replaced the horse and buggy for purposes of mobile courtship. Jazz,
North America's unique though African-inspired contribution to the
arts of European culture, continued to captivate and evolve. The
assembly line produced motion picture of mass emotional appeal
was well on its flickering way to influencing the mores of adolescents
who had discarded grandfather's Edison phonograph for the increased technological fidelity of the gramophone. Radio transmission, no
longer a new-fangled thing, was soon to become lucrative business
in Saskatchewan. While audacious, barnstorming pilots in their light
and sometimes improvised aeroplanes continued to provide spectacles
at local fairs and city exhibitions, a passenger airline service was in
operation between Winnipeg and Calgary, and word came out of
the northland concerning the intrepid daring and skill of bush-pilots
opening up hitherto inaccessible, potentially mineral-rich country of
the Pre-Cambrian Shield.

And yet, four full months before the bubble of uninhibited prosperity and seemingly unending progress burst, a restless Saskatchewan

electorate voted out the Liberal Party, which had been in office since the inception of the province, and voted in a majority of Conservatives, Independents, and Progressives. This was the emergent political fact after the ballots were counted on the night of June 6, 1929. Seemingly buried beneath the lure of prosperity and actual physical expansion of Saskatchewan's restless 1920's, were shifting but potent factors of post-war unrest in uneasy economic psychological combination. Despite the success of the much publicized pools (farmers' marketing co-operatives), agrarian unrest had continued. Increasingly emergent had been the war veterans' demand for further recognition of those who had rallied "to the colours" for overseas service, backed by patriotic civilians who had kept "the home fires burning . . . until the boys come home". Whatever the individual and composite motives, sentimental ties to Great Britain, "the old land" ("for King and Country") had been a considerable factor in the ready enlistment and early patriotic fervour of those "of British stock".

Some immigrants to Saskatchewan's prairie scene who were "without benefit of British ancestry" had failed, in the critically scrutinizing eyes of the patriots, to make proper response to the call. The (Canadian) Great War Veterans' Association, which became the Canadian Legion, British Empire Service League, and which was headed mainly by former front line soldiers of British stock, was relatively strong in Saskatchewan.

Germanic peoples in Saskatchewan, who were numerically a large group of the non-Anglo-Saxon category, had not generally felt the urge to enlist in the war against Germany. A considerable percentage of the "Germans" were Mennonites of Dutch and German origin who, prior to their arrival in Saskatchewan, had migrated to Russia where during several generations, they had lived under the alternate sunshine and shadow of Tsarist despotism. Yet when Tsarist Russia, allied with the British cause, collapsed in 1917 and the Bolsheviks took over, the revolution did nothing to endear the Mennonites to the "mad Russians". Moreover, the Mennonites were a pacifist religious sect, intent on bettering their economic position in prairie Canada by diligent application to agriculture.

A second large group of non-Anglo-Saxon immigrants to Saskatchewan were the Ukrainians, who came mainly from Galicia and Bukovina provinces of the Austro-Hungarian Empire allied with Germany in World War I. Though the majority of Slavic Ukrainians showed loyalty to, rather than love for, the Austrian Emperor, they had learned to look to Austria-Hungary as a shield against the overwhelming might of Russia, which might crush their nationality and destroy their church. They had emigrated to prairie Canada, not to extend a British Empire with which they were only vaguely conversant, but to grasp the offered opportunity for free ("$10 for 160 acres") homestead land. In addition there was the chance to avoid excessive governmental control, compulsory military service, and other obstacles to a freer life for their families.

The Doukhobors, an inexplicable Russian peasant pacifist sect obviously devoid of British tradition, and stubbornly and unequivocally opposed to the Russia of the Tsars, had, like the Mennonites before them, been granted exemption from military service by the Canadian Government anxious for agricultural immigrants to settle the prairie west at a time when large scale international war was generally considered "a thing of the past".

There were other continental European immigrants to prairie Canada who had left their homeland, not with a hope they might someday return there, but to make a new and permanent home in the peaceful, opportunity-offering, new world "free from landlords and too many officials wearing uniforms and riding on the backs of the people".

Thus a situation had existed which gave to some sensitive veterans and patriots of British origin a sense of grievance that they had carried the large share of the burden of war, while others had stayed home and got more land and money for themselves. This feeling was reflected in a growing criticism of governmental authority, particularly with respect to immigration. While the province did not have control of immigration, the Liberal Party had been associated with the policy which had originally brought so many continental folk to Canada and which continued to encourage further immigration from the same source.

In Saskatchewan's urban centres, labour, though numerically small and less well organized than the agrarians, was inclined to view with latent hostility the competition of immigrants; thus a further element of critical opinion existed toward the government in power.

Though European immigrant groups were inclined to put what little political faith they had in the Liberal Party, an emergent minority of Slavs and others, long opposed to the oppressions of Tsardom, became enamoured of the initially idealistic, pitchfork and machine-gun reforms of the Bolshevik revolution. At the same time, indigenous reformers-in-a-hurry of Anglo-Saxon heritage, including some militant leaders in the Saskatchewan agrarian movement, were mouthing Marxist phrases fed them by dedicated members of the Communist Party of Canada, most of whom would see Bolshevik Russia only in books and illustrated propaganda pamphlets.

The political potential of the restlessness was realized by a successful educator, J. T. M. Anderson, leader of Saskatchewan's Conservative Party, and by other more sophisticated politicians. Dr. Anderson, who had won a reputation by his study of the "New Canadians", at the same time represented "the solid, substantial, and patriotic Anglo-Saxon". Striking, fluent, and individualistically tailored, Anderson, who on street and hustings wore a billycock hat and wing collar, had campaigned on the slogan, "It's time for a change." Supported by war veteran Harris Turner of *Turner's Weekly*, a newspaper of comment which had ceased publication in 1920, Anderson, with his hastily assembled supporters, referred to Liberal maladministration during the Prohibition era, and effectively placed himself as champion of the returned soldiers. Under pressure from the Liberals, he dissociated himself publicly from the Anglo-Saxon supremacy and anti-Roman Catholic pronouncements of the Ku Klux Klan, an importation from south of the 49th parallel adapted to the Saskatchewan scene at the time, which had appeared prominently during the year previous to the election. But the Klan was recognized as an important factor in the 1929 election, after the ballots were counted.

Premier Gardiner and his cohorts had campaigned on "the record of the Liberal Party" and had frankly admitted that whomever the anti-foreign and politically active Ku Klux Klan was supporting, it was evidently not the Liberal Party, under whose federal auspices the great immigration from central Europe had taken place.

As word from the polls was telegraphed and telephoned to newspaper and radio stations on the night of June 6, 1929, it became evident that the Liberal Party had lost its supremacy. When the ballots were counted, the result was: Liberals 26, Conservatives 25, Progressives 5, and Independents 5, while the elections in the two constituencies embracing Saskatchewan's Pre-Cambrian Region were, as usual, deferred until July.

Unlike the resilient and politically omnivorous Prime Minister King in Ottawa, politically rigid and selective Premier Gardiner in Regina was unable to gain the Progressives' support, requisite in an attempt to form a government with a minority of Liberal members. Instead, the Progressives met with the Conservatives and Independents and agreed that Anderson should resign as Conservative leader to become leader of the three minority groups in the legislature. The meeting carried a resolution requesting the Gardiner government to resign in the face of the numerically superior combined opposition. The result was that the Gardiner administration was defeated in the legislature by a vote of 35 to 28, and, on September 9, J. T. M. Anderson became Premier of Saskatchewan. Premier Anderson's cabinet included these men: M. A. McPherson, Attorney General; W. C. Buckle, Minister of Agriculture; Howard McConnell, Provincial Treasurer and Minister of Municipal Affairs; J. F. Bryant, Minister of Public Works and Minister of Telephones; F. D. Munroe, Minister of Public Health and Minister in charge of

Child Welfare; A. C. Stewart, Minister of Highways; J. A. Merkley, Provincial Secretary and Minister of Railways, Labour, and Industries. Ministers without portfolio, that is, minus responsibility for administration of a cabinet department, were Dr. R. Stipe and W. W. Smith.

The Anderson government, sometimes known as the "Group" or "Co-operative" Government, appeared, in the eyes of its well-wishers, to have arrived in office at an opportune time. Business boosters were vociferous in their optimism as the stock-market continued to boom throughout North America from the Rio Grande to the Saskatchewan River. On business and financial fronts "credit was easy", and Canada's chartered banks readily loaned money to casual holders of established company and promotional stocks, thus enabling investors and speculators to pyramid their purchases on margin buying. The prairie wheat pools experienced little difficulty in borrowing from the banks to finance an initial payment to producers of the 1929 crop. Boom-time optimism was reflected even in the reports of staid financial institutions and of course in the feverish and luring bulletins of brokerage houses and the columns of publications devoted to the involved and fascinating witchcraft in the realm of finance.

10

Depression, Dust, and Defiance

THE selected names "Group Government" and "Co-operative Government" remained mainly in the record of the meeting at which the Conservative, Progressive, and Independent coalition was formed. Saskatchewan's new administration became known in the press and in popular parlance simply as "The Anderson Government".

While the distinguished-appearing Anderson, together with his hastily collected colleagues, had campaigned on the slogan "It's time for a change", there seems little if any indication that the candidates for office had anticipated the drastic economic and devastating climatic change—that conjunction of depression and drouth—soon to strain governmental contrivance and to test the temper of a perplexed electorate.

The impact of economic débâcle, apparent in the autumn of 1929 and the following winter, was felt in rapidly falling prices for farm products, in unemployment in the towns and cities, and in a growing "scarcity of money" reflected in a generally declining purchasing power amidst a psychological atmosphere of uncertainty and doubt. Drouth—that is, below average rainfall, accompanied by hot, dry winds in the growing season—began in 1929 and was accentuated throughout the dry and dusty summer of 1930. The resulting predicament, following an inflationary and financially expansive period in which crops had been considered "fair to good", was regarded initially as a "temporary setback", as indicated in what was to become a famous phrase of the period, "Prosperity is just around the corner."

But this elusive "corner" did not appear for a decade. Over an expanding area of Saskatchewan one crop failure followed another in distressing sequence while, as elsewhere in the world of European civilization, money—once presumed to be a somewhat readily available medium of exchange—remained a bewilderingly scarce commodity.

Whatever the "better next year" proclamations of the optimists were or the promulgations of pessimists critical of an "economic set-up that has broken down", the final dependence of Saskatchewan's wheat economy on export sales to the United Kingdom and continental European countries was grimly underlined. While Saskatchewan's farmers, and consequently most urban people, were adversely affected by depressed prices for grain, livestock, and other farm products, the Saskatchewan Wheat Pool experienced an insolvency which annihilated the pool's original purpose of farmer-controlled "orderly marketing for a fair price to the producer in accord with the cost of production". Wheat pool officials in Saskatchewan— along with those in the adjoining provinces of Manitoba and Alberta— were, in common with most men engaged in commerce, taken by surprise when the economic crash of 1929 resounded throughout the western world. On the 1929 crop, at a time when the open market registered around $1.50 per bushel for wheat (Number 1 Northern, Fort William), the pool made to its farmer members an initial payment of $1 per bushel. During December, 1930, the price of top grade wheat fell to a round figure of 50 cents per bushel on the open market at Winnipeg. The Saskatchewan Wheat Pool's final accounting of its 1929 crop transaction revealed an overpayment of more than 13 million dollars to its grower members. While individual wheat pool members benefited temporarily as a result of the miscalculation of their elected and appointed officers, the prairie wheat pools suffered staggering blows to their financial position and prestige. The three provincial governments of Manitoba, Saskatchewan, and Alberta, in turn guaranteed by the Canadian Government, came to the rescue of three prairie wheat pools by loans to the extent of 25 million dollars. While the governments were guaranteeing the existence of the wheat pools, not as co-operative marketing concerns but as grain-handling agencies, the chartered banks, which had loaned money to the pools to make the initial crop payment to the growers, benefited accordingly. The Saskatchewan Legislature in its 1930 session passed an act authorizing the Saskatchewan Government to guarantee advances made by chartered banks to the Saskatchewan Wheat Pool.

In addition to the unprecedented low price of wheat, there occurred the climatic phenomenom of less than average rainfall and moisture-sucking winds. The drouth, which had earlier become ominous in the vicinity of the Rio Grande, spread northward over the Great Plains through Texas, Oklahoma, Kansas, Nebraska, the Dakota states, and Montana to envelop Canada's southern prairies in dust driven by dry and relentless winds.

Long prior to the advent of the "dirty thirties", Saskatchewan and Alberta had been asking for control of public lands and natural resources retained by the Canadian Government. The eventual transfer to the provinces occurred at a time when the "natural resources", no matter how well administered, could not easily be made an asset. On March 20, 1930, the Saskatchewan Government received control of its natural resources when an agreement was signed with the Canadian Government.

Depression and drouth, with their consequent relief expenditures and unemployment, reversed the attitude toward immigration. Farmers' organizations joined with labour unions in opposing the entry of immigrants until "work and wages are found for our hundreds of thousands of unemployed". Under the circumstances leaders of all political parties declared themselves opposed to further large scale immigration.

During the windy summer of 1930, Prime Minister William Lyon Mackenzie King and Opposition Leader Richard Bedford Bennett appeared on the prairie scene to campaign in the general election of that year. In Saskatchewan much of the burden of the Liberal effort to arouse public opinion in support of the party was borne by two of King's cabinet ministers, "Tom" Crerar and "Charlie" Dunning, both of whom had emerged to national prominence following auspicious beginnings in the prairie farmers' movement. Dunning, as Minister of Finance, had concentrated increasingly on actuarial figures and statistical totals requisite to "balancing the budget". In his campaign speeches he concerned himself with justification of what, among advocates of "free trade", became critically known as "The Dunning Budget". While King and his Liberal Party colleagues were accused of ignoring or sidestepping the problems of alarmingly low prices for agricultural products, and mounting unemployment, Conservative leader R. B. Bennett came forth with bold pronouncements. Declared the redoubtable, impulsive, and personally forceful Bennett: "Mr. King tells you he will consider the problem of unemployment. I tell you I will solve the problem of unemployment . . . . I will blast my way into the markets of the world."

On the political hustings cautious, many-sided Mackenzie King, the student who combined an academic training with a political intuition carefully nurtured, may have sensed something of what was to become the "Great Depression". In the course of the campaign, much less emphatic than his politically uninhibited opponent, King made few bold pronouncements, offered no panacea to a restive electorate yet to feel the full impact of prolonged economic difficulty and social readjustment. Speaking in Regina, King accused Saskatchewan's Anderson government of delaying public works with the intention of projecting the problem of unemployment into politics. Subsequently, Saskatchewan's Premier Anderson announced his intention of openly supporting Bennett and opposing King. Said Anderson, "It will be my pleasant duty from now on to do all in my power to bring about the defeat of the King Government."

A potent factor in the defeat of the King administration was an economic condition theoretically within the bounds of human control.

When the ballots across Canada were counted on the evening of July 28, Bennett and his supporters were swept into office. In traditionally Liberal Saskatchewan the Conservative victory was less in evidence: Liberals 11, Conservatives 8, Progressives 2. But significant was the defeat of two outstanding cabinet ministers, Dunning and Crerar, who had represented prairie constituencies in the King administration. In R. B. Bennett's Conservative administration, Robert Weir, a successful prairie farmer elected in Saskatchewan's Melfort constituency, became Minister of Agriculture.

The new Canadian Government, from its inception obviously dominated by purposeful Prime Minister Bennett, was to fail in blasting its way into the markets of the world. The Conservatives, in accord with pre-election promises, began by revising the tariff upward. But by 1932, whittling at their own protective legislation, the Canadian Government signed the Ottawa agreements designed to lower tariffs and facilitate trade between British Commonwealth countries. Prior to the end of its term of office the Conservative administration was to find itself negotiating for reciprocal tariff reductions between Canada and the United States.

Protective tariff pronouncements, so prominent during the election campaign, became less in evidence as the new government was confronted with pressing problems on the domestic scene, accompanied by a popular clamour for their immediate solution. On September 22, less than two months after its election, the administration passed the Unemployment Relief Act.

At the outset of the depression and drouth, Saskatchewan's municipal governments attempted to take care of the essential needs of distressed persons within their respective boundaries in accordance with their normal responsibility. But as thousands of families required direct relief in the form of food, clothing, and fuel to keep warm in winter, the problem of relief rapidly became the joint concern of municipal, provincial, and federal governments. Moreover, many farmers were unable to provide feed for their livestock and lacked money to buy tractor fuel or binder twine, or to pay for repairs for their farm implements. Both the Saskatchewan Government and the Canadian Government assumed some responsibility for relief as early as 1929. In the autumn of that year, the Saskatchewan Government, with the assistance of grants-in-aid from the Canadian Government, began a programme of road building as a relief project designed for farmers in most urgent need. Thus about four million dollars was spent during 1929, 1930, and 1931, and a basis was laid for better roads in Saskatchewan, a sparsely settled province with the distinction of having more road mileage per person than any other province of Canada.

In 1931 the Saskatchewan Government, by order-in-council, set up the Saskatchewan Relief Commission. This commission functioned through its appointed relief officers, who worked with local relief committees. Food and clothing for human beings and feed for livestock were distributed to individuals and families after an application had been approved by the Saskatchewan Relief Commission, and on the understanding that the recipient of relief would repay the government when able to do so. For purposes of administration in the "dried-out area", Saskatchewan was divided into three zones: A, B, and C. In the A zone were 93 municipalities and local improvement districts in which the population had suffered three successive crop failures. In B area were 73 rural municipalities beset by two successive crop failures, while C zone contained some 70 municipalities wherein there had been one crop failure.

Prompted largely by distress in southern agricultural Saskatchewan, the Canadian Government in 1931 introduced the Unemployment and Farm Relief Act. Owing to the inability of municipalities and the Saskatchewan Government to meet relief expenses involved in the A zone, the Canadian Government agreed to pay the entire cost of relief expenditures in that zone for the fiscal year 1931-32.

While drouth was most manifest on the prairies, the economic depression—that is, a drastically reduced purchasing power concomitant with a bewildering disappearance of money accompanied by trade stagnation and unemployment—was a condition evident across Canada. In the Maritime provinces fishermen, who were well aware that the fish had not disappeared from the ocean, were made conscious of the fact that people elsewhere were unable to find the money to buy fish. In Ontario and Quebec, vegetables continued to grow in profusion, but there was "no market" for them. In British Columbia, the evergreen forests had not vanished, but mills and men were idle because "the bottom has gone out of the lumber industry". A small percentage of the "surplus vegetables" of central Canada and the "surplus cod fish" of the Maritimes was purchased by the Canadian Government and transported to the prairies, there to be distributed by relief officials. Special recipes for the preparation of dried cod fish were provided for prairie housewives.

In addition to government relief, various voluntary associations, including church groups, came to the aid of people in need. The Canadian Red Cross Society contributed clothing, blankets, and bedding, and in some instances donated money for the medical care of impoverished persons. Voluntary relief shipments, contributed by residents of other provinces, were distributed by the Saskatchewan Voluntary Relief Committee, and such consignments were handled free of charge by the railways.

Bennett buggy.

With little money available to buy gasoline for tractor, truck, and car, farmers turned back to horses in those areas where they could at least grow enough feed for the horses. Buggies, democrats, and buckboards had become virtually non-existent, but usually a farmer did have an old automobile on the place or "a car we can't afford to buy gas or repairs for". So he lifted the motor out of the family car, removed the windshield, attached a set of double-trees and a wagon tongue to the front axle, and hitched up a team of horses to what was designed originally as a "horseless carriage". These mobile innovations, appearing in increasing numbers on side roads and highways, soon became known as "Bennett buggies".

Where lignite coal was exposed on the sides of coulees in the Plains Region, farmers equipped with pick and shovel dug the low grade fuel and loaded it into their wagons for winter use. Small

Farmers digging coal

near-surface mines provided lignite coal for around $2 a ton at the minehead.

The privations of the period drew neighbours together for spontaneous co-operation most needed in harvest time, and reminiscent of the proud interdependence of the early agricultural pioneers.

In the Plains Region and to some extent along the southern rim of the Parklands, Russian thistle thrived despite little or no rainfall. Spring melting of the scantiest winter snowfall invariably provided sufficient moisture for the germination of the widespread seed of this annual weed native to the Russian steppe, where climate, terrain, and soils are similar to those of prairie Canada. With the force of the winds of late summer or autumn, roundish brown balls of mature weeds broke from their brittle stems and bounded in seemingly endless march across the land, scattering their multitudinous seeds along the way. As the wind changed direction, so did the massed ranks of rolling thistles, which even seemed designed to overcome the fences of man. As if possessed of a relentless strategy in collusion with the wind, the first ranks piled up against the fence, forming a ramp for the main army to roll over the top and continue on its way through the fields beyond. When severe dust-storms accompanied the line of march, or subsequently followed it, drifting soil lodged in the ramp of thistle, and in some instances both barbed wire and fenceposts disappeared from sight in a shroud of topsoil.

But farmers found that Russian thistle could be cut green, cured in stacks, and fed safely to horses and cattle as a substitute for the hay and grain that could not grow. On previously tilled but temporarily abandoned lands this persistent weed "took over", to provide a cover which reduced soil-drifting in summer and "held" the scant snows of winter.

The square dance

Prevailing winds, which in the years of early settlement had been caught in iron-bladed windmills for pumping water from deep wells, now provided power to turn the electric generator for the family radio. Often the improvised generator was a dismantled one from the automobile engine removed from "the old car", which had been fashioned into a Bennett buggy. On popular radio programmes were dance bands and hockey broadcasts. "Shortage of cash" resulted in less purchased amusement and spectator sport and in more local effort, in which more people participated for their own entertainment. Dances in community halls and empty barn-lofts, with music by local talent, were relatively inexpensive and well attended. Community hockey was played with a minimum of equipment, and there were budding young goalkeepers who folded newspapers over their legs as a substitute for felt-padded leg-guards.

There was a revival of the "open forum" initiated in earlier
pioneer days. More people attended meetings which included dis-
cussions of Capitalism, Socialism, Communism, and Technocracy,
and where "the gold standard", "planned economy", "debt-free
money", and "practical Christianity" were variously advocated by
advertised and impromptu speakers. Question periods and open
forum sessions—resulting in a rising demand on public libraries for
books concerning finance, banking, economics, and political philoso-
phy—continued at times until midnight and after. The diverse solutions offered and panaceas put forth were reflected in newspaper
reports and letter columns.

Both less wordy and less spectacular was the steady growth of
consumer co-operative endeavour and accomplishment. At country
points where no local co-operative existed, the Saskatchewan Co-operative Wholesale Society and the Saskatchewan Wheat Pool entered
into a tentative arrangement, whereby local pool elevator agents
would handle bulk commodities such as coal and binder twine "on
a strictly cash basis to the consumer". The cash basis included
acceptance of relief vouchers. At most points, coal consigned to a
local co-op was unloaded, at the railway siding, directly into farmers'
wagons, since the embryo co-ops did not have coal-sheds. This practice, termed "snow-birding" by local merchants who had invested
in coal-sheds, was considered "unfair to the trade". In consequence
hard pressed retail merchants through their association prevailed upon
the Saskatchewan Government to have coal relief orders honoured
only when presented to coal dealers equipped with coal-sheds. To
comply with the order of the Saskatchewan Relief Commission, local
co-ops, often with voluntary labour, began building "useless" coal-
sheds. The first co-op coal-shed was built at Blucher, the second at
Clarkboro, and an expanding building programme gave impetus to
further co-operative development as various "coal-shed co-ops" developed into retail co-operative stores. When at the instigation of the
Retail Merchants' Association coal mining companies declined to
sell coal to the Saskatchewan Co-operative Wholesale Society, the
co-operatives painfully proceeded to acquire their own mines in
Alberta, where bituminous coal was available in quantity.

In the Plains Region, in the vicinity of Moose Jaw and Regina,
farmer shareholders in local oil co-operatives became incensed with

the Canadian Government's gallonage tax on gasoline imported from the United States, and accused Prime Minister Bennett of "favouring the Imperial Oil Company by his unwarranted legislation".

Apprehension was increased when, during the autumn of 1933 and the spring of 1934, independent refineries supplying local co-operatives either were bought out by major oil companies or simply ceased operations. When subsequently the tankcar price of gasoline was raised as much as three cents a gallon, a few defiant farmers launched a campaign to "build our own refinery". During the dusty summer of 1934 determined votaries of the idea canvassed depression-ridden farmers for capital. By harvest time $32,000 was paid up in shares in the Consumers Co-operative Refineries Limited. On May 27 the following year at Regina, "the world's first co-operative oil refinery", a 500-barrel skimming plant, "went on stream". Sales in 1935 amounted to more than $250,000.

Credit, a continuing financial problem of the prairie economy, was increasingly difficult to obtain during the 1930's. Consequently the credit union or "people's bank" technique, introduced from Europe to Quebec in 1900, received more attention in Saskatchewan. The Saskatchewan Legislature in its session of 1937 passed The Credit Union Act, which enabled 10 or more persons to form a credit union for the purpose of saving or borrowing money. The first credit union in Saskatchewan to receive a charter under the act was the Regina Hebrew Savings and Credit Union incorporated August 2, 1937. Ten days later the Pioneer Savings and Credit Union of Moose Jaw was formed. Incorporation of subsequent credit unions resulted in the formation, in 1938, of the Credit Union Federation, a co-ordinating organization.

While various methods of "self-help" were initiated by individuals and minority groups, most people concerned themselves with their own day to day problems. Only after an innovation or a new technique had been proved obviously advantageous, did it attract popular support.

In the Plains Region tormenting days and nights of blowing dust caused the abandonment of farmsteads. Some families loaded their household equipment, together with chickens and a pig or two, on wagons and makeshift vehicles constructed from old implement wheels and boards torn from an empty granary. Driving their

A dust-storm

cattle on the hoof, they trekked northward to the Parklands Region and as far as the southern fringe of the Forest Region—"to anywhere we can find water, firewood, and shelter to stop a garden plot blowing away in the wind". Since much of the good farming land had been settled previously, the weary newcomers found themselves often on marginal soil. Once more the log cabin with earthern floor swept by a broom made of willows became a reality in Saskatchewan. Wives and daughters made dresses from flour sacks. Dad ploughed the grey bush soil for a garden plot. The lads tracked and snared bush-rabbits, and rabbit pie appeared with monotonous regularity on the family table.

In July, 1931, Premier Anderson and his hard pressed administration had asked the Liberal Party in opposition for a 12-month truce until "this period of human suffering is over". But the redoubtable J. G. Gardiner, Opposition Leader, persisted in his telling criticism of the Anderson regime. In the legislature and on the political hustings tireless "Jimmy" Gardiner demanded an appeal to the electorate in a provincial election. Supported by colleagues who were former cabinet ministers and "who knew their departments", he led an unrelenting Opposition, the more effective because not one member of the Anderson cabinet had prior experience as a cabinet minister. Moreover, the Progressives, on whom the Ander-

son government was dependent for support to maintain a majority in the legislature, became increasingly restive after formation of a new agrarian political party in Saskatchewan. Some of the Progressives had joined the Anderson government not so much in an enthusiasm for the "Group Government" but as a result of their dissatisfaction with the Liberal Party.

An emergent political party, which petitioned and criticized the Anderson government, had arisen from the United Farmers of Canada, Saskatchewan Section. This Saskatchewan organization, a lineal descendant of the Territorial Grain Growers' Association, had in the annual convention of 1931 voted to discard the non-political participation clause of its constitution and to take direct political action. Within this farmers' organization an aggressive minority of "Marxists" had, whether by scientific analysis or coincidental guessing, apparently accurately forecast the Great Depression. As a result of their prognostications, confirmed by the events, their prestige within the farmers' organization rose.

In the lead of the movement to form a new political party was George H. Williams, of Semans, president of the United Farmers of Canada, Saskatchewan Section. Of United Empire Loyalist background, he had, in World War I, enlisted in the Lord Strathcona Horse, a cavalry regiment which attracted volunteers from the prairie west. On the battlefields of France, Williams became a commissioned officer, was wounded in a cavalry charge, and was recognized for bravery in action. He returned to Saskatchewan to take a farm, near Semans on the Canadian National Railways' mainline, under the Canadian Government Soldier Settler Scheme. Following his re-establishment in civilian life, stocky, broad-chested, blue-eyed, and round-headed George Williams, who walked with a slight limp from his war wounds, became a student of such diverse thinkers as Karl Marx, G. D. H. Cole, and Edward Bellamy. Largely unheeded by his fellow farmers, he had advocated a "planned economy" through legislation. In 1931, amidst economic depression, drouth-stricken crops, and dust-ridden skies, the egotistical and determined George Williams came to the centre of a stage provided by a minority of defiant farmers who were "through with all the old parties" (includ-ing "the old Progressives"). After forming the Saskatchewan Farmer-Labour Group, these ardent votaries insisted theirs was not a political party.

It was the militant and controlling element of the United Farmers of Canada, Saskatchewan Section, which had sought an alliance with organized labour in Saskatchewan. But organized labour, such as it was in this predominantly agricultural province, was represented mainly in numerically small affiliates of the American Federation of Labor and in the Railway Brotherhoods, both traditionally opposed to direct political action. In Saskatchewan cities and towns the Trades and Labour Congress (AFL) rejected the overtures of the radical farmers' political group.

In Regina there was a recently organized, isolated branch of the (British) Independent Labour Party, a sort of Fabian discussion group headed by an able debater and Regina school principal (and lay reader in the Anglican Church), M. J. Coldwell. English-born and educated, this broad-shouldered, brown-eyed man of medium height who walked with lithe step had served as president and, subsequently, as secretary-treasurer of the Canadian Teachers Federation. An alderman of the City of Regina, 1922-25, he was defeated when he stood as a Progressive candidate in Regina constituency in 1925. Associated with Coldwell in both civic activities and the discussion of public affairs beyond the confines of Regina was suave, alert, and dapper Clarence M. Fines, another Regina school teacher intellectually displeased by the untidiness evident in the economic depression of

European civilization and accentuated, in Saskatchewan, by below average rainfall.

At the instigation of the United Farmers of Canada, Saskatchewan Section, the Coldwell and Fines tiny Independent Labour Party merged with the farm organization to form the Saskatchewan Farmer-Labour Group contrived to bring about a planned economy.

U. F. C. Secretary Frank Eliason, who as a young man in his native Sweden had eagerly participated in a national movement that was eventually to result in the "right to vote" for all male adults regardless of individual property status, became secretary-treasurer of the Saskatchewan Farmer-Labour Group, "which hardly had enough money in the treasury to buy stamps for mailing out the meeting posters we got printed on credit at the Modern Press".

Once again, but with less cash for travelling expenses than during the previous crusades, determined proselytizers "took to the road" to find converts for the most recent economic and political gospel put forth by a militant minority of farmers.

The precipitate step into politics, spurred on by a prairie agrarian revolt which had unequivocally abandoned the Liberal Party, did not endear the fledgling Saskatchewan Farmer-Labour Group to the majority of farmers. Membership in the United Farmers of Canada, Saskatchewan Section, declined. Various U.F.C. local lodges, torn by dissension and doubt, ceased to function. Business people, the traders and merchants of the towns and cities, were for the most part hostile to these new "politicians" categorized as "a bunch of Reds".

In August, 1932, at Calgary, the Saskatchewan Farmer-Labour Group became affiliated with the newly formed Co-operative Commonwealth Federation, which elected as its leader James Shaver Woodsworth of United Empire Loyalist background, an uncompromising reformer and crusading humanitarian, representing Winnipeg North Centre in the House of Commons. In 1933 in Regina, the Co-operative Commonwealth Federation held its first annual national convention and issued its manifesto for the abolition of the profit system and the establishment of a planned economy in Canada.

When the Anderson government, after five difficult years in office, called an election for June 19, 1934, there were three parties contending. The government party campaigned on its record in office. The

Liberals accused the government of inadequacy of policy and inefficiency in practice, and linked Anderson and his colleagues with Prime Minister Bennett, who had not endeared himself to the people of the prairie west. Both parties warned the electorate against the "Radicals" of the third party. The third party, proclaiming that there was no difference between the two old parties, urged the electorate to defeat both and to elect a "Socialist Government for Humanity First".

After the final ballot count the result was Liberal, 50; Farmer-Labour, 5. Not one of the previous government members or supporters in the legislature was re-elected. The vote was Liberal, 206,191; Conservative, 114,973; Farmer-Labour, 103,582; others, 4,134.

On July 19, the Anderson government resigned and J. G. Gardiner once more became Premier of Saskatchewan. On July 27, the Saskatchewan Farmer-Labour Group, led by George H. Williams, changed its name to Co-operative Commonwealth Federation, Saskatchewan Section.

The Social Credit Party, with its fluid mixture of monetary reform and religiosity, which in the summer of 1935 swept into office in Alberta, was attempting to gain a foothold in Saskatchewan, when Prime Minister R. B. Bennett announced a general election for October 14, 1935. During the much publicized campaign the Conservative and Liberal parties strenuously put forth proposals for ending the economic depression, and so did the Co-operative Commonwealth Federation (C.C.F.), the Social Credit Party, and the Reconstruction Party. W. L. Mackenzie King, with the advantage of being out of office during some five years of depression, led his party to a victory which gave the Liberal Party a majority of 97 seats over all other parties combined. In Saskatchewan 16 Liberals were elected to the House of Commons, two C.C.F., two Social Credit, and one Conservative, E. E. Perley, a Wolseley district farmer, first elected in 1930. One of the C.C.F. members elected was M. J. Coldwell of Regina, who stood for election in the rural constituency of Rosetown-Biggar. Dunning and Crerar once more became cabinet ministers in a King administration. At the insistence of Prime Minister Mackenzie King, J. G. Gardiner resigned as Premier of Saskatchewan to become Minister of Agriculture at Ottawa. Gardiner subsequently stood for election to the House of Commons in Assiniboia constituency, vacated for him by a Liberal M.P., and was elected. The Liberal cabinet in Saskatchewan selected prudent, amicable William John Patterson to lead the government. Saskatchewan's sixth premier, he was the first to be born within the boundaries of the province.

During the growing season of 1934 a grasshopper infestation, predicted by entomologists at the University of Saskatchewan, became obvious to the farmers, who fought this menace with poison bait supplied by Saskatchewan's Department of Agriculture. The continuing drouth and added ravages of grasshoppers made inevitable another crop failure. In August the Saskatchewan Government announced the abolition of the Saskatchewan Relief Commission. Effective September 1, the responsibility for the purchase and distribution of fodder and grain for winter maintenance of livestock, together with the purchase and distribution of grain for seed and feed, and the granting of credits for tractor fuel and machinery repairs, devolved on the Saskatchewan Department of Agriculture, of which J. G. Taggart was minister and F. H. Auld deputy minister. Moreover, the Liberal administration looked to municipal officials for guidance and placed on the municipal authorities the chief task of the local distribution of government relief.

By joint arrangement with the Canadian Government, the Canadian Pacific Railway and the Canadian National Railways, Canada Packers, Swift Canadian Company, and Burns and Company, farmers in areas most seriously affected by drouth were given the opportunity to dispose of cattle in poor condition, at a price guaranteed. The price was 50 cents per hundredweight with a promise of a further payment of whatever monetary surplus might be realized on the sale of the meat to the ultimate consumer. The second and final payment of 55 cents per 100 pounds made a total return of $1.05 per hundredweight net to the farmer.

Financial stringency in rural areas was not conducive to encouraging medical doctors to continue practice in the smaller centres. As doctors abandoned the countryside for the larger towns and cities, and as farm and village people became less able financially to go to the centres for medical treatment or to pay for the treatment, the problem of medical care was accentuated. The Saskatchewan Government, in an effort to avoid the complete disappearance of medical and dental services from the rural community, guaranteed a certain cash income to doctors and dentists and an additional travelling allowance. Hospitals, in addition to the statutory grant of 50 cents per patient per day, were further assisted.

Though some medical doctors had a minimum guaranteed income as a result of the Municipal Doctor Plan, the medical practitioners were, in many instances, financially hard pressed as patients lacked cash to pay bills. Dentists, with a capital investment in their instruments and the expensive material necessary to their function, also found it difficult to replace these requisites, when many persons requiring dental care were unable to pay for the services. There was, moreover, no effective way in which a lawyer could pay for his fixed overhead, except in money, the scarce commodity. Various other professional persons such as surveyors, civil engineers, architects, and accountants—especially those who were younger or for any reason less well established—found themselves in difficult financial circumstances in accordance with their actual or virtual degree of unemployment. University professors, and certain other professional persons on fixed salaries, suffered severe cuts in their monthly cheques. Yet in some instances they were "better off", because—though their salaries had been reduced—their income was not subject to the day to day fluctuations of free enterprise in a deflated economy. Moreover, though such salaries were reduced, the purchasing power of the dollar had increased. In a relatively affluent position were locomotive engineers, railway conductors, and other members of the "running trades" who possessed seniority of service sufficient to enable them to work a near maximum number of "hours and miles". Likewise, station agents, together with senior shop and roundhouse employees, did not suffer drastic reduction of income.

Grain elevator agents at country points, for the most part, had their salaries slashed, and many Saskatchewan Wheat Pool agents supplemented their meagre wages by handling coal, binder twine, and other bulk commodities for local co-operatives affiliated with the growing Saskatchewan Co-operative Wholesale Society. In depressed economic circumstance were school teachers, more especially those who were subject to annual contract in rural areas where men and women agreed to teach school for as little as $300, and then did not always receive their salaries in full. There were instances where teachers did not receive final payment of their "back wages" in arrears until the good crop years and the wartime prosperity of the 1940's. The adverse conditions of the 1930's accelerated organization of the Saskatchewan Teachers' Federation, of which J. H. Sturdy was secretary. Ontario-born, amiable, but persistent "Jack" Sturdy early in World War I enlisted as a "private soldier" and saw service on the battlefields of France. When he returned to civilian life he became principal of Fort Qu'Appelle High School. When subsequently he, with a number of others, accepted a pioneering task in building the Saskatchewan Teachers' Federation, he was recognized as a tenacious champion for "decent wages for our teachers".

Retail merchants, most of whom had "customers' accounts on their books" prior to the economic crash of 1929, were hard pressed by wholesalers, who in turn were pressed by manufacturers, in turn under pressure from chartered banks demanding payment of loans. Various local merchants, that is, "storekeepers", who by long service in the community knew well each individual customer's personal circumstances and preferences, helped heads of families "tide over" the prolonged period of depression and drouth. There were storekeepers who accepted farm produce, in exchange for store goods, only from those considered to be most in need. There was the storekeeper who in time of economic and moral stress became known as a practical and friendly counsellor, a protector in a shifting sea of uncertainty and distress. In Prince Albert, for instance, there was a successful, community-minded, philosophical furniture merchant, a Latvian-Jewish immigrant of the early 1900's, who let his hard pressed customers know that they would receive from him neither monthly statement nor request for payment of overdue accounts so long as the depression continued. During the prosperous 1940's this merchant was receiving final payments of old accounts incurred in the 1930's and before. In his words, "They just came in and paid me, though some of the accounts had gone seven years without a payment and so were therefore legally uncollectable."

Canada's chartered banks with their transcontinental diversification of both accounts and investment, together with the benefit of a bank act designed to protect the depositors, did not become insolvent or "go bust" as did many contemporary banks in the United States of America. As Canada's banks weathered the storm, there were certain criticisms directed against them. A vociferous protest from the prairies "for banking reform" so that currency might become a "medium of exchange" rather than "a commodity" gathered momentum across the land and had bearing on a revision of the Bank Act and the establishment of the Bank of Canada, whereby the control of credit and the issuance of currency became to a greater extent a matter of national policy.

Saskatchewan's most recent agrarian revolt, made spectacular in the rise of the Saskatchewan Farmer-Labour Group (C.C.F.), was from its inception editorially opposed by daily newspapers in the province, and remained for the most part unsupported by weekly newspapers, both provincial and local. In contrast to the rebellious and crusading pronouncements of editors in the 1880's, most newspapers of the 1930's declared themselves in support of the *status quo,* and berated the economic and political innovators. Though the *Saskatoon Star-Phoenix* was, in that regard, no exception in its editorial columns, this daily newspaper was recognized for its fair and factual news coverage of meetings and events.

In Saskatchewan's towns and cities casual labourers were among the first to "go on relief". Generally next to feel the impact of depression were semi-skilled workers, and soon a number of skilled artisans or mechanics—that is, carpenters, bricklayers, tinsmiths, and the like—were, with other heads of families, lining up at the relief office to receive a weekly dole for food, rent, and clothing. Some artisans and others whose services had ceased to be in demand had saved sufficient money to tide themselves over the depression, or at least a part of this period.

Though statistics exist concerning the numbers of persons "on relief", both urban and rural, there was no official tabulation concerning the percentage who readily "went on relief" and those "who held out" until acceptance of relief was for them imperative. In the opinion of some relief administrators, many heads of families initially struggled proudly to "keep off relief", even when the need existed. Their eventual and reluctant application for assistance was followed by a passive acceptance of the inevitability of the situation, and later there developed "a tendency to demand all they think they should have".

In least onerous financial position were individuals who, at the outset of the depression, had no pressing debts and who possessed cash, or its equivalent. These men and women, relatively few in number, in possession of the most sought after and scarce commodity—money, were able to purchase their needs at much reduced prices, reflecting the deflationary period.

Riding the freights

For unemployed single men there were relief camps financed by the Canadian Government. But many young men did not desire to remain in the relief camps, or to enter the camps. Thousands of men throughout Canada drifted back and forth across the country, riding boxcars of transcontinental freight trains, both C.P.R. and C.N.R. Some of these transients were looking for work, others were travelling to specified points where relatives or friends might find work for them, or care for them, and many were, in a semi-adventurous way, "on the move" in defiance of the stagnation of the economy. A few got into serious trouble with the law, but there were many who gained an education aside from the academic training they might have received under orthodox scholastic methods. In summer-time the transients, while living in boxcars and "jungles" adjacent to the railway, had no rent to pay. They could exist, for food, on about 30 cents a day. If they were willing to do a little work along the way they could often get vegetables and fruit in season in exchange for a few hours labour. In the "jungles"—that is, the transient camping places along the railway right of way, generally near a railway divisional point and handy to a lake or freshwater stream—the transients evolved a rough code of their own. "Green" teen-agers were made to wash themselves and their clothing, and also to respect other unwritten "rules of the road". Thus emerged a semblance of order in an unorganized and dispossessed segment of society. To the transients many non-itinerant persons were sympathetic and kindly, giving to these "rod-riders of the thirties" food, cast-off clothing, and sometimes shelter. For many of the transients there was a harsh and primitive sense of adventure spiritually elevated by a comradeship of the road that the more prudent and sedentary element of society knew neither by experience nor by intuition.

Prime Minister Bennett during the summer of 1932 became alarmed at the number of men riding boxcars. On October 1 of that year, the "Bennett ban" went into effect, and the Royal Canadian Mounted Police patrolled the railway yards in force and rode freight trains out of divisional points in the course of obeying their instructions to clear the trains of transients.

But while the Royal Canadian Mounted Police was faithfully, and rigorously, attempting to carry out its orders, village, town, and city policemen were telling the temporarily stranded transients to "get out of town". Moreover the jails became filled with transients and in consequence there was little or no accommodation for ordinary offenders.

Many transients, by their nature, youth, or conditioning, not anxious to stay in any one centre for long, again boarded the freights. And after a period of frantic enforcement the "Bennett ban" ceased to function and once more the transient flow back and forth across Canada was resumed. Out of this situation arose incidents which caused considerable concern. For instance, early in June, 1935, about 1,000 young men left government relief camps in British Columbia and boarded freight trains to present their grievances to the Canadian

Government at Ottawa. As these unemployed men proceeded eastward, their number grew.

Bennett's fear concerning fruition of "a plan for armed revolution", plus his determination to avoid the political embarrassment of several thousand unemployed transients demanding an audience on Parliament Hill, prompted him to have orders issued to Commissioner MacBrien of the Royal Canadian Mounted Police that the march was to be stopped at Regina. On June 14, the trekkers, reportedly numbering nearly 2,000, were at Regina, where with the consent of civic authorities they proceeded to organize a "tag day". From the proceeds of tag day contributions they purchased food and dispatched some of their leaders as a delegation to Ottawa. They refused an offer from the Canadian Government for provision of a temporary relief camp at Lumsden. On the evening of July 1, Canada's national holiday, they converged in an orderly manner for an open air meeting, which was attended by thousands of Regina citizens and farmers in the area. While the meeting was in progress, the R.C.M.P., assisted by Regina City Police, marched toward the rostrum to arrest the leaders. In the ensuing riot about 100 persons were injured, a city policeman was clubbed to death, much property damage resulted, and some 80 men were arrested. Arrests subsequently totalled 130; 24 were charged with rioting, wounding, and assaulting; nine were convicted and sentenced to prison terms of up to 14 months.

Premier Gardiner and Attorney General Davis protested the action of the Canadian Government as an invasion of provincial jurisdiction. The Saskatchewan Government negotiated with representatives of the transient unemployed, and on July 5, 1,500 men were moving westward on special trains provided by the Saskatchewan Government. On the same day the Saskatchewan Government announced the appointment of a royal commission to inquire into the riot. The commission, of which Chief Justice J. T. Brown, Court of King's Bench, was chairman, exonerated the Canadian Government and the R.C.M.P., found the food provided in the relief camps good food, and blamed the Ottawa-bound trek and the Regina Riot on Moscow-inspired Communism. But neither the violence of the riot nor the findings of the learned judges comprising the royal commission put an end to the appearance of transient unemployed on transcontinental trains.

A dug-out

The continuing social instability was accentuated by the continuing hostility of climatic conditions. Much of the populace regarded the dry and windy summers with their vicious dust-storms as a climatic phenomenon completely beyond the control of man: "Nothing could be done about it." Little in the news was the persistent work of a few scientists on the government experimental farms and in the universities and departments of agriculture. As a result of patient studies and experiments, limited by lack of funds, they were convinced "something could be done". In response to proposals put forth, the Canadian Parliament in April, 1935, passed the Prairie Farm Rehabilitation Act. The act provided for an expenditure of $750,000 during the fiscal year of 1935-36, and a sum not to exceed one million dollars a year for the four succeeding years. These expenditures were regarded not as direct relief but as part of a long term policy for rehabilitation of the severely stricken Plains Region of prairie Canada. The act was designed to provide assistance and encouragement on a self-help basis, whereby individual farmers and ranchers would conserve surface water for household use, stock-watering, regrassing, tree-planting, and reclamation of land eroded by wind.

A community pasture

Under an amendment to the act, in 1937, non-arable lands, selected by the three provincial governments, were to be withdrawn from cultivation and developed for the establishment of community or reserve pastures. Settlers on the lands considered non-arable were to be assisted in moving to arable land.

The act included assistance to universities for the extension of soil surveys and for an economic survey in co-operation with the provincial governments.

The work began in the summer of 1935 with the provision of engineering services, plus financial assistance to farmers whose applications had been accepted. In Saskatchewan during 1937, 16 community pastures were established, varying in size from 6,000 to 25,000 acres and involving an area of some 180,000 acres. In 1937, George Spence, an able enthusiast for the land rehabilitation project, resigned as Saskatchewan's Minister of Public Works to accept the appointment as director of Prairie Farm Rehabilitation for the three provinces. To an acknowledged extent likeable, talkative, grey-haired George Spence, with his weather-lined face and practical love of the prairie land, personified officially an emergent demand for soil and water conservation in contrast to the ruthless exploitation "of those acres you don't take with you when you die".

Further in accord with a trend toward long term rehabilitation policies, the Saskatchewan Government's Department of Municipal Affairs in September, 1935, set up the Northern Settlers' Re-establishment Branch to assist the many settlers who had trekked from the open plains to northern agricultural Saskatchewan, where both the drouth and its effects were less severe. In some northern areas the new settlers were assisted with drainage projects necessary for cultivation.

Meadow Lake, initially a logging town, was well within Saskatchewan's northern agricultural fringe. Some 350 air miles north of Meadow Lake, The Consolidated Mining and Smelting Company of Canada Limited produced gold from medium and low grade ore on the north shore of Lake Athabaska. Here was situated Goldfields, a wilderness mining camp, which was to become—before its eventual abandonment—an outpost supply base for prospectors seeking mineral-bearing ore in this area of the Pre-Cambrian Region.

In the summer of 1935, drouth was severe in western agricultural

Goldfields

Saskatchewan, but rain in the south and east—which at first gave promise of a fair crop—resulted in an epidemic of stem rust, which virulently attacked standard wheat varieties including Marquis wheat. The rust in turn led to increased experimentation in rust-resistant wheats and the development of Apex and Thatcher wheats.

Partly to encourage youthful farmers in the methods of scientific agriculture, the Dominion-Provincial Youth Training Programmes for Rural Young Men, 18 to 30 years of age, were introduced in 1937. During the winter of 1938-39, more than 5,000 applicants participated in the programme, which included courses at the University of Saskatchewan, the School of Agriculture at Regina, and courses at local centres in the province.

In 1937, the worst of the drouth years, Saskatchewan's wheat yield averaged 2.7 bushels per acre, as compared to a long term average of about 15 bushels per acre. The total wheat yield from the stunted stand with poorly filled heads was about 37 million bushels from some 14 million acres seeded to wheat. Considered the lowest total yield since 1908, when a much smaller acreage was under cultivation, the monetary value of the 1937 wheat crop was estimated at 16 million dollars, or three million dollars less than the total amount expended on government relief during the fiscal year 1937-38. Moreover, in 1937, the drouth extended further northward deep into the Parklands, where noisy but rainless electrical storms punctuated the dry winds which blew hot from the southeast and cold from the northwest, but where nothing brought the relief of moisture. In southern agricultural Saskatchewan an infestation of army worms and an expanding epidemic of encephalomyelitis, not only dangerous to horses (of which 1,500 died in 1938) but also communicable to human beings, added to the ravages of severe drouth during the growing season.

For both the 1936 and 1937 crops, the Canadian Wheat Board, which had in 1935 been reinstituted in a modified form, declared its intention to guarantee the grower 87½ cents per bushel (Number 1 Northern at Fort William) if the market price declined below that figure. But as the market price remained above $1, the wheat board accepted no wheat from the growers in either crop year.

Varying degrees of rust, drouth, and grasshopper damage curtailed the 1938 crop, and some farmers were supplied with relief feed for their livestock and seed for the 1939 crop. Though the seed was in short supply as yet, Thatcher, Apex, and Renown wheats withstood the ravages of the disease.

As the burden of relief expenditure and administration was pressing on provincial and municipal governments to an increasing extent, some form of a long term and self-liquidating method was sought. On the recommendation of J. G. Gardiner, Minister of Agriculture in the Canadian Government, the Prairie Farm Assistance Act was passed on June 3, 1939, and became operative for the crop year beginning August 1. The act was designed essentially as a form of compulsory crop insurance covering the entire grain-growing area of the prairie provinces. A one per cent levy was collected, by the Board of Grain Commissioners, on the sales of wheat, oats, rye, and barley. Subsequently farmers in municipalities declared within a crop failure area received assistance from the fund, to which the growers themselves had contributed.

Despite the differences between political groups in power on various levels of government, there was considerable evidence of flexibility in coping with the problems of depression and drouth, together with a pragmatic approach further reflected in the various recommendations received by the Royal Commission on Dominion Provincial Relations, which reported to the Canadian Government in 1938.

In the election of June, 1938, the Liberal government led by Premier Patterson was returned to office, though with a reduced majority. The Co-operative Commonwealth Federation, Saskatchewan Section, (C.C.F.) doubled its representation in the legislature.

With the inclusion of the deferred elections, the result was: Liberal 38, C.C.F. 10, Social Credit 2, and others 2.

Despite the exigencies of the period there was in evidence more defiance than defeat. Among examples of tenacity was the holding of the World's Grain Exhibition and Conference, July 24 to August 5, 1933, at Regina. Scheduled originally for 1932, this ambitious project had been postponed for a year in the hope of "better conditions" in 1933. In the steel and stucco exhibition building was a decorative theme of grains, grasses, and seeds. Adjacent to the building was a paved area for an extensive machinery exhibit. Among conference papers presented was "The Present World Wheat Situation and Trends". An exhibit of live beavers symbolized the merits of work and industry. Greetings were heard from representatives of participating countries, which included Great Britain, Holland, India, Australia, Mexico, Siam, South Africa, Spain, Hungary, Italy, and Germany.

In a speech to the conference, William Lyon Mackenzie King referred to the world disarmament conference then in progress and expressed the hope that it "may also be occasion for furthering good mutual-well-being and for the promotion of international goodwill".

During the summer of 1932, the World Economic Conference was being held in London, England, with a view to finding a solution to the economic difficulties of European civilization, and more especially in the hope of arriving at some sort of an agreement for the removal of tariff barriers.

But in Germany, on the other hand, the defiance of economic depression was evident in precipitate action which exceeded educational and political conferences hopefully designed for practical adjustments within an established society. In that country a hitherto obscure fanatic, Adolph Hitler, was gaining an increasing following for his virulent exhortations to action for a new order in which Germans, as a superior race, would at all costs gain greater living space. Two years after Hitler's Germany and Mussolini's Italy had, at Franco's request, intervened in Spain to destroy Spain's elected government and there set up yet another Fascist state, Germany—after absorbing Austria—marched on Czechoslovakia and smashed the remnants of that state in March of 1939. In the face of these bold and violent moves in the wake of broken promises to maintain the peace, the democracies seemed paralyzed by lack of unity and indecision.

The European shocks resulted in corresponding tremors among Saskatchewan's ethnic groups associated through kinship, nationality, or ideology with various sensitive areas of the European continent. Like leaves carried by a premonitory gust preceding a storm, a few European refugees, including those of Jewish, Czech, Ukrainian, Austrian, and German extraction, arrived in Saskatchewan.

It was against this ominous background of turbulence, uncertainty, and apathy that King George VI and his Queen Elizabeth left England for a tour of Canada. In May of 1939 their Majesties received an enthusiastic welcome in Saskatchewan.

Indicative of the attitude of Canadians to the Royal Visit was the tribute paid by Gustave Lanctot, Curator, Public Archives of Canada, who when writing in the *Canadian Geographical Journal* of July, 1939, said, "As to Canada, the Royal presence lifted the people out of the morass of business depression, war scares, and contentious politics, to the nobler level of national exaltation and solidarity, uniting the whole country in a spirit of loyalty to its highest ideals of freedom and justice, symbolized in the persons of its Sovereigns."

In August, Hitler's powerfully rearmed Germany made a treaty with Stalin's Soviet Russia, in which it was agreed that neither power would attack the other. At dawn on September 1, Germany invaded Poland. As an immediate result, Soviet troops marched into Poland, and subsequently a line was drawn partitioning Poland between the two powers.

On September 3, the United Kingdom and France, in accord with their pledge to protect the sovereignty of Poland, so that the totalitarian states should not advance from menacing power to overwhelming preponderance, declared war on Germany. Seven days later, September 10, the Canadian Parliament, in an emergency session called by Prime Minister Mackenzie King, independently declared war on Germany. Thus began a new chapter of history in which Saskatchewan, along with Canada's eight other provinces, was deeply involved.

11

Men and Machines

"Now therefore We do hereby Declare and Proclaim that a State of War with the German Reich exists and has existed in our Dominion of Canada as from the tenth day of September 1939." These fateful words, proclaimed in the King's name, appeared in the *Canada Gazette*. Yet to become a reality were the men and machines of mechanized warfare. On the day of war's declaration, Canada's professional soldiers numbered 4,500, air force personnel 3,100, and the navy 1,800. The army possessed two light tanks received from England in 1938, and 14 more arrived on the eve of war. The Non-permanent Active Militia had access to rifles of the 1914-18 pattern and was virtually without transport. Bullets, boots, blankets, and other necessaries were in short supply or non-existent.

Yet, 18 days after Canada's declaration of war, the Minister of National Defence publicly confirmed that the First Canadian Division would be sent overseas at the earliest possible date. Early in October, Saskatchewan-born Major General A. G. L. McNaughton was appointed Inspector General of the units of the First Canadian Division. Soon after Christmas the First Canadian Division, for the most part an army of volunteers, was in the United Kingdom. There, invasion was soon to be feared as a result of the German penetration of Denmark and Norway, followed by the invasion of Belgium and Holland, and the subsequent fall of France in a war in which ideological differences, apathy, and defeatism cut across and negated national loyalties, to reveal uneasy alliances and indecisive military strategy in the face of Nazi Germany's military might and totalitarian advantage. In June, 1940, the fall of France and the evacuation of British and some French troops from Dunkirk shocked the homogeneous people of the United Kingdom into action for the immediate defence of the British Isles and revealed the probability of a long and costly war of attrition. While Canadian troops were digging trenches and stringing barbed wire through the countryside of southern England, President Roosevelt stripped the U. S. Army of its reserve equipment and shipped rifles, machine and field guns, and related accoutrement to Britain.

Recruiting in Canada was stepped up. Yet, aware of various European attitudes reflected in Canada's non-homogeneous population, and especially conscious of traditional isolationist opinion in the Province of Quebec, the Canadian Parliament made no haste to introduce military conscription. Prime Minister Mackenzie King had indicated that the day of large expeditionary forces might have passed and that Canada's main contribution to the war effort might consequently well be in the realm of production for war rather than the dispatch of many men abroad. But the threatened annihilation of Britain's factories, oil refineries, and airfields by Germany's intensive bombing from the air stirred Canada to take energetic steps both for intensive recruiting and the training of army, air force, and naval personnel, and for a rapid retooling to produce the machines of war. The effect of this acceleration on Saskatchewan was an exodus of manpower into the armed and ancillary forces and to industrial centres of Canada, where the demands of a wartime economy ended the unemployment of the 1930's. On the farms and in the villages, towns, and cities of Saskatchewan, young women responded to the call for non-combatant service in Canada's armed forces and to the demand for wage earners in expanding factories and offices.

Canada's declaration of war in 1939 did not— as did the outbreak of war in 1914—result in heavy demands for wheat. But coincidental with the gathering war clouds over Europe was an increased rainfall over Canada's prairies during the growing season of 1939, marking the end of the severe drouth of the 1930's. Though in 1939 areas of crop failure comprised 260 townships, in which almost 40,000 farmers received $500,000 through the compulsory and contributory crop insurance of the Prairie Farm Assistance Act, the wheat harvest throughout the province exceeded 270 million bushels. The 1940 wheat yield of 17.5 bushels per seeded acre resulted in increased problems of storage and finance. By mid-1941 Canada's wheat carry-over was, in round figures, 500 million bushels in the face of virtually no European market other than that of the United Kingdom whose urgent agricultural demand was for bacon, butter, cheese, beef, dried milk, and eggs no longer obtainable from Scandinavian countries under Nazi domination. With continental European supplies cut off and long distance shipping from Australia, New Zealand, and Argentina hampered by increasing German U-boat destruction of merchant shipping, Britain looked to Canada for essential food in the form of animal products. Thus the Canadian Government, in an effort to encourage prairie farmers to turn from straight grain-growing to mixed farming, introduced a policy of bonus and subsidy to bring about a reduction of acreage seeded to wheat and, in its place, an increased seeding of coarse grains along with a shift to the production of livestock and dairy and poultry products.

Of Canada's nine provinces, Saskatchewan was recognized as possessing the greatest potential for agricultural expansion. While several years were required to build up a herd of cattle, the prolific nature of hogs, plus their relative rapidity in reaching maturity, made for a quick increase in hog production. Moreover, coarse grains and other fodder could be readily grown and fed on the spot. Saskatchewan became Canada's first province to pass the "eggs for export" production quota, and poultry raising, second only to Ontario's, became "one of this province's chief war industries". Wartime demands for sugar gave impetus to honey production. Saskatchewan beekeepers produced almost three million pounds of honey in 1941. In 1942 honey production increased to 4,947,110 pounds. Production of dairy products exceeded that of any previous year when, in 1942, more than two billion pounds of milk was produced in the province. Almost two million hogs were marketed in the peak year of 1944, or three times the number marketed in 1940.

In 1940 the Canadian Bacon Board had been set up to administer the bacon agreement between the British and Canadian governments. The Dairy Products Board was formed to facilitate a similar agreement concerning cheese and other dairy products. Early in 1941 the Special Products Board was organized to fill all contracts for Canadian food supplies to Britain not already handled by other government boards.

The lessened export demand for wheat, in evidence prior to the war, was indicated by the quota system of the Canadian Wheat Board. Concerning the 1939 crop, the board had agreed to accept from any one farmer a maximum of 5,000 bushels of wheat at a price of 70 cents a bushel basis Number 1 Northern at Fort William. All quotas for acceptance of the 1940 crop were cancelled in April 1941. Canadian Government policy with regard to the 1941 crop included limitation of wheat deliveries by farmers to 230 million bushels during the crop year August 1, 1941, to July 31, 1942; and payment of storage on farm-held wheat at the rate of 1/45th of a cent per bushel per day, payable on the amount of the undelivered quota only. Payments to prairie farmers for reduction of wheat acreage were announced as follows: $4 per acre if reduced acreage devoted to summer-fallow, payable July, 1941, or soon after; $2 per acre if reduced acreage sown to coarse grains, payable upon proof of such sowing; $2 per acre if reduced acreage devoted to grass or clover. Additional summer-fallow land seeded to grass or clover in 1942 was to warrant a payment of $2 per acre.

On Saskatchewan farms the wartime labour shortage was manifested in the effort to shift the emphasis from grain-growing to mixed farming. At the same time there was decreased availability of farm machinery and repairs, owing to wartime restrictions on material plus the fact that farm implement manufacturers were increasingly engaged in the production of the engines of war. Again the struggle of men and machines was accentuated. With Soviet Russia's entry into the world war as a result of Nazi Germany's invasion of Russia in June, 1941, there developed an accelerated demand for Canadian tanks, transport, armament, and ammunition, which, with United States supplies, were shipped to Soviet forces and a technologically backward Chinese people resisting Japanese aggression. Japan's stunning attack, that December Sunday morning, on the U. S. Pacific fleet stationed at Pearl Harbor, followed immediately by declaration of war on the United States by Germany and Italy, gave further impetus to Canada's industrial production of the machines of war.

Technological development of farm machinery had resulted in more tractors and implements "riding on rubber". Rubber tires meant a greater speed in field work and a smoother operation requiring less fuel consumption per acre than were obtainable from "the old iron-wheeled implements". The wartime demand for rubber in short supply caused some farmers to supplement their mechanical motive power with horses. This situation was reflected in a temporary "rise in prices for work horses", while gasoline shortages added to the momentary and limited reversion.

Although farmers responded to the Canadian Government's policy of reducing wheat acreage, the weather during the growing season of 1942 was conducive to a record wheat crop of 335 million bushels, for which neither ready market nor adequate storage facilities existed. The harvesting of the heavy crop, retarded by insufficient harvesting machinery and interrupted by unfavourable weather, was made more difficult by a shortage of skilled farm labour, though high school boys and girls from Saskatchewan centres and students from the towns and cities of central Canada made a valuable contribution.

Ten-year-old farm boys were taking their turn at tractor wheels and teen-age girls were driving trucks. Under the pressure of the war years "old folks", both men and women, some of whom had retired,

returned to tasks of production and tried to forget
their aches and ignore their "shortness of breath"
in the rush of seed-time and harvest plus the daily
grind of producing much needed meat and milk.

While Saskatchewan men and women were
active in the Royal Canadian Navy, Royal Canadian Air Force, and merchant ships sailing under
various Allied and neutral flags, other Saskatchewan men in the Canadian Army, on guard in
the United Kingdom, were to participate in action for the first time on August 19, 1942, when
men of several Canadian regiments, including the
South Saskatchewan Regiment, made a heroic
but costly assault on the Dieppe beaches of
France. The following spring Canadian soldiers
embarked from England for the Sicilian and
Italian campaigns. In the summer of 1944 Canadians were in the thick of the fighting in Holland,
France, and Germany, in conjunction with
British and American troops. German troops,
caught between the advancing forces of the
Western Allies and those of Soviet Russia, were being pressed to the
point of defeat.

Prairie lads like Ernest McNab, who served in the Royal Air
Force before and during the Battle of Britain and in the Royal Cana-

dian Air Force, were recognized for their aptitude both in the air and on the ground. The superior visibility in the prairie skies and the sparse inhabitation of the land combined to provide desirable conditions for training air crew personnel in both flying and bombing. Under the British Commonwealth Air Training Plan agreement signed at Ottawa on December 17, 1939, by the governments of the United Kingdom, Canada, Australia, and New Zealand, the Royal Canadian Air Force accepted the responsibility of training pilots, observers, navigators, wireless operators, air gunners, and bombers. During the war, R.C.A.F. and R.A.F. units were stationed at 15 sites in Saskatchewan: Assiniboia, Caron, Dafoe, Davidson, Estevan, Moose Jaw, Mossbank, North Battleford, Prince Albert, Regina, Saskatoon, Swift Current, Weyburn, Wilcox, and Yorkton. Nationals of France, Poland, Holland, Czechoslovakia, Belgium, and other European countries, attached to R.A.F. units, found in Saskatchewan an understanding of their various languages and ways. Moreover, World War II brought many of the younger generation of Saskatchewan's heterogeneous population together as Canadians in a common cause and conditioning, virtually ending the invidious distinctions of previous years.

The ready adaptation of prairie lads to seafaring ways was summed up later by Vice-Admiral E. R. Mainguy, R.C.N. Chief of Naval Staff. Speaking at the University of Saskatchewan (May 9, 1952), Vice-Admiral Mainguy said:

There have been various theories put forward to explain both the size and vigour of the contribution of the prairie provinces to the Navy. Some say that it arises from a desire to find out what the sea looks like. Others insist that it is because the men of the prairies have a natural affinity with the great open spaces. It's even been said that the boys just want to get away from the farm. . . . I think there is a simpler explanation than those. I can put it in a single sentence. It takes a he-man to make a good sailor, and that is the kind of men that the prairies produce. The more of them we get the happier we shall be. Added to this essential quality is the further quality, which is to be found in great abundance on the prairies, that of being able to do the best that you can with what you have, no matter what the circumstances are, and maintaining good humour whilst you are doing it. This quality is an essential to successful existence at sea, and in the wide spaces of the prairies.

Anticipating the end of the war, the Canadian Parliament had set up a Special Committee of the House of Commons on Reconstruction and Re-establishment, designed to meet the economic and social problems that would confront the nation in its transition to conditions of peace.

In anticipation of the problems of peace the Saskatchewan Legislature had, during its session of 1943, passed the Saskatchewan Reconstruction Council Act. Under this act, in October, 1943, the Saskatchewan Government by order-in-council appointed the Saskatchewan Reconstruction Council, composed of seven members with Dean F. C. Cronkite, College of Law, University of Saskatchewan, as chairman. While the council was, in accord with its instructions, studying "possible post-war problems" with a view to developing and recommending "plans, policies, and activities for the purpose of meeting such conditions and problems", Premier Patterson submitted a brief to the Special Committee of the House of Commons on Reconstruction and Re-establishment.

Premier Patterson's submission, on behalf of the Saskatchewan Government, dated April 19, 1944, began:

Saskatchewan has approached the problem of the post-war period with a view to providing for all her citizens, who are physically able, the opportunity to provide themselves with that security that is necessary to realize the four freedoms. Keeping this end always in mind, we are endeavouring to work out plans for the development of our natural resources, for the placing of our basic industry, agriculture, on stable foundations, and for the establishment of social services and guarantees for those of our citizens who, through no fault of their own, are unable by their own efforts to guarantee themselves or their families security.

With reference to works projects the Premier said his government had no intention of "creating work" but would construct "necessary and useful buildings".

"At the present time," Premier Patterson continued, "somewhat over 70,000 Saskatchewan men and women are reported as members of the various Armed Services; so it is evident that with general demobilization a considerable body of labour will be available for a period of expansion and development in this province. . . ."

The Department of Public Works had a $9,950,000 construction and repair programme in mind.

In addition the University of Saskatchewan has proposed an extensive building program that will be necessary in the near future if the University is to be in a position to continue its useful work in the community and be in a position to provide higher education for returned men and women.

This is a $2,970,000 building program which will necessitate an increase of approximately $150,000 to the present annual provincial grant to the University.

Premier Patterson's brief, released for publication during the political crossfire of an undeclared provincial election campaign, proposed further expenditures for projects which included these items: school buildings and equipment, $2,642,200; highway construction, $87,-805,000; telephones, $1,000,000; forest protection and culture, $6,600,000; provincial parks, $1,127,000. It was inferred there might be unstated sums for the improvement of commercial and sport fishing, fur farming, trapping, game preserves, topographical mapping, geological surveys, industrial development, rural electrification, housing, and social services. Moreover, it was "estimated that rural telephone companies would spend up to $5,000,000 for renewal and construction", and "cities, towns, villages and rural municipalities are expected to provide employment for many with expenditures of $30,000,000[,] of which much would be paid to labour". After an estimate that agriculture accounted for 95 per cent of production in the province, farm improvement was suggested through extension of soil surveys, P.F.R.A. projects, marketing facilities, agricultural schools for boys and girls, and a "form of intermediate term credit".

To conclude his brief, Premier Patterson stated in part:

. . . we in Saskatchewan believe that for the so-called reconstruction period we must have for an objective, an economy which will offer to everyone who may be reasonably expected to work, an opportunity for productive labour with a reward which, when coupled with such social services as are provided, will enable him and his dependants to enjoy a standard of living such as our resources reasonably warrant. For the aged or incapacitated, special services must be provided, and against the accident of unemployment, there must be provided an adequate insurance. We have little doubt that the economy of Canada will support a taxation policy to defray the necessary expenditures involved.

We believe this ideal is quite possible of achievement, but we fear it will not be achieved unless there is evolved an improvement in Dominion-Provincial relations so as to permit of more effective co-operation among the governmental agencies of Canada. We suggest that this is the most serious problem facing the country on the eve of what has come to be called the reconstruction period, if anything like the objective I have just mentioned is to be achieved without a regimentation of people's lives such as we do not wish to tolerate.

Saskatchewan's Liberal government led by Premier Patterson had, by an unprecedented proclamation concerned with wartime exigencies, extended its term of office beyond both the four-year period customarily observed and the five-year period allowed by the constitution. Thus, after six years in power, the government on May 10, 1944, called an election for June 15 and the political campaign—which in fact was already underway—officially began for the votes of a restless electorate conscious that Allied victory now seemed inevitable, while feeling itself on the verge of post-war adjustment.

On May 11, Thomas Clement Douglas, M.P. for the Saskatchewan constituency of Weyburn, was travelling west to lead the Co-operative Commonwealth Federation (C.C.F.) on the provincial hustings. Scottish-born, 39-year-old Douglas had, while a Baptist minister in Weyburn during the early 1930's, become imbued with the "practical Christianity" promulgated by Chicago-born Saskatchewan farm wife Louise Lucas and other reformist crusaders of the United Farmers of Canada, Saskatchewan Section, which had launched the Saskatchewan Farmer-Labour Group, a new and radical political party which subsequently changed its name to Co-operative Commonwealth Federation, Saskatchewan Section.

The Reverend Douglas had, in the Saskatchewan general election of 1934, stood as Saskatchewan Farmer-Labour Group candidate in Weyburn constituency, where a Liberal Party candidate was elected. Nevertheless Mr. Douglas, while carrying on his church work, continued to speak at Farmer-Labour (C.C.F.) meetings, and in 1935 was elected as C.C.F. candidate (Weyburn) to the House of Commons, where he proved himself apt and vigorous in debate and fast in rebuttal. When Saskatchewan C.C.F. adherents became apprehensive concerning what they felt was a "factionalism" involving the (C.C.F. Saskatchewan Section) leadership of George Williams, there arose a concerted move to draft "Tommy" Douglas as leader of the Saskatchewan C.C.F. At the 1941 Saskatchewan C.C.F. annual convention in Saskatoon, Douglas was elected leader over Williams. The physically diminutive, cheerful, quick-witted "Tommy" had earned his living as a linotype operator for the *Winnipeg Free Press,* and had attended Brandon College, Manitoba, and, for post-graduate studies, Chicago University. In college he had excelled in debating, oratory, dramatics, and boxing.

In contrast to George Williams with his personal concept of Marxist Socialism—a dogmatic presentation that alienated various of his fellow farmers—Douglas appeared as one who would draw diverse elements of the Saskatchewan C.C.F. into a crusade for definite reform minus certain elements of socialism, such as state ownership and leasing of land, of which the electorate in general was apprehensive.

Readily at home on the hustings, Douglas agreed "in principle" with Premier Patterson's proposals for post-war projects, but declared his non-confidence "in the Liberal Party for carrying out the proposals".

Patterson, speaking at Lloydminster, offered the electorate a choice between "regimentation" by the C.C.F. and "individual liberty" under the Liberals with their unsurpassed record in the administration of the affairs of Saskatchewan. Liberals accused the C.C.F. of being lukewarm concerning the war effort. Douglas spoke in favour of the Sixth Victory Loan, but said, "The C.C.F. has differed from other political parties with reference to the most effective way to conduct the war and as to the fairest distribution of sacrifices involved." Douglas, an officer in Canada's reserve army, had volunteered for active service but had been rejected by the medical authorities.

Throughout a political campaign which called forth mainly loyalties to the two current major Saskatchewan parties, Liberal and C.C.F., there was a lively interest on hustings, in public meeting hall, in the press, over the radio, and in the homes of the people.

Added to the electorate's restiveness, caused by wartime exertions and the anticipated end of the war, was the fact that the active element of the farmers' movement in a predominantly agricultural province conditioned to voluntary but virile organization had abandoned, temporarily at least, the Liberal Party. From farmstead, village, and urban home individual men and women variously associated in an electoral campaign for "a better way of life" went forth to "visit with", persuade, cajole, and exhort the voters to "vote C.C.F.". In this election the accent was on unity for the attainment of office so as to implement modified C.C.F. policies. In large, Marxist, pacifist, moralist, and other factional minorities had receded or were bypassed in the area of practical politics.

When the ballots were counted the electoral result was: C.C.F., 47; Liberal, 5; and Active Service Voters' Representatives, 3. Of ballots cast the C.C.F. received 211,308, the Liberal Party 139,183, Progressive-Conservatives 44,197, and others 3,026.

The 12 members of the new cabinet were T. C. Douglas, Premier and Minister of Public Health; C. M. Fines, Provincial Treasurer; J. W. Corman, Attorney General; G. H. Williams, Minister of Agriculture; J. H. Brockelbank, Minister of Municipal Affairs; O. W. Valleau, Provincial Secretary and Minister of Social Welfare; J. L. Phelps, Minister of Natural Resources and Industrial Development; J. T. Douglas, Minister of Highways and Minister of Public Works; W. S. Lloyd, Minister of Education; J. H. Sturdy, Minister of Reconstruction and Rehabilitation; C. C. Williams, Minister of Telephones and Telegraphs and Minister of Labour; and L. F. McIntosh, Minister of Co-operation and Co-operative Development.

The former premier, W. J. Patterson, one of the five Liberal Party members elected, won by a margin of six votes over Mrs. Gladys Strum, farm wife and candidate for the C.C.F., and became leader of the Opposition.

While the election of Saskatchewan's "Socialist" government was viewed with both amazement and alarm in most newspapers and periodicals published in the province and elsewhere in Canada, the administration, whose members were uninhibited by previous experience in office, confidently set about to introduce reforms and innovations related to the Regina Manifesto of 1933 and promised during the political campaign.

Though leaders of Canada's Co-operative Commonwealth Federation (C.C.F.) were, from their party's inception, conversant with the evolution of the British Labour Party and, in some instances, enamoured of its aims and policies, British men of Labour paid scant attention to a C.C.F. success in a far-off, thinly populated, agrarian province of Canada "mainly concerned with the price of wheat". At the same time, Canada's Moscow-line Communists, who had once declared the Saskatchewan C.C.F. "a social Fascist party" were without influence in Saskatchewan's new government. Though U. S. Congressmen were vociferous concerning a "Red Menace" within the borders of their country, and though in Canada Communists had been elected to sit in the provincial legislature of "loyal old Anglo-Saxon Ontario", and an industrial constituency of "the ancient Province of Quebec" had elected a Communist (Labour-Progressive) to the Canadian Parliament, Communists who, under any name, stood for election to the Saskatchewan Legislature all lost their deposits. Yet, when the newly elected government was suspiciously examined in hectic and entertainment-vending periodicals published in the United States of America, Saskatchewan was singled out as North America's "Red" province, where a politically immature electorate had become hoaxed and subverted by local Communists financed with Moscow gold.

In Canada's federal political field, the Liberal Party under the guiding hand of Prime Minister Mackenzie King was returned to power in the election of 1945.

Though Fuehrer Adolph Hitler had disappeared and Nazi Germany had on May 7 accepted unconditional surrender terms from Allied officers, Japan refused demands for unconditional surrender. On August 6, the United States of America shattered Hiroshima with the explosion of the world's first atomic bomb used as a weapon of war, and on August 9 dropped a second atomic bomb on Nagasaki.

Impressed with this new and
vastly destructive power in the
hands of its principal opponent,
Japan sent delegates to accept
terms of unconditional surrender
aboard the U. S. battleship
Missouri anchored in Tokyo Bay,
September 2. And so World
War II came to an end in a
reverberating, world-s h a k i n g
flourish of scientific endeavour
co-ordinated with an unsurpass-
e d technological know-how.
Outstanding scientists of various
racial and national backgrounds,

The Geiger counter

together with able technicians whose combined work was facilitated by
government funds and direction, had produced "the bomb". They
became aware of its initial detonation and of the proved power of its
devastation only in the same manner as most other people—that is,
through radio newscasts and in newspaper columns.

To the evolution and realization of atomic power, physicists of the
University of Saskatchewan had contributed in "a very hush-hush"
government-sponsored programme unknown to other faculty members and not remotely suspected by the people generally, including
the men and women serving in Canada's armed forces.

Prairie men, for the most part "machine-conditioned" prior to their enlistment in this war of men and machines, returned to Saskatchewan with the additional experience of mechanized warfare on land, on sea, and in the air. In France, Holland, Sicily, Italy, and Germany, and in and over the Asian jungles, men of the army and air force had fought and flown while sailors traversed the seven seas. Returning with a proud sense of a job well done, they were determined to reorientate themselves rapidly in civilian life, using their war-gained skills and financial endowments to this end. While governments, both federal and provincial, with the post-war experiments of World War I behind them, were better prepared for the inevitable period of readjustment, the men and women returning from World War II held few, if any, illusions concerning wars to end wars for a new and better world. Moreover, they came home to Saskatchewan at a time of buoyant economy, when many farmers found themselves free of indebtedness for the first time and when "business generally was good". The "civilian army [and air force and navy] of volunteers" disbanded to merge into a civilian scene of individuals striving for a better house equipped with the latest radio, record-player, refrigerator, and vacuum cleaner, plus a garage for the already attained, or planned for, family automobile. With their re-establishment credits, numbers of men and women attended university to fit themselves further for civilian careers. Of the 4,195 students registered at the University of Saskatchewan for the year 1946-47, 2,543 students had served in the armed forces.

12

Epilogue

HISTORICAL perspective, always an elusive quality, becomes even less likely of attainment when the writer is in the midst of events concerning living personalities and fluid situations all of which will someday be evaluated by historians in a position to "look back" on what, by then, will have ceased to be the current scene. Accordingly, this epilogue is little more than a statement of some of the facts and an indication of some of the developments which characterized the 10 years immediately preceding 1955, when the 50-year period as a Province of Canada is marked by Saskatchewan's Golden Jubilee.

Throughout these 10 years, Premier Douglas continued to lead both the Saskatchewan Government and the Co-operative Commonwealth Federation, Saskatchewan Section. In the election of 1948 there were elected to the legislature 31 C.C.F. members, 19 Liberals, one Conservative-Liberal, and one Independent. In subsequent by-elections prior to the 1952 election, the results were C.C.F. 2, and Liberals 2. In the election of 1952 the result was C.C.F. 42, Liberals 11. In subsequent by-elections held in 1953, one Liberal was successful and one Progressive-Conservative.

In 1946, William John Patterson resigned as head of the Saskatchewan Liberal Party although he continued to lead the Opposition in the legislature. Walter Adam Tucker, member of Parliament for the Rosthern federal constituency became the leader of the party in Saskatchewan in August, 1946. He resigned his seat in the House of Commons in June, 1948, and successfully contested the Rosthern provincial constituency in the election of that year. He then succeeded Mr. Patterson also as Liberal leader in the legislature. He continued to lead the Opposition till 1953 when he resigned, and was once more elected to the House of Commons in his home constituency. Mr. Tucker had for many years practised law in the town of Rosthern, centre of a prosperous farming community containing a large percentage of men and women of Mennonite persuasion.

Mr. Patterson was appointed Lieutenant Governor of Saskatchewan by the Liberal government at Ottawa, in June, 1951. After Mr. Tucker's resignation, Mr. Asmundur A. Loptson, M.L.A., elected in Saltcoats constituency, became leader of the Opposition in the Saskatchewan Legislature. In November, 1954, A. H. McDonald, M.L.A., was elected by the convention of the Liberal Association of Saskatchewan to succeed Mr. Tucker.

Organized labour, especially that part represented in unions affiliated with the Canadian Congress of Labour (C.I.O.), supported the C.C.F. in its political campaigns and thus was a factor in C.C.F. success in the cities. While the Trades and Labour Congress of Canada (A.F.L.) did not affiliate with the C.C.F., many individual union members voted for this party, whose pro-labour policy was an integral part of its political platform.

While several socialist-conceived government ventures, including a boot and shoe factory which specialized in "Sturdy Work Boots", were eventually discontinued as unprofitable, the Saskatchewan Trans-

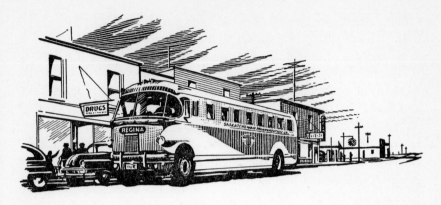

portation Company continued to operate successfully a highway bus service.

As the number and speed of automobiles increased, so did the traffic accidents, but the number of car and truck owners providing themselves with public liability insurance remained a minority. Compulsory public liability insurance was introduced in 1946 when the Saskatchewan Legislature passed The Automobile Accident Insurance Act whereby the cost of the insurance was added to the annual registration and licence plate fee. The act, drafted by The Saskatchewan Government Insurance Office, provided for compensation to victims of automobile accident without regard to fault. Thus another social and economic concept without precedent in North America became a reality in Saskatchewan. While The Saskatchewan Government Insurance Office developed an expansive business in writing fire insurance of various types, it was restricted from expanding beyond the boundaries of the province. To overcome this restriction the Saskatchewan Government purchased, in 1949, The Saskatchewan Guarantee and Fidelity Company Limited and, in 1954, this company was writing a variety of insurance risks in more than 20 countries.

Over the Forest and Pre-Cambrian regions the Saskatchewan Government Airways emerged as a profitable venture both from the balance sheet standpoint and that of opening "Saskatchewan's North" to accelerated mineral prospecting and development. Aircraft, equipped with pontoons in summer and skis in winter, made more practical a policy of forest conservation whereby Saskatchewan became

Canada's first province to use plane and parachute for fighting forest fires. "Smoke-jumpers" answered radio-telephone calls from remote areas and parachuted down to a fire prior to the arrival of fire-fighting trucks and bulldozers, or into an area where no wheeled or tracked mechanical equipment could penetrate the wilderness of lake, bush, and rock. In this most recently expansive phase of a 300-year-old record of exploration and transportation, the internal combustion engine, driving a whirring airscrew, lifted the Whiteman's winged carriage far above the rugged terrain and, with unprecedented rapidity, transported him to where no man of European heritage may have set foot before.

The plashing of a voyageur's canoe paddle in a forest stream, the squealing of a wooden-axled Red River cart along a rutted prairie trail, the rumbling approach of iron railway wheels on shining steel rails—these sounds of "here they come" became, in the new northland, transformed into the welcome drone of bush-piloted aeroplane, the "Whiteman's pelican" flying in the trackless sky. But the eager, wolfish yelping of husky dogs continued in familiar chorus at outpost settlement and isolated camp. Advancing technology was far from eliminating dogsled travel for routine trapline inspection, neighbourly visit, or emergency trip when wind-driven snow blanketed a frozen terrain.

Smoke-jumpers

Following recommendations of a Royal Commission on Forestry, appointed by the Saskatchewan Legislature, the Department of Natural Resources in 1946 proceeded to implement further its policy for forest conservation and marketing of forest products. This included increased fire protection; cutting white spruce saw-timber on a quota basis;

thinning immature stands to encourage better growth; sale of spruce and pine saw-timber regulated by the Saskatchewan Timber Board, which developed contract logging and manufacturing practices for "orderly marketing", building new roads to bring more remote areas of saw-timber under production; marking of standing saw-timber for removal; accelerated publicity for the prevention of forest fires; and decreased waste of cut timber by increased use for by-products. The more important stands of white spruce came under management plans to "provide for orderly removal, over a fixed period, with the assurance that the area will continue to yield a crop in perpetuity". A forest inventory indicated the possibility of a pulp milling industry.

The Saskatchewan Government Airways was initiated when one small commercial "bush flying" company only was in operation. This private enterprise concern, desirous of selling out, was purchased by the Saskatchewan Government. By 1954, Saskatchewan Government Airways had in service 20 aircraft ranging from Cessna 140 to Douglas C47. While most aircraft were on pontoons in summer and skis in winter, the provincial Department of Natural Resources constructed landing strips at Lac la Ronge, Stony Rapids, Ile à la Crosse, and Buffalo Narrows.

To link remote settlements of northern Saskatchewan, where telephone and telegraph were virtually non-existent, the Radio Branch of the Department of Natural Resources developed a radio-telephone system which, from the mid-1940's, became indispensable to government and other agencies. In 1954, Saskatchewan's Natural Resources Department operated nearly 500 two-way radio sets throughout the north, as compared to 62 in 1945. Seven of these were key monitor stations at Goldfields, LaLoche, Stony Rapids, Lac la Ronge, Meadow Lake, Hudson Bay, and Prince Albert. Messages from outlying areas were funnelled through the nearest key stations.

Prior to World War II, radio equipment operated by the department required qualified telegraphers. Switching to radio-telephone, as telegraphers were absorbed into the armed forces, the radio operators were able to communicate by voice in the place of Morse code. The director of the Radio Branch, assisted by five technicians, maintained a construction and repair workshop at Prince Albert. A policy of renting radio equipment to individuals, groups, and enterprises not directly served by the department's radio system proved valuable to prospectors, mining companies, trappers, logging camps, and tourist resorts. The radio-telephone became the "wireless party-line telephone" of the northland.

Goldfields, on the north shore of Lake Athabaska, had become a ghost town during World War II, when a combination of low grade ore and wartime labour shortages led to the abandonment of the gold mining project, but in 1950 Goldfields began to revive as an outpost exploration centre of pitchblende ore, source of radium and uranium—and atomic energy. Adjacent to Goldfields, the Canadian Government's Eldorado Mining and Refining Corporation began mining uranium ore in 1952. In the same year the Saskatchewan Government completed a road from Black Bay via Uranium City to Eldorado, and Chipewyan Indians who worked on the road construction and who had never seen a horse, rode in an automobile for the first time.

For the northern trapper of wild fur, muskrat, beaver, weasel, mink, and fox pelts were of leading commercial value. For various types of fur the fluctuating demand continued to be dependent, as had been dramatically demonstrated 100 years before, on fashion's whim in far-off centres of population. Fur conservation, on a co-operative basis, was carried out by councils elected by resident trappers and acting under Saskatchewan Government legislation. Representative five-member councils were to include Indian, Métis, and White trappers when individuals of the three groups were trapping in an area. The Saskatchewan Fur Marketing Service, only government-operated fur agency in North America, marketed pelts at Regina by public

auction, to which buyers came from as far away as Montreal and
New York. The trapper-endorsed non-compulsory government agency
charged the trapper a five per cent commission for grading and selling
his fur. Some local fur traders also used the marketing service to
dispose of their purchases from trappers. While White trappers
initially favoured the new marketing system, many Métis and Indians,
less able to cope with cash in their pockets, "were better off" under
the old system of selling to the Hudson's Bay Company and independent traders who customarily extended credit from season to season.
Most trappers were of Cree, Chipewyan, or Halfbreed origin, but the
combination fisherman-trapper, possessing a considerable investment
in motorized canoes, nets, traps, and dog teams, was often of Scandinavian background and inclined to favour "orderly marketing".

Fish filleting

Of the more than 40 fish species found in the cool, clear northern
lakes, whitefish, lake trout, pickerel, and tullibee were of leading
commercial value. Production exceeded 10 million pounds in a year.
Of the many lakes fished, the chief producers were Athabaska,
Reindeer, Wollaston, Peter Pond, Primrose, Dore, and the chain of
lakes comprising a stretch of the Churchill river system contiguous

to Lac la Ronge and, more recently, Cree Lake. Increasing demand for filleted fish resulted in the establishment of government and privately owned filleting plants, from which fish were transported in winter by caterpillar-tractor-train and truck to railhead, and, both summer and winter, by aeroplane for consignment to the larger markets of central Canada and to New York, Chicago, and Buffalo.

Grayling fly-fishing in the rapids and clear pools of Fond du Lac River, within 50 miles of the Northwest Territories, and south along the rocky shores of the Cree River, made Saskatchewan famous to wealthy sport fishermen of the United States. Arctic grayling, like rainbow trout, rise to the fly, jumping clear of the water.

The Hudson's Bay Company maintained outpost general stores in Saskatchewan's north and opened a store in the much publicized, wilderness-surrounded, uniquely urban community of Uranium City. But modern department stores in the cities of the Parklands and Plains regions constituted the venerable company's chief retail business in the province. Marking its 284th anniversary in May of 1954, this long-lived commercial enterprise—known to resident and tourist alike for its Fort Garry brand coffee and Hudson's Bay blankets—held profusely advertised sales in its department stores. On that occasion it was remarked that one item bearing the Hudson's Bay Company trademark, but neither advertised nor reduced in price, was Hudson's Bay (Jamaica) rum, procurable in the province only in Saskatchewan Government liquor stores at the government-controlled price of $5.15 per 26-ounce bottle, "of which amount four dollars went in customs and taxes to West Indies and Canadian provincial and federal governments".

While "hardrock" geologists were delineating the glacier-exposed rugged surface of the Pre-Cambrian Region and examining rock samples from trenching and core-drilling, geologists specializing in sedimentary formations left by the southwestward grinding of the glaciers and resultant inland seas, searched scientifically for oil in the Plains and Parklands regions. Much of Saskatchewan's Plains and Parklands was recognized as "potential oil and gas country", but surface geology in Saskatchewan was more difficult than in the foothills of Alberta and Montana, because of Saskatchewan's heavier overlay of glacial drift and sedimentation.

Previously successful and expanding crude oil exploration and production in Alberta had a bearing on subsequent development in Saskatchewan. Lloydminster, initially an agricultural distributing centre straddling the Saskatchewan-Alberta boundary—"the town where you get mail at the post office in Saskatchewan and buy your railway ticket at the station in Alberta"—became Saskatchewan's "first oil town". Saskatchewan's crude oil production in 1940 was 331 barrels; in 1945, more than 16,000 barrels; in 1947, 150,000 barrels; in 1954, some 5,000,000 barrels as exploration involving millions of dollars resulted in new oilfields near Coleville, Fosterton, Smiley, Kindersley, and elsewhere.

An oil rig

After natural gas was struck near Kindersley and Unity, local coal stoves and furnaces were converted for burning gas, and subsequently a 10-inch gas pipeline, originating at Brock, was built to supply Saskatoon and intervening points. The exploration and development of crude oil and natural gas was left to free enterprise in view of the initial risk entailed. The Minister of Natural Resources and Industrial Development defined Saskatchewan Government policy as "encouragement to legitimate development. . . . there is no place in the field for lease hounds. . . ."

Exploratory drilling for oil in the Unity-Vera area revealed a deposit of common salt (sodium chloride) laid down by ancient inland seas. In 1946 the Saskatchewan Government signed an agreement with the Prairie Salt Company (subsidiary of Dominion Tar and Chemical Company, Montreal), whereby the company was to invest one million dollars in a plant with a capacity of 25 tons minimum daily.

In the Plains Region more than 200 "alkali" deposits, composed mainly of sodium sulphate, had been located, and Saskatchewan was Canada's only province shipping sodium sulphate from naturally occurring deposits. Midwest Chemicals Limited, a free enterprise company financed largely in Edmonton, operated "the salt mine" at Palo, while a similar mine at Chaplin was an enterprise of the Saskatchewan Government. Principal markets were in industrial Ontario and Quebec, where the salt was used in the manufacture of paper and to a lesser extent in glass making, tanning, dyeing, nickel and copper refining, and as a constituent in some fertilizers. When in summer moisture-sucking winds evaporate the shallow water from an "alkali" lake, the bone-dry surface gleams as the sun shines on the snowlike sheets of salt crystals. "Alkali soil" meant "bad lands" and "poor land" to the prairie farmer, but a combination of science, technology, and commerce sought alkaline substances for removal and sale elsewhere. Potash, a crude form of salt which, when refined, is used as fertilizer and utilized also in several manufacturing processes, was searched for by deep drilling beneath the soil of Saskatchewan farm lands. In 1954, exploration companies registered in Carlsbad (New Mexico), Houston (Texas), and Calgary (Alberta), were seeking potash in Saskatchewan "where deposits were estimated to be the largest in the world".

While several exploration concerns, seeking mineral wealth in Saskatchewan's Plains Region, were corporations based in southwestern U. S. financial centres of the Great North American Plains, Saskatchewan farm lads learned something of "the grain farming country down there" when they took the family combine-harvester across the 49th parallel for the earlier harvest occurring north of the Rio Grande. Some "outfits starting in to harvest a thousand miles from home, in Texas in June," worked northward through Oklahoma, Kansas, Nebraska, South Dakota, North Dakota, and other states "to be home for our own harvest in August and September". These Saskatchewan men, more often younger members of the family, adept at operating motorized farm equipment, drove their combine-harvesters over immense tracts of grain land, "slept in trailers and auto-camps, and saw places where there were no farm houses, no local community, no schools or churches—just grain land run by operators who lived in town and maybe in the nearest city". Thus did these venturesome and contract-conditioned men see extreme examples of large unit farming operations which, to some extent, were reflected on Saskatchewan's open plains. The "custom work combining" south of the 49th parallel began during the latter part of World War II when a shortage of farm machinery and skilled labour, plus wartime demands for grain, "temporarily eliminated the border for harvesting purposes"; and thereafter for several years the work increased. By "taking on custom work [contract harvesting] across the line" a few Canadian prairie farmers found a way, " if rates were right and the weather with us", to pay off more rapidly the indebtedness incurred in the purchase of their machinery, or "just to make a few hundred dollars extra". In the annual southward trek a technological factor was the increased use of the self-propelled combine-harvester, with which two men working two shifts, and aided by electric lights for night-time operation, could, with a 14-foot-cut machine harvest 60 acres of wheat, threshing 1,800 or more bushels within the span of a 24-hour day.

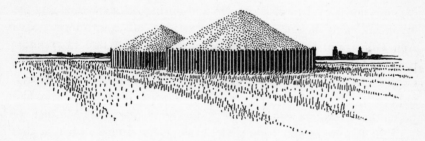

A "wheat glut granary"

During the 1950-54 period, moisture conditions in Saskatchewan were average or above, though frost, wet autumns, and early snows retarded harvesting operations and resulted in reduced grain grades in some areas. The "bumper" 1953 crop of 375 million bushels of wheat had not readily moved to world markets. Country and terminal grain elevators became filled, and farmers, restricted in delivery to country elevators by a quota system, constructed in their fields temporary granaries often improvised from snow-fencing, "laths held by hay wire," and lined with tarpaper.

But neither uncertain markets nor unseasonable wet weather dampened the enthusiasm of ardent advocates "for a dam across the South Saskatchewan River in the vicinity of Outlook". Dr. W. B. Tufts, medical practitioner of Outlook and president of the Saskatchewan Rivers Development Association, pointed out that the fast-flowing water of the river continued to empty into the salt water sea of Hudson Bay without, en route, providing either irrigation or hydro power for the prairie land through which it passed. Particularly in Saskatchewan, and also in the neighbouring prairie provinces, there was almost unanimous support for "the Saskatchewan river dam project requiring Federal financial aid".

Meanwhile, the decline of wartime and "Marshall Plan rehabilitation" demand for wheat and other prairie farm products gave impetus to a revivification of "grassroots movements" of protest and agitation, evidenced in the rapid growth of farm union membership from 1950. Immediately prior to 1950, the United Farmers of Canada, Saskatchewan Section—lineal descendant of the Territorial Grain Growers' Association—met in annual convention at Saskatoon. Membership had dwindled prior to and during the war years, and the organization with one full-time permanent office employee, Miss Ann Gilbertson, listed as secretary, owed some $10,000 to creditors pressing for payment. Delegates to the 1949 convention unanimously elected Ontario-born Joseph Lee Phelps as their president. Driving, impatient, idea-and-action man "Joe" Phelps, of Wilkie, who had been the Saskatchewan (C.C.F.) Government's first Minister of Natural Resources and Industrial Development, and who had at that time initiated the Saskatchewan Government Airways and other "socialist and statist" projects, ceased to be a cabinet minister when, in the provincial election of 1948, he was defeated by Iceland-born Asmundur A. "Minty" Loptson, well known farmer and folksy Liberal candidate in Saltcoats constituency.

While electing Mr. Phelps as president of their organization, the 100 or so farmer delegates assembled voted unanimously to change the name from United Farmers of Canada, Saskatchewan Section, to that of Saskatchewan Farmers Union. Not an unprecedented departure in Saskatchewan farm movement practice, the change of name was this time considered necessary because many farmers continued to regard the "old U.F.C. as too close to the C.C.F.

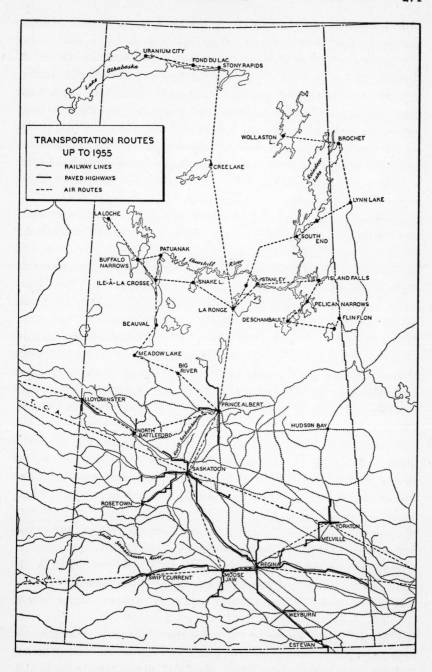

TRANSPORTATION ROUTES
UP TO 1955

RAILWAY LINES
PAVED HIGHWAYS
AIR ROUTES

when we now have to build a new grassroots farmers' movement from
the bottom up".

A rapid rise in membership of the newly proclaimed Saskatchewan
Farmers Union and an equally rapid liquidation of the lingering
$10,000 debt resulted from Phelps's dynamic leadership at a time
when farmers were "not too hard up" but were apprehensive concerning markets and prices. As it became evident that the Saskatchewan Farmers Union was not a "left arm of the C.C.F. political
party", various non-C.C.F. farm union advocates were drawn into the
revivified organization, including "the new women's president", energetic and voluble Saskatchewan-born Mrs. Bernice Norman of
Paddockwood, who became, almost overnight, a province-wide platform attraction in rural meeting places. At the S.F.U. annual
convention in 1954, in Regina, when Phelps had completed the
maximum presidential term of five years allowed by the farm organization's constitution, Saskatchewan-born Frederick W. Woloshyn,
North Battleford farmer, of Ukrainian and Dutch parentage, was
elected president.

The "wheat glut"—that is, a lack of ready markets for prairie
wheat—and a consequent "farmers' shortage of cash" became reflected
in the curtailment of credit by retail merchants throughout rural
Saskatchewan. In November, 1954, R. E. Walker, Saskatchewan
secretary of the Retail Merchants' Association, announced that almost
5,000 Saskatchewan retail merchants "now are operating on a cash
only basis", and "Ituna was the first town to agree to the no credit
system advocated by the Retail Merchants' Association." In its
membership this association included independent grocers, butchers,
lumber dealers, garage operators, and farm implement agents faced
with increasing "cash purchase" competition from cash-and-carry
chain stores, including Canada Safeway, Red and White Stores, and
Saskatchewan's O. K. Economy Stores owned by Shelly Brothers
Wholesale, and retail co-operatives and, to a lesser extent, from the
more recently organized Canadian Co-operative Implements Limited.

Retail co-operative store officials, acting on the somewhat reluctant
decision of elected board members and appointed managers, were
conditioned to the theory and practice that "this prairie country was
built on credit". But bolstered by exhortations from the Saskatchewan
Federated Co-operatives Limited, the local co-ops largely adopted a

policy of advising seekers of credit to approach "your local credit
union for a loan". In other words, the co-op merchandisers, who did
somewhat less than 10 per cent of the retail store business in the province, proclaimed themselves "not in the banking business". In this regard curtailment, or virtual elimination, of "credit across the counter"
was in general the policy of co-op outlets, chain stores, independent
retail merchants, and dealers alike. Reviewing the situation, Alfred
Gleave, farming 1,280 acres and president of the Biggar Co-operative
Association, laconically remarked, "Well, if this country was built
on credit, by the looks of things it's built."

The increasing sales volume of both the Saskatchewan Co-operative
Wholesale Society and the Consumers Co-operative Refineries, plus the
interdependent relationship of the two co-operative enterprises, had
resulted in yet closer co-ordination of distribution and administration.
Various local co-ops concerned mainly with handling petroleum
products desired to retail hardware and other lines, while coal and
wood co-ops had expanded into bulk petroleum outlets. With individual local membership in both the refineries and the wholesale being
in many instances identical, the advantage of amalgamation was
realized at a joint meeting of the respective delegates at Saskatoon,
June 8, 1944, and formal amalgamation became effective in November
of that year under the new name of Saskatchewan Federated Co-operatives Limited, whose business turnover for the year 1953 amounted to
about 29 million dollars.

Saskatchewan farmers initiated the Canadian Co-operative Implements Limited, incorporated under federal charter in 1940. Wartime
restrictions of materials delayed a practical realization of the machinery co-operative aims, but once again individual farmers "got in their
cars and took to the road" to persuade their fellow farmers to invest
in the "machinery co-op . . . to reduce the price of farm machinery . . .
and ourselves manufacture the kind of implements we need". This
co-operative enterprise started an implement factory of limited capacity near Winnipeg. In December, 1944, Canadian Co-operative
Implements, with shareholders in the neighbouring provinces of
Manitoba and Alberta, had a contract with the Cockshutt Plow
Company whereby that major farm machine company would manufacture tractors, combines, and other machines, under the co-op label.
In its financial year ending October 31, 1953, Canadian Co-operative

Implements Limited sold farm machinery to the value of $6,328,000, and almost half the sales were to Saskatchewan farmers.

Evolution of farm implements continued largely through a combination of the improvisation of alert and experienced farmers and more precise mechanical principles applied by agricultural engineers, plus the commercial competitive drive of farm machinery manufacturers and local sales agencies.

At the same time, advanced scientists and technicians "combined to produce hitherto unheard of machines". In response to an undercurrent of popular demand "to make some constructive use of atomic energy in our province rich in uranium-bearing ore", the University of Saskatchewan, recognized for its outstanding physicists, became Canada's first institution to install a cobalt therapy unit for radiation treatment of cancer and other diseases. Free treatment (paid by the taxpayers generally) for cancer patients had been introduced subsequent to free tuberculosis treatment instituted in 1929. After free treatment for tuberculosis patients came the establishment of free treatment for mental patients. This institutional care, paid for by the taxpayers as a whole, relieved the patients' next of kin from the obligation of incurring a financial burden most often beyond the capacity of the individual or family concerned.

Nearing completion in 1954 was the university hospital, planned for 500 beds and attached to the College of Medicine, University of Saskatchewan.

Compulsory prepaid hospitalization care, a form of government insurance popular with the electorate, became general early in 1947. In 1954 the annual rates were these: adults (18 years and over), $15; children (under 18 years of age), $5; maximum for a family of any size, $40. The holder of a hospitalization card was entitled to a hospital bed without further charge, upon the recommendation of a medical practitioner. In 1953, 803,941 individuals were covered by this insurance plan.

For reduced costs and increased efficiency in smaller hospitals, by application of the "larger unit principle", the "union hospital idea" became a method whereby two or more municipalities co-operated for construction and operation of a hospital in a town central to the area so organized. In such hospitals serving an intimate community "everybody soon gets to know who else is in there", and so a visitor who comes to see a member of the family or close friend "is likely to stay on to visit with a neighbour".

The air ambulance

There was the problem of rapid transportation for emergency patients to medical centres. Saskatchewan's Golden Jubilee year, 1955, marked the seventh year of operation for the Saskatchewan Air Ambulance Service, first of its kind in North America, whereby emergency cases of illness or accident, vouched for by a municipal councillor or other responsible local resident, were transported to a medical centre at a flat rate fee of $25, regardless of distance within the province. Landing in stubble fields, summer-fallow, and open stretches of prairie, alert and efficient air ambulance pilots became "the bush-pilots of the prairie". Following an emergency call for an ambulance plane, farm folk, villagers, or townspeople gathered at a nearby spot which they considered would "be a good place for the plane to land". Often they signalled with bedsheets or blankets as they saw the plane approaching. The pilot, having taken his map bearings from railway lines and highways leading to the general location, banked low over the impromptu "landing field" to search for stones, meadow hummocks, barbed wire fences, abandoned machinery, or other impediments. Despite the sometimes hazardous nature of such landing and take-off, no patients had been injured in aircraft accidents as the province entered its Golden Jubilee year. The provincial welfare programme of homes and care for aged citizens included the issuance of a hospitalization card without payment and free false teeth and optical glasses.

That the "social legislation" was, in general, well received by the populace was indicated during election campaigns when few, if any, candidates, regardless of their respective political loyalties, advocated abandonment of the principle of such social legislation. Candidates standing for office in opposition to the party in power almost invariably stated their intention to retain the legislation, while at the same time pointing out that the administration of it should become more efficient in the interests of the taxpayers.

A new school unit

Not unrelated to the emergence of larger farm units, together with increased transportation facilities and the evident decline of the once closely knit rural community, was the introduction of the larger school unit developed previously in Alberta but not so readily accepted in Saskatchewan. Nevertheless, the larger school unit plan became generally accepted in rural areas where a number of school-houses were closed and subsequently sold to the highest bidder. In some instances, pupils were transported each school day by larger unit school bus between their homes and a more centrally located school-house, sometimes enlarged and often better equipped, at least in the physical sense. While all rural ratepayers were concerned about increasing administrative costs, a minority hoped for increased educational advantages.

"Disintegration of the rural community" accompanied by a trend toward "urbanization of farm folk" was largely attributed to the automobile and related technological development. Altering modes and changing conditions were reflected in the voluminous, comprehensive, and controversial report of the Royal Commission on Agriculture and Rural Life, published in 1955. The royal commission, authorized by the Saskatchewan Legislature in 1952, was concerned with ". . . the requirements for the maintenance of a sound farm economy and the improvement of social conditions and amenities in rural Saskatchewan". Chairman of the six-member commission was Professor W. B. Baker, Department of Agriculture, University of Saskatchewan.

While the rural population declined, the rise in the expanding larger towns and cities was evidenced in an urban housing shortage and a rapid construction of houses, apartment blocks, and schools, accompanied by the appearance of new retail stores and branch banks. City and town engineering departments were under pressure to keep up with the demand for water mains, sewage system extension, electricity, and pavement. Regina, Moose Jaw, and Saskatoon "almost overnight blossomed forth with intersection signal lights of the stop, go, wait, walk, hesitate variety so that anybody who is colour blind or can't read might as well stay home". Parking meters, initially a controversial innovation, had been installed seemingly to stay, and there were a growing number of advocates for commercial or civic parking lots.

Though there was less "bread basket of the world" boasting in Canada's leading wheat producing province, Saskatchewan's economy continued to be vitally dependent on agriculture, with wheat, as the principal source of revenue, "seeking an export market in restricted world markets". Apart from agriculture, industries within the province were topped in monetary value by petroleum products, both in crude oil production and in refining. Following, in monetary value, came these: flour milling, slaughtering and meat packing, butter and cheese making, beer brewing, bread and related baking, printing and publishing, sawmilling, aerated water manufacturing, processing of feeds for livestock and poultry, and sash and door planing.

The Canadian Government census of 1951 indicated Saskatchewan had the most motor trucks in use on farms and more farm tractors and combine-harvesters than any other province. At the same time, according to the census, Saskatchewan had less rural electric power than Manitoba or Alberta, where hydro power was available, and one-third of Saskatchewan's electrified farms had wind-driven or gasoline engine generators. But rural electrification in Saskatchewan, dependent on steam or internal combustion plants, was steadily expanding. Thus were rural people being assimilated further into the ways of town and city.

Saskatchewan, "mainly without millionaires living or dead" to endow places of learning or institutions of culture, remained dependent on the taxpayers for an expanding university whose interest and influence reached beyond campus confines. Though professorial specialization in an era of unprecedented scientific and technological development tended toward increasing departmentalization, not so evident at the university's inception, faculty members continued, for the most part, to keep in touch with the people of the province and to be aware of their problems, needs, and aspirations. Original and scholarly work by men and women largely unfettered by tradition—yet conscious of tradition's value—was reflected in an article in *Science*, the official publication of the American Association for the Advancement of Science. According to *Science*, the University of Saskatchewan, in the production of distinguished scientists, stood eighth among the hundreds of institutions of higher learning on the North American continent. "Only eight Canadian institutions ranked among the first hundred on the continent; only one stood higher than

Saskatchewan (University of British Columbia); the next stood 21st; the two largest universities in Canada ranked 150th and 238th."

The first president of the University of Saskatchewan, aware of the advantages of an Edinburgh tradition modified and adapted in Canada's Maritime provinces, had viewed western Canada's emergent prairie scene with a mind's eye admirably adapted to evaluate the present and to visualize a future. He was, for example, concerned with the development of the arts—and encouragement to aspiring artists—in an area emerging from frontier attitudes and conceivably rich in artistic potential. To painters from Scotland, England, Austria, and other lands, he gave his backing and found for these pioneers much needed financial support on a minimum bread and butter basis in times of both boom and depression. Such painters, struggling at first in an environment more unconcerned than hostile, became teachers to infuse hundreds of Saskatchewan-born boys and girls with a desire for expression in line and colour, and eventually to create with a combination of freshness and maturity.

A welcome gathering place for artist-painters and the public alike was the Saskatoon Art Centre in the King George Hotel basement, where a poolroom had previously been accommodated. When the poolroom gave way to an art centre and the hotel management named its basement an "Arcade", aged and respected Chi Struthers, whose mother was a plantation slave "freed by Lincoln", continued his shoeshine stand. Said Chi, "Them art centah folks don't buy no shines— not like the poolroom boys used to . . . but art's educational and you don't want to knock art." Commenting on a painting by Franz Marc, famous for his formal rhythms, loaned for exhibition by Fred S. Mendel, proprietor of Intercontinental Packers Limited, Saskatoon, Chi said, "Them pigs in that picture never made no money for Intercontinental—sleepy hawgs with snouts that sharp." Significant it was that neither at the Saskatoon Art Centre nor at the Art Gallery of Regina College were comments such as Chi's written off as of no consequence.

Since territorial times and during the formative years of a new and expansive province, books by various authors in many lands had influenced Saskatchewan's leaders, dreamers, and rebels. In 1950 the rural people of the Prince Albert-Melfort vicinity voted to add to their municipal taxes a fraction of a mill to pay, in part, for a regional circulating library, the North Central Saskatchewan Regional Library, with headquarters in Prince Albert and branches in towns and villages. The cost of books was shared among the urban centres, rural municipalities, and the Saskatchewan Government. A Nipawin farm woman remarked: "It's not a question of whether we can afford this library. We can't afford to be without it."

Bruce Hutchison, author and capable Canadian commentator on the changing scene *A Mari Usque Ad Mare,* has remarked on Saskatchewan's penchant for meetings and organization. As a result of meetings attended by Saskatchewan music teachers from widely separated, and often isolated, points, The Canadian Federation of Music Teachers' Associations was ultimately formed. Music teachers and musicians, mainly from other lands, had given instruction and encouragement to students in the province, and eventually Saskatchewan-born musicians made their mark with the Canadian Broadcasting Corporation, with the National Film Board, and in concert halls of London, Minneapolis, and Budapest. Back of this development was the Saskatchewan Association of Music Festivals, born in the earlier years of the province, plus a variegated populace for whom music was not always a formal accomplishment, but a necessity both for emotional expression and cheerful living.

The Little Theatre movement, encouraged by the university, sent graduates to drama centres elsewhere in Canada and to the stages of London and New York.

Contributing to cultural evolution was the ethnic background of Saskatchewan's people in the process of becoming homogeneous without "forced draft compulsion". In 1954 less than 50 per cent of the population was of Anglo-Saxon, or British Isles, background. Approximately 50 per cent had their origin in Germany, Holland, the Ukraine, the Scandinavian countries, Russia, Hungary, Poland, and other areas of Europe, and in French-Canada.

The government-sponsored Saskatchewan Arts Board, interested in furthering the arts and crafts, adopted a policy of helping young musicians by the arrangement of public recitals. It also purchased paintings by Saskatchewan artists and held exhibits of arts and crafts.

In the realm of sport, both spectator-commercial and amateur-participation, hockey and football with their mass appeal flourished without state subsidy. The Saskatchewan Roughriders rugby team in their hometown, Regina, credited by a sports writer with "crazy, unswerving enthusiasm" for football spectacles, drew crowds of 15,000 to Taylor Field. If all these spectators were residents of Regina, one out of every five citizens—inclusive of newborn babies— must have attended a capacity crowd game. But many of the ardent fans converged on the capital city from other Saskatchewan cities and from towns, villages, and farmsteads as far distant as 200 miles and more.

In Humboldt, a purchasing centre of 2,500 population, located amidst a lively agricultural community largely of German background, Russian-born Mayor Bures T. Laskin, a local merchant, headed a successful campaign to raise money for artificial ice in the rink. As a result, junior and minor hockey received added impetus in Humboldt town and vicinity.

Melville's community rink, equipped with an artificial ice plant, burned down, for the second time, one mid-November night in 1954, "just as the hockey season was about to get going". Shortly after midnight, as citizens watched the fiery demolition which defied combined town and railway fire-fighting equipment, tears came to eyes of hockey-imbued youngsters who had scrambled out of bed to follow their elders to the fire. As the quonset-style aluminum roof disintegrated in the heat of the flames, someone remarked, "Too bad, but we'll build it again."

PRESERVE OUR HERITAGE

"YOUR OLD MEN SHALL DREAM DREAMS,
AND YOUR YOUNG MEN SHALL SEE VISIONS"
— JOEL 2:28

Selected Bibliographical References

In view of the limited amount of monograph material published on Saskatchewan's history, especially on the period since Saskatchewan became a province, it has been necessary in the production of this history to consult a great variety of references: annual reports of provincial and federal government departments, reports of crown corporations, reports of committees and royal commissions appointed by the Saskatchewan government, newspapers and periodicals, unpublished masters and doctoral theses, the Parliamentary Guide, and the Canadian Annual Review, as well as many incidental government and private papers, publications, maps, and charts. Because of this, it is not considered practical to attempt to give a bibliography here. What follows is a selected list of bibliographical and general references.

BIBLIOGRAPHICAL REFERENCES:

Kupsch, W. O., *Annotated Bibliography of Saskatchewan Geology,* Regina, Queen's Printer, 1952.

MacDonald, Christine, *Publications of the Governments of the North-West Territories, 1876-1905, and of the Province of Saskatchewan, 1905-1952,* Regina, Legislative Library, 1952.

Peel, Bruce B., *Bibliography of the Prairie Provinces,* Toronto, University of Toronto Press, 1955.

PERIODICALS:

The Beaver, Winnipeg, Hudson's Bay Company.

Canadian Historical Review, Toronto, University of Toronto Press.

Canadian Journal of Economics and Political Science, Toronto, University of Toronto Press.

Saskatchewan History, Saskatoon, Saskatchewan Archives Board.

GENERAL REFERENCES:

Black, N. F., *History of Saskatchewan,* Regina, Saskatchewan Historical Company, 1913.

Britnell, G. E., *The Wheat Economy,* Toronto, University of Toronto Press, 1939.

Dawson, C. A., *Group Settlement; Ethnic Communities in Western Canada,* Toronto, Macmillan Co., 1936.

Dawson, C. A., and Younge, E. R., *Pioneering in the Prairie Provinces: The Social Side of the Settlement Process,* Toronto, Macmillan Co., 1940.

Fowke, V. C., *Canadian Agricultural Policy,* Toronto, University of Toronto Press, 1946.

Giraud, Marcel, *Les Métis Canadiens,* Paris, Institut d'ethnologie, 1945.

Hawkes, John, *The Story of Saskatchewan and Its People,* Chicago, S. J. Clarke Publishing Co., 1924.

Howard, J. K., *Strange Empire,* New York, William Morrow & Co., 1952.

Hedges, J. B., *Building The Canadian West,* New York, Macmillan Co., 1939.

Jenness, D., *The Indians of Canada,* Ottawa, King's Printer, 1932.

Lipset, S. M. *Agrarian Socialism,* Berkeley, University of California Press, 1950.

Moorhouse, H. J., *Deep Furrows,* Toronto, George J. McLeod, 1918.

Morris, A., *The Treaties of Canada with the Indians of Manitoba and the North-West Territories,* Toronto, Belfords, Clarke & Co., 1880.

Morton, A. S., *A History of the Canadian West to 1870-71,* London, Thomas Nelson and Sons, Ltd., 1939.

Morton, A. S., and Martin, C., *History of Prairie Settlement and "Dominion Lands" Policy,* Toronto, Macmillan Co., 1938.

Oliver, E. H., *The Canadian North-West* (documents), Ottawa, Government Printing Bureau, 1914-15.

Patton, H. S., *Grain Growers' Cooperation In Western Canada,* Cambridge, Harvard University Press, 1928.

Shortt, Adam, and Doughty, A. G. (Editors), *Canada and Its Provinces,* Vols. 19 & 20, Toronto, Publishers' Association of Canada, Ltd., 1914.

Stanley, G. F. G., *Birth of Western Canada,* Toronto, Longmans, Green & Co., 1936.

Turner, J. P., *The North-West Mounted Police,* Ottawa, King's Printer, 1950.

Wood, L. A., *A History of Farmers' Movements in Canada,* Toronto, Ryerson Press, 1924.

Yates, S. W., *Saskatchewan Wheat Pool,* Saskatoon, United Farmers of Canada (Saskatchewan Section), 1947.

Index

Abernethy, 117
Advance Rumley Thresher Company, 159
Agriculture, Canadian Council of, 190, 198
Agriculture, College of, 153
Agriculture, Department of, 117, 133, 150, 162, 174, 189, 201, 231
Agriculture, School of, 240
Air Ambulance Service, Saskatchewan, 275
Airways, Saskatchewan Government, 261, 263, 270
Alaska, 14, 51, 75
Albany River, 34
Alberta, 2, 8, 40, 57, 58, 69, 90, 108, 111, 121, 123, 126, 129, 147, 159, 179, 190, 192, 198, 199, 200, 216, 217, 224, 230, 266, 267, 273, 276, 278
American Abell tractor, 132
American Association for the Advancement of Science, 279
American Federation of Labor, 228
Amisk Lake, 203
Anderson, J. T. M., 202, 212, 213, 214, 215, 218, 226, 227, 229, 230
André, Father, 55, 81, 82, 86, 95
Apex wheat, 240, 241
Archibald, Lieutenant Governor, 53, 56, 64
Army Service Corps, Canadian, 171
Assiniboia, 43, 69, 107, 112, 192, 231, 250
Assiniboine River, 42
Athabaska Lake, 36, 43, 203, 239, 264, 265
Atomic energy, 257, 274
Auld, F. H., 231
Avonlea, 169

Bacon Board, Canadian, 247
Baker, Professor W. B., 277
Baker, W. G., 182
Baker Company, I. G., 60
Balgonie, 105
Bank of Canada, 234
Bank of Montreal, 143
Barr, Reverend I. M., 118
Batoche, 55, 80, 86, 87, 91, 93
Battle River, 64, 93
Battleford, 63, 64, 70, 74, 87, 89, 92, 93, 94, 118
Beardy, James, 45

Beaver Lake, 203
Beaverdale, 148
Begg, Alexander, 118
Bell, Major, 111
Bell, farm, 73
Belly River, 59
Bennett, Richard Bedford, 109, 218, 219, 225, 230, 236, 237
Bering Straits, 5, 14
Big Bear (Indian warrior), 85, 90, 93, 94, 95
Biggar Co-operative Association, 273
Black, Rev. John, 45
Black Bay, 264
Blucher, 224
Borden, Robert Laird, 154, 155, 181, 182, 188, 190
Bradshaw, J. E., 180
Brandon, 114
British Columbia, 49, 51, 220, 236
British Commonwealth Air Training Plan, 250
British Empire Service League, 210
British Labour Party, 256
British North America Act (1867), 51, 124
Brock, 267
Brockelbank, J. H., 255
Brouillette, Louis C., 197, 199
Brown, J. T., 237
Bryant, J. F., 213
Buckle, W. C., 213
Budd, Reverend Henry, 45
buffalo, 22, 23, 24, 46, 47, 54, 55, 56, 80
Buffalo Narrows, 45, 263
Bulletin, The, 83
Burdett-Coutts, Baroness, 73
Burgess, M.C., Captain D. L., 202
Burns and Company, 231
Butler, Lieutenant, 64

Cabot, John, 31
Cairns, V.C., Hugh, 172
Cairns' Store, 159
Calder, James A., 126, 160, 180, 181, 188
Calgary, 93, 109, 145, 209, 229, 268
Canada Gazette, 244
Canada Packers, 231
Canada Safeway Stores, 272
Canadian Bank of Commerce, 143
Canadian Broadcasting Corporation, 280
Canadian Congress of Labour, 260

284